MEXICAN COOKERY

MEXICAN
COOKERY
Lourdes Nichols

COLLINS

First published in 1984 by
William Collins Sons & Co Ltd
London · Glasgow · Sydney · Auckland · Toronto · Johannesburg

Editor: Robin Wood
Cookery editor: Veronica Sperling
Designer: Janet James
Photography: Peter Myers
Line illustrations: Brenda Armit

ISBN 0 00 411279 2

Text set in Century Schoolbook by Wyvern Typesetting Ltd, Bristol
Colour reproduction by Dot Gradations Ltd, Essex
Printed and bound by W. S. Cowell, Ipswich

Contents

Acknowledgements

This book has been a real pleasure to write, so my first acknowledgement is to Robin Wood and Collins Publishers who have made it possible.

I must then thank my dear mother, without whose patient guidance, encouragement and determination I would never have learnt to cook; not to mention my grandmother, without whose cookery book, carefully compiled, these recipes would have been lost! Also Ana Clipstone for her great support and understanding and J. C. Paget for his interest and assistance in keeping the tortilla factory going while this book was being written.

To Alison Wormleighton I owe thanks for her participation in helping me with the manuscript. To Veronica Sperling, my thanks for doing such a good job of the editing, which could not have been easy. To Joyce Orr who, believing in me and my enthusiasm to introduce a true Mexican cuisine to Europe, has offered me continuous help and support. Another great help has been Shelagh Jagger, assisting me by trying out the recipes. She has got to be the best connoisseur of Mexican food ever to learn about it, whilst she avidly prepared each dish wondering if it would turn out at all!

I must also thank the Mexican Embassy, the Mexican Tourist Council, the British Mexican Society and Roberto Latapí of the Mexican Bank Intermex for their support and enthusiasm; Intermex also for their generous assistance with the cost of the illustrations; the Mexican nationals who have given me recipes and encouragement, in particular Lilly Courtney, Cristina Rohlfs and María Teresa Carrera. Also the Americans living in England, especially Linda Smith, Ruth Sundell, Tessa McDonald and Alice Portnoy, who have supported my efforts right from the beginning.

And finally, thanks to my husband Peter, and my son Richard and daughters Linda and Elena who patiently tried umpteen versions of *tamales*, *salsas*, *antojitos* and the like in my eagerness to refine and simplify these recipes—for being supportive when things went wrong, enticing me to try again and again, and for the many 'not as good as yours, Mum' which were sent to me in letters whenever they were abroad.

Foreword

It gives me special pleasure to write a foreword to Lourdes Nichols'
Mexican Cookery as, apart from the esteem in which I hold Lourdes, I
think it is very important to have books on food that are honest and real,
not gimmicky. Hers is.

She is as much in love with this wonderfully festive food as I am. She
wants to share her knowledge of it with others, as indeed I did. It is too
good a cuisine not to be more widely known. For far too long it has been
beyond the reach of people in Britain, largely because so many of the
vital ingredients were not available until Lourdes took up the challenge
of bringing or producing them here.

It is ironical because so many European cuisines depend on foods that
were first cultivated in the Valley of Mexico from about 7000 BC, roughly
the same time as agriculture began in the Middle East. We owe to those
early American agriculturists the tomato, *tomatillo*, corn (maize), all of
the chillies, the common bean (green or dried), red kidney and other
beans, avocados, courgettes, cho-chos, pumpkins, chocolate, vanilla,
pineapples, papaya (paw-paw), guavas, pecans and turkeys. They were
all unknown outside the Americas until Columbus, looking for a quick
way to the Spice Islands, made landfall in the New World in 1492. Most of
these foods migrated rapidly. Others were accepted more slowly.

Though the Mexican cuisine still rests firmly on its Aztec and Maya
foundations, today's kitchen derives from the colonial kitchen. This
resulted from the unique culinary marriage that took place when the
foods and cooking techniques of Europe met the foods and cooking
techniques of Mexico. Modern cooking equipment and kitchen tools, like
the food processor and the blender, and modern agriculture and
marketing have made the cuisine more accessible. In the past, when the
only way to grind corn (maize) or chillies was by hand, it was very
time-consuming.

Reading Lourdes' book reminds me of my own early adventures into
the Mexican cuisine when I married and went to live in Mexico, finding
myself plunged into a very foreign world. I knew about cooking in the
West Indies where I spent some years of my childhood, and of India where
we had a family connection through my grandfather's work. My mother

7

was a brilliant cook in the French and British tradition, and my father, whose work took him abroad a great deal, always brought back recipes. So I had, in fact, some knowledge of most of the world's food. But Mexico came as a revelation—exotic and delicious, different from any cuisine I had encountered. I started on a voyage of discovery that resulted in my own book, *The Complete Book of Mexican Cooking*, which has been in print in the USA since 1967.

Lourdes had the happy advantage of growing up with this highly sophisticated yet forthright cuisine. Her book has a wide range of sensible recipes that can be cooked in any ordinary, reasonably well-equipped kitchen. There are useful headnotes which explain unfamiliar aspects of the cooking, and a helpful section on special ingredients and equipment. She brings us authentic Mexican dishes in recipes which are well tested and within the reach of anyone prepared to follow her clearly written instructions. This is a splendid introduction to a fascinating cuisine. Adventurous cooks everywhere will be grateful.

Elisabeth Lambert Ortiz

Introduction

As a home-sick Mexican living abroad, one of the most difficult things for me to cope with was the lack of Mexican foods and ingredients in Britain. Like other people who live away from their native countries, I missed the familiar smells and flavours that reminded me of home. Unfortunately, restaurants supply only a very limited menu of what they think people will eat, and people eat it because they do not know any better. This was certainly the case when I visited some of the Mexican restaurants, where I sadly realized that the only thing Mexican in there was me!

It was this longing for authentic Mexican food which started me on my search for basic ingredients and which has culminated in my efforts to make it available to people in Britain and to the Mexicans who, like me, are longing to eat the real thing. While it appears that some of the ingredients are difficult to find, once you know where to look your task is simple. Indian, Chinese and West Indian shops all contribute to the Mexican pantry overseas, aided by Italian, Spanish or Greek shops. The most difficult thing to find is a good corn or wheat tortilla, for which you need not only the proper ingredients but also expertise. Fortunately tortillas are now sold frozen by a few exclusive shops and hopefully the supermarket chains will soon realize that the popularity of the food warrants the sale of its ingredients. In the meantime, you will find step-by-step instructions in this book on how to make your own tortillas at home, and if you persevere you will no doubt reap the benefits of your efforts as I did.

Mexico is a very international country and it has adapted popular international dishes to its own tastes and needs. The great variety of ingredients available there, combined with the flair and ingenuity of its cooks, has earned Mexico a well-deserved place in the world of cookery. The Mexican cuisine is varied and tasty, featuring dishes with colour, texture and interest.

How has all this come about? I hope that the following brief explanation of the Mexican geographical and historical features will assist in your understanding and help you to cook a Mexican meal with confidence.

THE LIE OF THE LAND

Mexico lies to the south of the United States of America with whom it shares a natural boundary—the *Rio Bravo*, also known as *Rio Grande*. The bordering states are California, Arizona, New Mexico and Texas. To the south, Mexico borders with the Central American States of Guatemala and Belize, to the west and south west lies the Pacific Ocean, to the east the Gulf of Mexico and the Caribbean Sea. It also has two large peninsulas—*Yucatán* in the south east and *Baja California* with its *Golfo de Cortés* in the north west.

Owing to its unique geographical location on both sides of the Tropic of Cancer and its wide range of elevation with the *Sierra Madre* cutting through the length of the country until it becomes the Rockies in America, Mexico enjoys a variety of climate unequalled in any other part of the world. The lands along the 10,000 kilometres of coast are tropical, supplying the country not only with a wide variety of fish and shellfish, but also with all the citrus and tropical fruit such as coconuts, sour-sop, sugar cane, paw-paw, avocados, mangoes and a wide variety of bananas and other fruits and vegetables native to Mexico which have yet to make their international debut.

As one ascends the mountain slopes from the low-lying lands, the heat is tempered by the altitude and thus a whole new range of agricultural products emerges, until upon reaching the highest inhabited points, the climate is that of the north temperate zone. After that lies the famous perpetual snow on the volcanoes known as *Popocatepetl* and *Iztaccihuatl*. These are located just outside Mexico City and their *lava* (volcanic rock) features in some of the native cookery implements like the *molcajete* and *tejolote* (mortar and pestle), *metate* (three-legged stone grinder) and *mexalpilli* (rolling pin).

Because of its varied climate—that of *tierra caliente* (tropical zone), *tierra templada* (semi-tropical zone) and *tierra fria* (cold zone)—Mexico exhibits a remarkable variety of flora and fauna. The flora includes valuable types of wood, medicinal plants and mushrooms and an extensive variety of fruits and vegetables. Of

the fauna, fish of many types are abundant both in the seas and in the rivers, lakes and mountain streams, and the birds are of brilliant plumage, varying in size from the tiny *chupamirto* (hummingbird) to the large *guajolote* (turkey) and *guacamalla* (macaw).

AGRICULTURAL PRODUCE

The agricultural resources in Mexico are of extraordinary value, variety and extent, though an agrarian system has yet to be devised to stimulate production, which is low. Of the total tillable area, only about one-quarter is used in crop production, irrigation being the main problem.

The main crop is *maíz* (maize or Indian corn) which is the food crop of the Mexican people from which *tortillas* (Mexican bread) are made. Maize is generally treated with lime before grinding and shaping into tortillas; they contain no gluten so are good for gluten-free diets. Maize depends on man for its propagation, since it is not self-planting; it grows well together with beans and pumpkin plants in the same furrow. Beans of many colours and sizes are still cultivated and are the main source of fibre and protein in the Mexican diet. Courgettes and pumpkins enjoy great popularity as vegetables as well as providing a welcome shade for the roots of the *milpa* (corn plant), allowing the roots to keep cool by providing cover with their large leaves. Other main crops are barley, rice, coffee, cotton, tobacco, sisal, sugar and rubber. Tomatoes, the green husk *tomatillos*, potatoes and chillies of many different varieties crowd the market stalls and are continually present in Mexican dishes.

Cattle, sheep and goats are raised in large quantities. In addition, pigs, turkeys and chickens are raised for human consumption, their by-products offering a wonderful contribution to the culinary and handicraft arts.

THE AZTECS

The early history of Mexico is obscure and is based on legends rather than fact but it appears that *Anahuac* (the Lake Country), now Mexico City, was populated by the noble, talented and religious *Nahua* people called *Toltecs*. As far back as the 7th century to them are ascribed all the arts, religions and the pyramids. In the 14th century came the *Chichimecas* who were excellent tradesmen and handicraft people. They were finally taken over by the *Aztecs*, who were warriors, but cultured people whose civilization flourished: they founded a powerful empire in the Valley of Mexico some three or four hundred years before the discovery of America.

The *Aztecs* had an organized way of living, with schools and codes of law. Their food was simple, mostly boiled or steamed, and they hand-patted their corn tortillas to eat at each meal. The markets were well attended and trading was done by barter. *Cacao* (cocoa) beans were used when necessary instead of money, and gold and silver had little value other than for their ornamental beauty. *Moctezuma*, the *Aztec* Emperor, lived in a palace with beautiful gardens, fountains, flowers and animals. He is said to have had one thousand dishes to choose from at every meal. Each dish was freshly cooked and prepared for his Royal Highness; pheasants from faraway *Yucatán* and fish from the Pacific coast were brought to Mexico by a relay of barefooted runners. He drank *xoco-latli* (chocolate), which was a bitter-sweet drink, and wore capes of brilliant colours which had feathers carefully sewn together in intricate patterns; his treasure consisted of rooms and rooms full of cocoa beans.

THE SPANISH INVASION

The defeat of the *Aztec* Empire by *Hernán Cortés* and a handful of Spanish adventurers is one of the most startling military feats in history. *Cortés* tricked the Indians into submission and burnt his boats so his men could not desert him.

It was only through a series of remarkable coincidences that *Moctezuma*, the almighty *Aztec* Emperor, did not destroy the intruders. But *Moctezuma* was a benevolent Emperor who granted the Spaniards the benefit of the doubt. They had in their favour their 'floating houses' (Spanish galleons), never seen by Mexicans before, their horses—no hoofed animals existed in the New World—and even more impressive, their 'thunder' which terrified as it killed the Indians by the thousands. To crown it all, they fulfilled the *Aztec* prophecy that such humans would one day govern the land.

Moctezuma sent the Spaniards presents of a sun the size of a cart-wheel made of gold, and a moon, even larger, of silver, and gold nuggets, food, drink and precious stones. He requested that they take their leave as soon as possible, denying them a meeting in *Tenochtitlán* (Mexico City).

Cortés was determined to get to the capital, imagining that gold and silver would be abundant. Had it not been that the smaller Indian tribes hated the *Aztec* supremacy, tax collectors and thirst for human life, *Cortés* would have gone down in history as an adventurer massacred on the beaches of Mexico. But these tribes had had enough and swore allegiance to the Spaniards, their king and their God. They made treaties to assist in the destruction of the *Aztecs* and so it was that 400 or so Spaniards aided by *Malinche* and thousands of Indians eventually occupied *Tenochtitlán*.

After the conquest of Mexico in 1519–21, the *conquistadores*, maintaining their traditional European eating habits, brought across to the New World pigs, chickens, cattle, cereals, vegetables, olive oil, sugar cane, fruits and wine. The Mexican Indians also continued with their native cuisine and it was some time before the two finally merged, forming a new and exciting way of cooking. The trade with China and the Philippines was responsible for other additions. Indeed it is now said that the 'X' in Mexico appears to embrace food from the four cardinal points. Over the years these influences have culminated in an extraordinary blend of textures, a kaleidoscope of flavours and extremely nutritious and colourful cuisine.

The first Spanish city on Mexican territory was called *Villa Rica de la Vera Cruz* (rich valley of the true cross). Rich it was indeed, with a large surplus of fowl, wild pigs, fish, fruits and vegetables as well as an abundance of wild and beautiful flowers, such as gardenias, camelias and orchids—the pods of an orchid found in these lands has given us vanilla. Veracruz is now one of the most important agricultural states in Mexico.

Chocolate, the drink of the *Aztec* Emperors, won acceptance in all the strata of European society and was established as the aromatic drink we now know. The drinking of chocolate became as popular in colonial Mexico as drinking tea was in Britain, to the point where special cups were made for it.

Food, like art, went through a 'baroque' stage and *mole* or *molli* (sauce) is a good example of this as it combines spices from the east with native dried chillies and is served with rice from the Philippines and beans from Mexico. Mexican artists of the period were producing paintings inspired by the newly introduced

Catholic religion, which proudly displayed Christ at the Last Supper with *cazuelas* (clay cooking pots) full of *molli* and a colourful Mexican kitchen in the background! In fact the Catholic church established itself so strongly that there were cases when the bishops or archbishops were Viceroys as well. The nuns in the many convents were responsible for the official banquets, which is probably the reason for the popularity in old Mexican cookery books of recipes using a lot of egg yolks—the egg whites were used in great quantities to glue the gold leaf to the church altars.

A century later some of the native dishes were being served at the Spaniards' tables. Because grapevines and olive trees had not been introduced into Mexico for commercial reasons, wine and olive oil had to be imported at great expense from Spain and so were only consumed by the very wealthy. The natives continued to use pork lard for cooking and drank *pulque* (fermented *agave* juice).

INDEPENDENCE FROM SPAIN

Mexican heroes like *Miguel Hidalgo y Costilla* (now called 'Father of Mexico'), a *Mestizo* (half-caste) priest with some education, encouraged his parishioners to plant olives and vines and taught the natives to read and write and to attain a high standard in music, the arts, metallurgy and other handicrafts. This upset the Spanish authorities and in 1810–21 came the Mexican War of Independence—three hundred years of Spanish rule had become quite unbearable. It was during this war that Mexico was opened up.

The whole country erupted in violence—peaceful, complacent Indians took whatever weapons they could find and criss-crossed the land, fighting, hiding or simply camping in the unexplored peaceful valleys. All the Mexicans became brothers unified by one aim—independence from Spain. At the call of *Viva México! Viva la Virgen de Guadalupe! Viva la Libertad!* (Long Live Mexico, Long Live our Lady of Guadaloupe and Long Live Freedom) they went into battle. The war meant walking miles from well-trodden paths and familiar surroundings and coming across new people and new ideas. The women following their men on their journeys met other women from all over Mexico and shared culinary secrets. They learned, for instance, of the wide range of chillies and beans and their different flavours and uses. In this way the many regional varieties of cooking travelled through Mexico enriching and enhancing other methods.

And when independence was finally achieved, in a country still licking its wounds, a new cuisine was born, a cuisine combining culinary expertise of a millennium of indigenous dishes with centuries-old European traditions from Spain.

THE FRENCH INFLUENCE

But that independence did not last long. From 1863 to 1867 the French, under an agreement with other European powers, occupied Mexico, and Ferdinand Maximilian Joseph of Hapsburg was crowned Emperor of Mexico. Thus it was that French customs and dishes came into the Mexican cuisine—though the rulers were influenced by the Mexican culture too.

The French occupation came to a sad and tragic end in 1867, but the French influence is noticeable to this day. Dishes like pâté, fricassée, croquettes, crêpes and crème-caramel, not to mention an array of delicious breads and cakes, baguettes, croissants and millefeuilles, are still sold all over Mexico. Bread was made with and without eggs and salt, and the art and imagination of the natives were soon manifested in complicated and colourful breads like *Pan de Muerto*, *Rosca de Reyes* and *Biscochos para Chocolate*.

Drinking habits were affected too, and along with the French food, the wine and champagne from France were incorporated into the meals of wealthier Mexicans. By the same token, at court banquets chocolate would be served instead of coffee in elegant porcelain Limoges cups.

DRINKING HABITS

Pulque was the only alcoholic drink of the Indian civilizations and it was considered sacred. It was made from the fermented sap of the *maguey*, a type of *agave* which grows wild. This produced a foamy, milky drink with an acrid odour which cannot be disguised even today, despite the efforts of the locals who 'cure' it with fresh fruits like strawberries or pineapple. It has a similar potency to beer and is in fact losing ground to the latter.

Tequila is thought of as 'the Mexican drink', but it was the product of the imaginative Spaniards who distilled the juice of another type of *agave* plant which is similar to a cactus with which it is often confused. In fact it is a member of the amaryllis family with spiky leaves growing straight up from the core close to the ground. The plant is called *tequilana* or blue *mezcal*. It takes 8–14 years to reach maturity and is grown in the land surrounding the township of *Tequila* from where it takes its name.

The *agaves* are allowed to reach maturity, then the plant is cut at the base, all the leaves cut off, leaving the core which looks like a gigantic pineapple and which weighs between 25 and 100 kilos (50 to 250 lb).

The *piñas*, as the cores are called, are steamed for seven hours until they become sweet and very stringy; then they are pressed between rollers to extract the juice which is fermented in vats. The waste is used in the manufacture of paper, bricks or fertilizer. When fermentation is completed, distillation begins. The Tequila is then stored for a minimum of three years in wax-lined casks for the colourless drink and in wooden casks for the *Añejo* (aged), which has a golden hue and a mellower taste. *Mezcal* is a similar drink. It comes from the same plant but only high-quality *Mezcals* can be called Tequila, whilst all Tequilas are a type of *Mezcal*.

With the introduction of sugar cane brought originally to the Americas by Christopher Columbus, rum was soon being distilled and Mexico has many excellent white and dark rums. Wines were always imported, but in latter years the growing Mexican wine industry is winning popularity.

Beer is made in the north of Mexico, mainly because it is there that the soil grows better barley. There are several types of excellent beer, lighter in alcoholic content than British beer and comparable to lager. The better-known makes are XX (Double X), XXX (Triple X), *Carta Blanca* and *Superior*. Mexican beer is always offered well chilled. You can find Mexican beer in some of the liquor stores around London. It is also exported to other European countries and, of course, is served in Mexican restaurants.

OTHER EUROPEAN INFLUENCES

The British saw the opportunities in the New World and, having commercial enterprise, soon settled in Mexico, bringing with them their beer, *bistec* (beef steak), roast beef, and parsley-buttered potatoes, as well as their delicate china to eat them off. As time went by, Mexico attracted people from every European country and their varied dishes have all contributed to the Mexican menu.

Once the country settled down again and the French were evacuated from Mexico, there was a period of relative affluence.

THE REVOLUTION

But in 1910 the Revolution began, ending the 30-year dictatorship of Porfirio Diaz. The ensuing 10 years, when *Madero*, *Carranza*, *Villa* and *Zapata* all emerged as heroes, were a confusing and destructive period in Mexico's history. The land was covered in blood—it was a war of Mexicans killing each other. Like all revolutions, it achieved only some of its aims, but again one of the by-products was that regional cooking methods became more and more widely known.

After the Revolution, Mexicans suffered a period of re-organization and it was not until some years later that Mexican art, architecture, music and food became of outstanding import-ance in their own right. These days, Mexicans take a great pride in their history and culture, and anything to do with the pre-colonial and colonial period, whether furniture, music, art, food or drink, is highly esteemed.

THE FOOD OF MEXICO TODAY

In Mexico, mealtimes are, above all, happy times, and the best sauce to a meal is loving preparation with some laughter for good measure. Mexicans are well known for their hospitality and the secret is the spontaneous offering of food and drink, however humble it might be, combined with friendly surroundings and cheerful background music, which creates the well-known *ambiente* or ambience.

For the past few years, Mexican food has been the largest-growing food industry in the United States. In fact, Mexican food has now become an American institution and I was very pleasantly surprised when I discovered that my American friends in Britain missed their Mexican food as much as I did. This is quite understandable since Mexicans have established themselves north of the border and have taken their eating habits with them. Los Angeles is now the second-largest Mexican city and California has excellent Mexican restaurants.

Texans have developed a style of cooking unique to them, which is now called Tex-Mex. Many of the tinned foods are 'Tex-Mex' and not Mexican. It is a cuisine in its own right, which is ideally suited to the fast-food trade. The main difference lies in the tortilla, which is mostly eaten fried, either as *taco* shells or as corn chips (*totopos*); their *Chili con Carne* is also unknown in Mexico and it appears they use cumin and cayenne to flavour their sauces instead of green hot chillies.

Mexican restaurants are also springing up all over North America and, judging by the number of enquiries I receive, they are starting to spread to Great Britain, Europe and elsewhere.

The ingredients for Mexican cooking are now available all round the world; some of the everyday vegetables, meats and fruits had their origin in the Americas. The Spanish, French and English galleons which took gold and silver to Europe also took something of more lasting value—the potato from Peru and many vegetables, fruits, fowl and spices from Mexico.

Vanilla, extracted from the pod of a wild Mexican orchid, now flavours our ice-creams and cakes. Turkeys are a true American and British tradition; tomatoes, red, rich and juicy, are now known in Britain as 'British tomatoes'. Avocados in a variety of sizes and colours, with thick or thin skins, green or black, are now widely available the world over. Peanuts have provided the world with innumerable by-products, from shoe polish to cooking oil. *Cacao* beans, used by the *Aztecs* as money, are now such a favourite in Europe that their consumption in the form of chocolate surpasses that of Mexico.

Maize, the staple food of Mexico, is now grown all over the world and feeds the populations of North and South America and Africa. Chillies of innumerable colours, shapes and sizes preserve and flavour our food. Beans, in a variety of sizes and colours, provide a valuable source of minerals and protein as well as dietary fibre, now considered of prime importance for healthy eating. Pumpkin and pumpkin seeds, along with courgettes and their blossoms add more variety and colour to the Mexican diet.

EATING THE MEXICAN WAY

Mexican menus are designed to make meat go a long way and are therefore an economical and healthy way of cooking. The carbohydrate from the maize, the vitamins from the vegetables and the protein and fibre from the beans offer a well-balanced daily diet. Mexican cuisine excels in striking the right balance in colour, texture, flavour and nutrition.

A typical Mexican day for a peasant would start at dawn with only a cup of strong black coffee and a few warm tortillas for *desayuno* (breakfast). He would then tend the animals and fields, returning at around 10 am for *almuerzo* (brunch); this would consist of *Huevos Rancheros* (fried eggs in a tomato sauce), beans, tortillas and perhaps *biscochos* (sweet buns) and more black coffee. He would then go out again and work until about 2 pm when *la comida* (midday meal), the main meal of the day, would be ready. For this he would have *sopa aguada* (soup), *frijoles* (beans), perhaps a little meat and lots of warm hand-patted corn tortillas with *salsa* (sauce) to moisten the meat inside, all washed down with cold beer. There would be nothing to eat until the evening when at about 8 or 9 pm a small meal of warm tortillas, beans and coffee would be had. The well-known *antojitos* (snacks) fit in beautifully in-between meals. In fact Mexicans are notorious for eating between meals. *Antojitos* are consumed in Mexico at all times of day or night. We go so far as to boast that he who doesn't eat *antojitos* between meals is not Mexican!

In contrast to the peasant, the city-dweller would have a more traditional *desayuno*, consisting of freshly squeezed orange juice, eggs or *chilaquiles* with *frijoles*, *biscochos*, hot chocolate or coffee before leaving for work—with a mid-morning break of coffee and sweet buns to be followed at around 1 pm by *la comida*, consisting of *sopa aguada* (soup), *sopa seca* (rice or pasta), meat, one vegetable, beans and salad, accompanied by innumerable warm corn tortillas and a *salsa* or *Guacamole* eaten between courses. For dessert, fresh fruit is as good as any prepared pudding, but in some homes prepared sweets are always available and *Flan* (crème caramel) is a great favourite. *La merienda* (supper) is usually an *antojito* with lots of black coffee or hot chocolate and *biscochos* of assorted types.

La copa y la botana—the pre-meal drink and snack—is offered by Mexican cooks before the main meal of the day, *la comida* or *la cena* (dinner), which can take place anywhere between 1 pm and 11 pm according to the occasion. *La merienda* is a light supper served after the mid-day main meal. Mexicans travelling abroad surely get a shock when they appear for lunch and all they can get is tea and scones.

The setting of the table is formal but simple, the style of eating more in the French custom than the British, in that conversation is usually animated and the meal can take hours, whilst discussions are taking place. The settings can vary from the very humble, to the very elegant. Tortillas are always eaten by hand, even on the most formal occasions, except when they are used as part of a made-up dish and covered with sauce, as is the case with *enchiladas*. Black coffee is more popular than milky coffee after the meal, but very milky coffee is often drunk for breakfast or supper.

Entertaining is casual and takes place very often. Whole families get together, enabling all ages to mingle. You can do no worse than to arrive at a friend's home whilst they are still eating because you will be sat at the table and offered a full meal even if you've just had one. *Vale mas llegar a tiempo que ser convidado* (it is better to arrive on time than to be invited) is a popular saying and a very true one. Everyone is welcome at a friend's table.

In short, you can entertain in the Mexican style very easily. The informal surroundings, the music in the background, the unusual dishes and the Tequila will speak for themselves even in the most traditional of homes. With this I take my leave: all I can say is thank you for your interest, I hope it is well rewarded and

'BUEN PROVECHO AMIGOS'

Suggested Menus

The Mexican menu combinations are as varied as you wish. For your guidance only, I am suggesting a few ideas in the hope that you will feel more confident in making your own choice. A selection of these dishes is illustrated in the colour photographs so you can see what the food actually looks like. I have also made appropriate serving suggestions in many of the recipe introductions.

I would, however, like to call your attention to just a few points which may be of assistance:

- warm soft tortillas may be offered all through the meal, instead of bread.
- a *salsa* or *Guacamole* is usually present at a Mexican table, either to fill warm tortillas with or to enliven any dish.
- I make it a point always to offer *Jalapeños en Vinagre* (Jalapeño-style pickles) separately so that each person can help themselves according to their own taste.
- beans should not be repeated in any one menu. Serving them either as a soup or a side-dish is enough. If re-fried, try and use them with a dish containing a sauce. As a general 'safe' rule I have found that people who are experiencing beans for the first time would rather see them whole.
- if your main course is complicated, use a cold starter.
- as Mexican food can be rich, choose a light dessert.
- if very hot and spicy, choose a cooling dessert like ice-cream or fruit salad.

Desayuno

Breakfast

Jugo de Fruta Fresca (Fresh Fruit Juice)
Huevos Rancheros Típicos (Ranch-Style Eggs with Tomato Sauce)
Café de Olla (Coffee with Cinnamon and Sugar)
Pan de Muerto (Halloween Bread)

■

Fruta Fresca (Fresh Fruit)
Tamales (Corn Dumplings Steamed in Maize Husks)
Frijoles (Beans)
Chocolate Caliente (Hot Chocolate) or *Atole* (Maize Drink)

■

Comida

Lunch

Cocktail de Camarones Almendrados (Prawn and Almond
Cocktail)
Enchiladas Anita (Stuffed Tortillas in Chilli Sauce)
Frijoles Refritos (Re-Fried Beans)
Helado de Vainilla con Kahlua (Vanilla Ice-Cream with Coffee
Liqueur)
Café Negro (Black Coffee)

■

Sopa de Frijol (Bean Soup)
Arroz con Pollo (Rice with Chicken and Vegetables)
Ensalada de Nopalitos (Nopal Cactus Salad)
Flan (Crème Caramel With a Difference)

Cena

Dinner

Margarita Cocktail (Tequila Mixed with Lime Juice)
Sangria (Red Wine Cup)
Nachos (Tortilla Chips with Cheese and Peppers)
Seviche (Fish Marinated in Lime Juice)
Pierna de Carnero Adobada (Leg of Lamb with Chilli Sauce)
Calabacitas con Rajas y Elote (Courgettes with Peppers and Corn)
Chilaquiles (Tortilla Chips in a Sauce)
Arroz con Jitomate (Rice with Tomatoes)
Crema de Mango (Mango Cream with Hazelnuts or Almonds)

■

Cena Vegetariana

Vegetarian Dinner

Quesadillas Mexicanas (Tortillas with Melted Cheese)
Coliflor Capeada (Cauliflower Fritters in Tomato Sauce)
Esquites (Fried Corn with Courgettes)
Budín de Camote (Sweet Potato Purée)
Arroz Blanco (White Rice, Mexican-Style)
Helado de Vainilla con Kahlua (Vanilla Ice-Cream with Coffee Liqueur)

■

Cocktail de Aguacate (Avocado Cocktail)
Enchiladas Suizas (Tortillas Stuffed with Chillies and Melted Cheese)
Quesadillas de Flor de Calabaza (Pumpkin Blossom Quesadillas)
Chiles Rellenos Zacatlán (Peppers Stuffed with Fruit)
Arroz con Frijoles (Rice and Beans)
Gelatina Blanca (Vanilla Jelly)

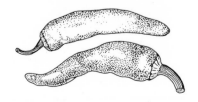

Asado

Barbecue

Costillitas Adobadas (Spare Ribs in Chilli and Cream Sauce)
Tacos al Carbón (Charcoal-Grilled Steak Wrapped in Warm Tortillas)
Elote Asado (Roast Corn on the Cob)
Cebollitas Asadas (Grilled Spring Onions)
Frijoles Borrachos (Tipsy Beans)
Salsa Típica (Raw Tomato Sauce)
Ensalada de Frutas (Fruit Salad)
Borrachitos (Tipsy Meringues)
Café Negro (Black Coffee)

Pescado

Fish

Jaibas en su Concha (Savoury Baked Crab)
Arroz con Rajas (Rice Casserole with Peppers, Cream and Cheese)
Huachinango a la Veracruzana (Cod in Tomato Sauce with Capers, Olives and Orange)
Calabacitas Rellenas (Courgettes Stuffed with Parsley)
Budín de Espinaca (Spinach and Potato Casserole)
Crepas con Cajeta (Banana and Milk Caramel Pancakes)

Buffet Frio

Cold Buffet

Rosca de Aguacate Doña Margarita (Avocado and Chicken
Ring)
Chiles en Vinagreta (Peppers Stuffed with Beans in an Onion
Vinaigrette)
Empanadas de Bacalao (Salted Cod and Tomato Turnover)
Ensalada de Papa (Potato and Herb Salad)
Helado de Mango (Mango Ice-Cream)
Cocada con Crema (Grated Coconut Dessert)
Café de Olla (Coffee with Cinnamon and Sugar)

■

Buffet Caliente

Hot Buffet

Budín Azteca (Tortilla and Chicken Pie)
Mole Poblano (Turkey in Rich Chilli, Nut and Spice Sauce)
Arroz Blanco (White Rice Mexican-Style)
Frijoles (Beans)
Dulce de Calabaza (Stewed Pumpkin with Cinnamon and
Orange)
Chongos Zamoranos (Junket in a Cinnamon Syrup)
Café de Olla (Coffee with Cinnamon and Sugar)

■

Cocktail Party

Cacahuates Enchilados (Peppered Peanuts)
Pepitas de Calabaza (Pumpkin Seeds)
Guacamole con Totopos (Avocado Dip with Corn Tortilla Chips)
Taquitos con Pollo (Miniature Taco Shells with Chicken)
Sopes (Maize Dough Shells with Beans and Chorizo)

■

Special Ingredients and Equipment

In this chapter I have included an a–z list of ingredients most commonly used in Mexican cooking, to help you identify them more easily and act as a guide to buying. (See also the Pronunciation Guide on page 230.)

In general, it is always worth looking in health food shops and Indian, West Indian or Chinese stores for the more unusual foods.

COOKING UTENSILS

The good news is that you do not really need any special cooking utensils in order to produce Mexican food. The only exception is the tortilla press (see page 39 for instructions on how to make your own), which is a must if you wish to make corn tortillas.

Electric mixers, blenders and food processors are of course helpful, and I have mentioned them when appropriate. Microwave ovens are also useful. In short, you can use most of the everyday pots and pans in your kitchen, and if you are lucky enough to possess the modern devices you will produce excellent food in a short period of time.

ANISEED *Anis* spice is easily available from health food shops. It adds flavour to sauces and *Jalapeños en Vinagre* (Jalapeño-style pickles).

ANNATTO *Achiote* is a small red seed from the annatto tree, used for colouring and flavouring, usually sold in Mexico already ground and mixed with spices. Its mildly spicy flavour is used for seasoning fish, fowl and meat. Most popular in the *Yucatán Península* where the Maya people live, it must be dissolved in Seville orange juice or vinegar before using. In Britain, substitute a Tandoori mixture from any Indian shop.

AVOCADO PEARS *Aguacates* Avocados are rarely sold ripe, so remember to buy them well in advance. To assist the ripening process, wrap them well in newspaper and keep in a warm place

27

away from direct light and heat. Turn them daily and check for ripeness. When they start to soften, they can be put in a cool place or even the refrigerator to delay further ripening. If they are to be used for *Guacamole*, the riper the better, but when they are very ripe they become too soft to handle for slicing. Avocados will start to turn black soon after cutting, so prepare them at the very last minute. If they are to be left standing for any period of time, it helps to cover them in lime or lemon juice immediately and sprinkle them with a little salt. I prefer the small knobbly-skinned black ones which are more tasty than the larger green ones. I do not recommend the larger round green hard-skinned avocados because they have a watery flavour despite their appealing appearance. In Mexico there is a variety of even smaller avocados the size of large plums with a soft speckly skin which can, if you wish, be eaten and adds to the flavour.

BANANA LEAVES *Hojas de plátano* Not readily available in Britain, these are used to wrap *tamales* in, but greaseproof paper and kitchen foil squares are good substitutes. However, should you manage to get some, immerse in boiling water for 10 minutes to soften them before use.

BEANS (PULSES) *Frijoles* The staple food of Mexico. There are very many varieties of beans and they are all very good. The most commonly used are the rosecoco (borlotti), red kidney, pinto and black beans. Of these, black beans are the most difficult to obtain, although I have occasionally found them in the market. Canned beans may be substituted to avoid the initial lengthy cooking process.

CHEESE *Queso* The Spaniards introduced cattle into Mexico and with them all the dairy by-products. It would be unthinkable to serve *enchiladas* without their crumbly white cheese, called *Queso Fresco*, which can be substituted by any of the white crumbly cheeses in this country like Wensleydale, Cheshire or Lancashire. The Greek *feta* is also very good. The arrival of the *Mennonites* in the Northern Mexican State of *Chihuahua* has given birth to the *Queso de Chihuahua*, now eaten all over Mexico. It is similar to a mild Cheddar cheese by which it can be substituted. I like to mix the Cheddar with Mozzarella to provide the stringy consistency which is a must in the Mexican cooked cheese dishes. I have found that some Italian shops sell what they call *Queso Pera*, which is a pear-shaped cheese covered in a layer of transparent wax. This cheese is a good substitute for *Queso de Oaxaca* or *Queso Asadero* used in *quesadillas*, though the Cheddar and Mozzarella mix is also excellent. *Queso Añejo* is an aged cheese which is often called for in *antojitos* and cooked dishes. I am not crazy about it, but Italian Parmesan can be used as a substitute.

The Mexican cheese industry has grown intensively in the last ten years and they now produce very acceptable French cheese imitations such as Camembert—delicious with *Rajas Poblanas* instead of Cheddar cheese or with *quesadillas*; there are Mexican varieties of Port Salut, Gruyère and cream cheese too.

CHILLIES *Chiles* These are the pride and joy of the Mexican cuisine. They grow abundantly in Mexico and are always available in a variety of sizes, shapes and colours.

Fresh chillies In Britain there are two main types of green hot chillies—some very thin tight-looking ones which are extremely hot and others imported from Kenya which are more fleshy and a little less hot. They can be obtained from some of the supermarket chains and Indian shops. The larger poblano chillies I have never come across in this country, but green capsicum peppers are a good substitute. If you wish them to be very hot, introduce a piece of small green chilli into the pepper before filling. I must confess I have managed to deceive even trained palates in the past.

Dealing with chillies It is important to remember that chillies are hot, and that the hottest parts are usually the seeds and veins. Often just by touching them your fingers will sting and so will your eyes, nose or any part of your skin you happen to touch. Therefore, I strongly recommend using rubber gloves when handling chillies. Always cut them on kitchen paper towels and wash your knives carefully after use.

How to control the sting To guide you in the control of the 'sting' or hotness you use, I emphasize that tasting as you go along is most important. Remember that people may insist that they love hot food but scarcely know what they are letting themselves in for. As a general guide I suggest:

1) Add small amounts of chilli at a time and taste. If you are not sure of how hot your guests will be able to take it, serve some *Jalapeños en Vinagre* in a small bowl and leave them on the table for people to help themselves.

2) To flavour without hotness, add the unbroken chillies during cooking and remove and discard them immediately after.

3) To allow for more 'sting', cut the chillies in half and remove and discard the seeds.

4) For full 'sting', chop the chillies, seeds and all. If it is not hot enough, just add more chillies until it is how you want it.

To suppress the 'burn'   It is awful to bite into a chilli by mistake as it can give a nasty shock. Nothing will really take the burn away, your eyes will fill with tears and you will feel like screaming. I find that chewing a piece of cheese is more efficient than drinking gallons of water! But . . . the burn certainly lasts for a long time.

To keep chillies fresh   Remove the stems and wrap the chillies in a paper bag inside a polythene bag, then seal and refrigerate. They will keep for about two weeks.

Dried chillies   There are many varieties, each with a distinctive flavour and colour. The most commonly used are *chile ancho, chile mulato, chile pasilla, chile chilpotle* and *chile cascabel*. It is difficult to distinguish the *ancho* from the *mulato* which gives a darker sauce, but whichever you manage to get will keep for a long time in a cool place. These chillies are sold dried at all times of the year and they make popular *salsas* to accompany meats, vegetables, beans, rice and tortillas. Instructions on how to use them are in each recipe.

CHOCOLATE   *Chocolate*   The most popular way of consuming chocolate in Mexico is as a drink. Unsweetened cooking chocolate is a good substitute.

CHORIZO   This is a spicy sausage made from pork. It can be obtained from delicatessens or you can make your own (see recipes on pages 156–7).

CHRISTOPHENE OR CHO-CHO   *Chayote*   A heart-shaped vegetable, light green in colour, about 13 cm (5 inches) long. Their flavour is watery and earthy and they can be obtained from Indian or West Indian shops. The best quality is the dark green and very prickly chayote which is not available in Britain. It is boiled in its skin and peeled before serving.

CINNAMON   *Canela*   Cinnamon sticks are more common than ground cinnamon but the latter is an excellent substitute. Use 1 teaspoon ground cinnamon for each 5 cm (2 inch) stick cinnamon.

COFFEE   *Café*   Your favourite ground coffee will be fine—for a different flavour try *Café de Olla* on page 227.

COOKING FATS   *Manteca*   Pork lard is used widely in Mexico for frying. *Antojitos* cooked in lard taste better too, but with health in mind I have substituted unsaturated oil for the animal fat. I particularly like corn oil. Please remember never to start frying in cold or lukewarm oil. Always heat the oil up first and by draining the food on absorbent kitchen paper your intake of oil will be less.

CORIANDER (FRESH) *Cilantro* or *Culantro* is used raw in vast amounts. This herb indisputably adds the magic to some Mexican dishes. It has no substitute when called for in raw sauces or *Guacamole*—it is best to do without than substitute. When a substitute is acceptable, I have mentioned it. Coriander can be bought from some good greengrocers as well as Indian, West Indian and Greek shops. It keeps well for about 10 days in the refrigerator. Cut off the roots, wrap it lightly in absorbent kitchen paper and keep in a sealed plastic container. Coriander may also be grown from seed in a semi-sunny position.

CORN (SWEET CORN) *Elote* is used as a vegetable and is normally found fresh in Mexican markets the whole year round. However, frozen corn kernels are a good substitute when fresh are not available.

CORN HUSKS *Hojas para tamal* These are the dried outer leaves of the corn on the cob. They are used to make *tamales* and can usually be bought ready dried. A good substitute is squares of waxed paper inside squares of kitchen foil.

COURGETTE BLOSSOMS *Flor de Calabaza* These are the blossoms from either courgette, pumpkin or marrow plants which are not sold commercially in Britain. I wait until my plants have pollinated and then carefully remove and freeze the blossoms until I have enough to cook.

COURGETTES *Calabacitas* are of two basic shapes in Mexico. The rounded ones which are young *spaghetti vegetal*, and the longer ones being young marrows, which are easily available in Britain.

CREAM *Crema agria* Slightly soured cream is called for in some of the recipes. If you prefer, you can make your own by adding 1 teaspoon of lime or lemon juice to 150 ml (5 fl oz) of single cream and allowing it to stand for 20 minutes. Otherwise the commercial varieties of soured cream are very good.

CUITLACOCHE Fungus which grows on the corn on the cob. It has a mushroomy flavour and is almost black when cooked. It is considered a delicacy, and may be obtained from some speciality shops.

EPAZOTE A herb used in many Mexican dishes. I have not been able to find it in the shops yet. However, I have succeeded in growing my own plant in a sheltered sunny spot in my own garden. I then dry the leaves in the autumn which carry me through the winter. Fresh coriander can substitute *epazote* sometimes.

GREEN TOMATILLOS *Tomatillos* or *Tomates Verdes* Not to be confused with ordinary green tomatoes, these are a relation of the Cape gooseberry which turn yellow when ripe. They have a transparent loose husk which must be removed before cooking. *Tomatillos* have no adequate substitute, but can occasionally be found canned. You can grow your own from seeds which may be purchased from seed merchants under the name of New Sugar Giant.

MAIZE MEAL *Masa harina* This is a specially treated type of flour made from maize. It is not yellow in colour or granular; it is just like a heavy type of flour. There is no substitute for *masa harina*, but some shops stock large packets of it.

MOLE POWDER *Polvo de mole* This is a convenient way to make *Salsa Adobada* and *Mole Poblano*—it is simply dried chillies ground to a fine powder which is then blended with stock and tomatoes to make a *salsa*. Its flavour is unique and there are no substitutes. However, if you are unable to find it, then use 1 tablespoon of ground chilli powder, mixed with 1 teaspoon of cornflour for every 50 g (2 oz) of chillies called for in your recipe (or for every two chillies).

NOPALES *Nopales* The oval fleshy paddles of the prickly pear tree are edible and are usually found already cleaned with all the sharp thorns cut off. The smaller, thinner paddles are nicer than the thicker, darker ones. They must be boiled before eating. Canned *nopales* are a good substitute but hard to find.

ONIONS *Cebollas* Spanish or English onions can be used for cooking, depending entirely on your choice. One strong feature of Mexican cooking is the use of raw onions as a garnish over cooked dishes. If you prefer a milder onion flavour, just soak the chopped or sliced onions in 1 teaspoon of salt to 150 ml (¼ pint) water for 10 minutes, then drain and use as directed. Spring onions are a good substitute.

PAW-PAW *Papaya* A huge elongated melon-shaped fruit, usually green or yellow skinned, with an orange fleshy inside. Often used as a starter for breakfast. In England tiny paw-paw can be found in speciality shops.

PECAN NUTS *Nuez encarcelada* Despite their popularity in Mexico and the United States, pecan nuts have not quite succeeded in gaining popularity over the better-established varieties. Walnuts are a good substitute though they are more oily. Pecan nuts can be found in health food shops.

PINE NUTS *Piñones* are a small nut about the size of a large grain of rice. Usually found in health food shops, they are used in desserts.

PLANTAIN *Plátano macho* These are often found in West Indian shops. They are twice as large as a large banana and for Mexican cookery must be very, very ripe, the skin black and soft to the touch. It pays to buy them ahead of time and ripen them in a warm place.

PULSES (see Beans)

PUMPKIN *Calabaza* Grows in the British Isles very successfully and it is usually large, round and yellow. Used as a dessert in Mexico, stewed with raw sugar, cinnamon and orange peel.

PUMPKIN SEEDS *Pepitas* are imported and sold in health food shops. They are usually shelled, of green-grey colouring. Eaten either roasted or salted as snacks or in sweet and savoury dishes as a thickening agent.

RICE *Arroz* Introduced into Mexico by Spain. The type used is normally the long grain white rice which is found in most supermarkets. I prefer the shops' own brand rather than the boxed type which I find is very starchy. However, should you prefer to use the boxed variety, I recommend that before using, you wash it under a hot tap for a minute to remove some of the extra starch which often makes the rice stick.

SESAME SEEDS *Ajonjolí* A fine seed, used as garnish and in small amounts in sauces. They can be obtained from health food shops.

SHRIMPS (DRIED) *Camarón seco* Can be bought, peeled and cleaned, from Chinese shops. They have a strong flavour and go well with rice.

SWEET BUNS *Biscochos* Sweet buns similar to Bath buns, Swiss rolls etc. *Pan de Muerto, Campechanas* or *Rosca de Reyes* are normally offered with hot chocolate.

SWEET POTATOES *Camote* A large tuber similar to a large red-skinned potato but not of the same family. They can be boiled or baked in their skin and their slightly sweet flesh used as a vegetable or dessert.

TOMATOES *Jitomates* Mexican tomatoes are large and irregularly shaped, having a stronger flavour than the smaller, round British or Dutch tomatoes. They are always sold ripe in the Mexican markets. I usually buy them ahead of time and allow them to ripen in a warm place before using. For the sake of convenience and economy, and because ripe tomatoes are often hard to get, I have substituted them with tinned peeled tomatoes and used fresh tomatoes only in salads and as garnish. The 'beef tomatoes' on sale in some vegetable shops are very much like the Mexican variety.

TORTILLAS (CORN) Tortillas are still hard to find and I am doing my best to get them introduced into health food shops and supermarkets. I cannot recommend the tinned ones or the dehydrated ones made with a strong yellow-coloured flour which are nothing like the real thing. Some exclusive shops now have frozen corn tortillas as good as the best in Mexico.

TORTILLAS (WHEAT) Not for sale yet in Britain. I strongly recommend you make your own (see recipe on page 40) as the ingredients are available and a little determination will produce good results.

VINEGAR *Vinagre* Malt vinegar is used in Mexico for most recipes, but it is less strong than British malt vinegar. I do not mind the difference but if you find it too strong, dilute it half and half with water. Distilled vinegar is better for pickles because it does not discolour the vegetables.

Recetas Basicas
Basic Recipes

The recipes in this chapter are those which are used again and again in Mexican cooking. Over there, of course, the ingredients are readily available in huge market places, the tortillas can be bought without any problem and the beans are a staple food, so none of these is ever missing in the home.

Living away from Mexico for so long, I have learned that the best alternative is to cook in bulk and freeze, so I can provide even complicated meals with relative ease. If you wish to prepare Mexican food often, and not take too long over it, you too can cook larger amounts of any of these recipes and freeze them. This applies particularly to recipes which take a relatively long time to prepare and cook, like the beans, tortillas and dried chilli sauces. However, I have found they all respond well to freezing and re-heating. In fact, this can often improve them. They can be the main ingredients to a meal or even the meal itself. You can also incorporate them into your menu without having to prepare it all on the day.

The tomato and *tomatillo* sauces are quick to prepare. However, I do freeze the cooked tomato sauces, because I find them very handy to produce *enchiladas*, *Huevos Rancheros* or *chilaquiles* for quick meals. The *Jalapeños en Vinagre* go with so many dishes, that I keep them in store all the time. I find that cold meats, cheese, and eggs are all enhanced by a small amount of the pickle.

The *Caldo* recipe is just for your guidance. I find that if the same water is used to boil several vegetables, and that water is then used for stock, sauces, soups or gravies, some of the vitamins are not lost, and you also stand to gain a little more flavour.

■

Masa harina

Treatment of dried maize for corn tortillas

This is a complicated method, and I for one am not keen to do it. However, many people who are desperate for corn tortillas and are unable to obtain the *masa harina*, are willing to start from scratch. But it is laborious, and it may take you a few times to master the procedure.

MAKES 1 kg (2lb) *masa harina*

1 kg (2 lb) dried maize kernels	*3 litres (5½ pints) water* *50 g (2 oz) garden lime*

Wash the kernels, then place in a large saucepan with the water. Dissolve the lime in a little cold water and strain into the pan. Bring to the boil, cover and simmer for 30 minutes. Remove from the heat and leave to cool. When cool enough to handle, rub the kernels between your hands to remove the outer skin and any 'eyes' (these are the pin-pricks at the end of each kernel where it is attached to the cob). Rinse in cold water, removing any bits left behind and washing off the lime. Place about 5 tablespoons of the maize at a time in a blender and blend to a smooth paste. Continue blending, in small amounts, until it is finished. You now have ready-mixed *masa harina* which can be used for *Tortillas de Maíz* (see opposite) or any of the *antojitos* on pages 87–109.

Tortillas de maíz

Corn tortillas

By far my favourite—I would go as far as to say that no Mexican meal is complete without them. Beans or even chillies may or may not be present, but if tortillas are there, the meal is identified as Mexican. Tortillas are served in Mexico at every meal instead of bread or even along with it. They are filling and nutritious as well as being easy to warm up, fry or casserole. Even very stale ones can be soaked in milk and then used again! You need never throw a tortilla away. They are also very versatile and can be served as cocktail snacks, starters, main courses or side dishes. The original *taco* is a warm soft tortilla filled with anything from hot rice to beans, meat or salad, then rolled up and eaten. 'Come for a *taco*' means literally come for a bite!

Making your own tortillas is fun, and the recipe is included here. If you prefer to buy them, however, you'll find fresh or frozen tortillas in some delicatessens and health food shops. In fact, as Mexican food grows in popularity, they are becoming more readily available.

To make about 45 tortillas approximately 13 cm (5 inches) in diameter, which is the most common size used, you will need:

MAKES 45

750 g (1½ lb) masa harina　　　*750 ml (1¼ pints) warm water*
175 g (6 oz) plain flour

Special equipment
Griddle or heavy-based　　　*1 tortilla press* (see diagram
　frying pan　　　　　　　　　　on page 39)
45 15 cm (6 inch) squares　　　*2 clean tea-towels*
　of waxed (not greaseproof)
　paper

Mix the flours together in a mixing bowl, then add the warm water gradually until it all sticks together leaving the sides of the bowl absolutely clean. This takes about 10 minutes with an electric mixer on slow speed or 20 minutes working by hand as in bread-making. If the sides of the bowl are sticky, add a little more *masa* and carry on mixing a little longer. (You cannot overmix *masa*.) Test the dough by squeezing between 2 fingers. If it cracks badly it may need a little more water. You will soon learn the right amount of water to use, as the temperature, humidity, age of the flour, etc., all affect it. When a small ball of dough immersed in a glass of cold water does not dissolve, the dough is ready to use. Keep the dough covered with a damp tea-towel while you press the tortillas.

Open the tortilla press and place a square of waxed paper on it, shiny side up. Take a small amount of dough, the size of a plum, and roll it in your hands, flattening it to make a thick round, about 4 cm (1½ inches) in diameter. Lay this on the waxed paper, about 1 cm (½ inch) closer to the bracket than the centre. Now place another square of waxed paper on top of the dough, shiny side down. Close the lid of the tortilla press and apply gentle pressure to the lever, holding the base of the lever with your left hand. The tortilla should be about as thin as a new penny, because it will get slightly thicker as it cooks. After you have done a few you'll know how much pressure you need—you can always press a little more if it comes out too thick. Give the tortilla a quarter or a half turn to ensure an even thickness.

Heat a dry griddle or heavy-based frying pan until a few drops of water will sizzle on it. Reduce the heat slightly and carefully peel off the top layer of waxed paper from the tortilla, keeping your hand close to the paper and taking care not to tear the dough. Gradually lower the tortilla, exposed side down, into the pan, leaving the top waxed disc in place. Take care not to do this too quickly, or trapped air bubbles will prevent even cooking. After about 1 minute, the top waxed paper will have loosened slightly and will be easy to pull off. Once removed, it can be used 3–4 more times. When the edges of the tortilla start to lift, turn it using a spatula and cook for 40 seconds. Turn again and cook for 30 seconds. If it fluffs up as you touch it with the spatula, you can congratulate yourself—you have produced a perfect tortilla. If on the other hand it does not puff up, don't be too disheartened— practice makes perfect, and even I had a hard time learning. Continue with the rest of the dough.

Stack the tortillas on a wire rack, protecting them from the wires with a tea-towel and keeping them covered with another tea-towel to prevent them drying out and becoming tough. The tortillas are

How to make your own tortilla press

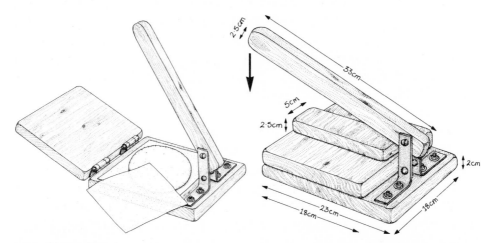

You will need:

One piece of close-grained hardwood (such as beech, as used for kitchen chopping boards) measuring 41 cm (16 in) long by 18 cm (7 in) wide by 2 cm (¾ in) thick, with the length running across the grain of the wood.
Cut this in two to give:

23 cm (9 in) by 18 cm (7 in) for the base.

18 cm (7 in) by 18 cm (7 in) for the top.

One piece measuring 17 cm (6½ in) by 5 cm (2 in) by 2.5 cm (1 in) for the block on the top.

One piece measuring 33 cm (13 in) by 2.5 cm (1 in) by 2 cm (¾ in) for the handle. For strength, the grain of the wood must run along the length of the handle.

2 x 4 cm (1½ in) butt hinges with 13 mm (½ in) screws.

2 x 13 cm (5 in) right-angle metal brackets.

5 x 4 cm (1½ in) bolts, nuts and washers.

Wood glue.

Join the base and the top together at one end with the hinges and screws. For strength, screw into the side grain of each piece of wood, as shown. Glue the block to the top piece.

Position the brackets on the base, allowing 2 cm (¾ in) gap for the handle. Drill 4 holes through the base for the bolts, and then widen the holes in the bottom of the base sufficiently to countersink the bolt heads so that the press will lie flat. Attach the brackets with the washers and nuts. For a smooth finish, file down the protruding bolt threads.

Drill a hole through the handle, 2.5 cm (1 in) from the end, for the final bolt. Secure with the washer and nut, but allow the handle to move freely.

For a neat finish, round off the sharp edges of the wood. Your tortilla press is now ready to use.

now ready to eat, fry, refrigerate or freeze. They will keep in a sealed plastic bag in the refrigerator for up to 10 days.

■

Tortillas de harina

Wheat tortillas

In the north of Mexico, near the U.S. border, the tortillas are made from wheat rather than corn, and, as a result, wheat flour tortillas—*Tortillas de Harina*—are consumed by the millions in the United States. More filling than corn tortillas, they are also more difficult to make. If overcooked they become brittle and will not fold—they must be supple and floppy when newly cooked. If you like *Tortillas de Harina*, I suggest you make more than you need and then store them. They keep well in the refrigerator in a sealed plastic bag for up to 5 days, but when frozen they will stick together unless you put waxed paper between each one. Be sure to protect them from being knocked about in the freezer as they become very brittle when frozen and will break easily. Because they do not separate easily after being frozen, thaw them at room temperature for a short time before using.

There are a number of recipes in this book for different ways of using *Tortillas de Harina*. You can make them with wholewheat flour if you want them to be more nutritious.

MAKES 14 tortillas 25 cm (10 inches) in diameter

500 g (1¼ lb) plain or wholewheat flour
1 tablespoon salt

75 g (3 oz) lard, cut up
300 ml (½ pint) hot water

Put the flour and salt in a large mixing bowl. Rub in the fat until it resembles breadcrumbs. An electric mixer makes this job easier, particularly if you wish to double the recipe. Place about half the mixture in another bowl and mix in half the hot water to make a soft, warm pliable dough. Knead on a floured board until no longer sticky, then cover with a warm damp tea-towel. Take about 50 g (2 oz) of the dough, shape it into a ball, then flatten it. Place on a floured board, and with a floured rolling pin roll it out until it is thin enough to see the board through the pastry. (This requires determination and gets easier with experience.) If your tortilla is not perfectly round, don't worry, just use a dinner plate of the desired size and cut around it. Carry on cutting the tortillas, putting them on a floured tray and making sure there is enough flour on them so they do not stick together. When you finish the first batch, mix the remainder of the mixture into a warm dough, incorporating any remaining scraps of dough. Make into tortillas in the same way as for the first batch.

Heat a griddle or heavy-based frying pan until a few drops of water will sizzle on it, then reduce the heat slightly. Pick up a tortilla and lay it in the palm of your hand, then place it carefully in the pan. Leave for about 30 seconds. As it cooks it will thicken a little. When it starts to bubble, turn it over and cook for 10 seconds. At this stage the tortilla will have lost its transparency, but will still look very pale. This doesn't matter, as it will cook a little more when you warm it up. If on the other hand you overcook it, it will become dry and brittle and will not be supple enough to fold. Stack the tortillas on a wire rack, protecting them from the wires with a tea-towel and keeping them covered with another tea-towel, to prevent too much moisture escaping as they cool.

When all the tortillas are cooked, allow to cool, then place a square of waxed paper between each one to prevent them from sticking together. Store in a sealed polythene bag. Wheat tortillas are used in the same way as corn ones and are reheated in the same manner. Never eat them cold, except when they have been deep fried.

■

Maíz cacahuazintle

Hominy

Maíz cacahuazintle is considered to be a superior quality of maize. It is treated with lime in order to remove the skin and speed up cooking. When the base of the kernel is also removed and the maize boiled, it bursts open and looks like small white flowers. *Cacahuazintle* is a popular addition to soups, especially as the 'flowers' look so pretty. It is occasionally possible to find canned *maíz cacahuazintle*, but you will almost certainly have to use dried maize instead. Garden lime is available from ironmongers. Preparation starts two days in advance.

MAKES 750 g–1 kg (1½–2 lb)

450 g (1 lb) dried maize   *1½ litres (2½ pints) water*
  kernels   *1 teaspoon garden lime*

Wash the kernels, then soak them in the cold water overnight. Drain and place in a saucepan with more cold water and bring to the boil. Cover and simmer for about 2 hours. Dilute the lime in a little cold water, strain onto the maize, then boil for 10 minutes. Remove from the heat, cover and leave for about 1 hour.

Drain off the lime water, and wash the kernels in warm water 3–4 times. Rub the kernels between your thumbs and forefingers to peel off the transparent skin. If the pin-prick base is still attached to the kernels, cut that off as well. (Often the maize has been cut off the cob in such a way that the kernels have no base.) Rinse again and use it in soup. Any remaining can be frozen.

■

Frijoles

Beans

In Mexico to be on the bread line is to be on *frijoles y tortillas* (beans and tortillas). Beans are the staple food and the source of protein for the majority of people. They are eaten morning, noon and night—simply stewed or lightly fried and re-fried. They have other uses: as a filling for *tacos* and *tortas*, in soups and added to meat stews like *Chili con Carne*. They are delicious and nutritious, contributing protein, iron and fibre to the diet. Each extra cooking actually improves the taste, as the liquid is reduced and the flavour becomes more concentrated.

Beans are always best one or two days after cooking. They keep well in the refrigerator for up to eight days and longer if re-fried often. They heat up easily and are an excellent stand-by. Because of the lengthy initial cooking time, it is a good idea to cook more than you need for one meal, say 450 g (1 lb) at one time; this will feed about eight people or six if the beans are to be re-fried.

It is essential when using red kidney beans to cook them at a rolling boil for the first 15 minutes of cooking time in order to neutralize the poisonous substances they contain. (In fact, Mexicans always cook all their beans at a rolling boil.)

SERVES 8

450 g (1 lb) dried black
pinto, red kidney or
rosecoco (borlotti) beans
2 cloves garlic, skewered on
cocktail stick for easy
removal

2 teaspoons salt
2 teaspoons granulated
sugar
2 tablespoons cooking oil
1 onion, chopped
2 green chillies

Examine the beans carefully, a handful at a time, for small stones, then place in a large saucepan. Cover the beans with cold water and wash them, changing the water several times until it is clear. Drain, then cover the beans with fresh cold water, to come about 15 cm (6 inches) above them. Leave to soak overnight. (Alternatively, after washing, place the beans in cold water, bring to the boil and boil uncovered for 10 minutes, then cover, remove from the heat and leave to stand for about 2 hours.)

When the beans are ready to cook, they will have absorbed the water and doubled in size. Top up with more water. (If you have boiled the beans rather than soaking them overnight, then top up with boiling water.) Add the garlic, and bring to the boil. Partly cover the pan and cook at a rolling boil for up to 3 hours, or until the beans feel very soft between the fingers. Top up with boiling water frequently—*never* use cold water on hot beans. Discard the garlic cloves and cocktail stick, add the salt and sugar and simmer gently for 10 minutes.

Heat the cooking oil, and fry half the onion until golden. Add the oil, onion and chillies to the beans, and simmer for 15 minutes or until the bean liquid thickens. To hasten this process, you can mash a few beans against the side of the pot to act as a thickening agent. Use immediately or allow to cool, discard the chillies (unless you want the beans to be hot), cover and refrigerate, or freeze for up to 3 months. To reheat, place the beans in a covered casserole and bake in a preheated oven at 180°C, 350°F, Gas Mark 4 for about 30 minutes. Garnish with the remaining onion if desired.

VARIATION:

Add 50 g (2 oz) grated cheese to the beans before reheating them.

USING TINNED BEANS

Tinned beans may be used if time is short. They will have more flavour if cooked in the following way:

2 tablespoons cooking oil
1 onion, finely chopped
2 cloves garlic, crushed
4 × 400 g (14 oz) cans cooked
  red kidney beans

2 green chillies, chopped
½ teaspoon sugar
½ teaspoon salt

Heat the oil in a frying pan and fry the onion and garlic until golden. Add the beans and their liquid and all the remaining ingredients. Simmer over medium heat until the liquid is reduced and the consistency of the beans is that of thick porridge.

■

Frijoles refritos

Re-fried beans

Re-fried beans make a good side dish with any Mexican meal. The texture is similar to that of mashed potatoes, but not quite as fluffy. So unless you know that people will enjoy the re-fried beans on their own, always include in your menu either *Salsa Típica* or dishes like *enchiladas* or *Chiles Rellenos* which have lots of sauce.

Re-fried beans must be mashed into a purée. You can either mash them as they are frying, which is the traditional way, or purée them beforehand in a food processor or liquidizer.

SERVES 4

2 tablespoons cooking oil
½ onion, very roughly
  chopped
½ quantity Frijoles

To garnish
½ onion, finely chopped
8 Totopos (see page 56)
  (optional)

Heat the oil in a large, heavy frying pan and fry the large onion pieces until well coloured. Discard the onion, add the beans and fry over medium heat, stirring frequently, and mashing with a potato masher (unless already mashed). The beans will tend to stick at the bottom and on the sides. If they stick when you are stirring, they require more oil. Make a well in the centre of the mixture and add another tablespoon of oil.

When the beans are thick, they are ready for spreading on *tostadas* or *tortas*, or for eating as a side dish, but if you like them truly re-fried, then carry on stirring until they stick together like a paste and you can actually toss them in the frying pan. Garnish with chopped onion and *totopos* and eat hot.

Should you want to re-fry these beans again, add a little water to soften them and then proceed as above.

■

Salsa de tomate verde

Green tomatillo sauce

The *tomatillo* is a special variety of fruit, a relative of the Cape gooseberry. It has a thin papery skin and when it ripens it is yellow, not red. Despite the similarity in names, it is not related to the tomato, and the taste of a green *tomatillo* is distinctly different from that of an ordinary green tomato. *Tomatillos* are often grown in greenhouses, and occasionally speciality shops stock tinned *tomatillos*. You might even find tins of the ready-made sauce. (If you wish to grow your own, New Sugar Giant is the best one to choose from British seedsmen's lists.)

Salsa de Tomate Verde can be served raw as a garnish for *tacos*, or cooked as a sauce for *tamales*, pork stews and other savoury dishes. I prefer it cooked because it has a lot more flavour. This sauce refrigerates well, and stews made with it will freeze equally well.

MAKES enough sauce for 10 *tamales*, and some left over to add before serving

2 × 275 g (10 oz) cans green
  tomatillos or 450 g (1 lb)
  fresh tomatillos, skinned
1 tablespoon cooking oil
½ onion, chopped

12 sprigs coriander
1 chicken stock cube
¼ teaspoon ground black
  pepper

To make the raw sauce, combine all the ingredients except the oil and liquidize for 1 minute. Serve cold.

To make the cooked sauce, if you are using fresh *tomatillos* peel and place them in a saucepan. Cover with water, bring to the boil and simmer for about 5 minutes. Heat the oil in a heavy-based frying pan and fry the onion for about 2 minutes. In a blender, purée the cooked or tinned *tomatillos* and their liquid with the remaining ingredients. Add to the frying pan, and simmer for about 25 minutes, until it starts to thicken.

Salsa para enchiladas

Cooked tomato sauce

This *salsa* is the base of most Mexican sauces and indeed of many Mexican dishes. It is so simple and tasty that you can use it for breakfast, lunch or dinner dishes. I make several batches at once and freeze it so that we can have *Huevos Rancheros* for breakfast with no difficulty. It calls for grilled and peeled tomatoes which in Mexico are cheap and plentiful; but in Britain, where fresh tomatoes are more expensive, you can substitute tinned peeled tomatoes. Bulgarian ones, which have been grilled before tinning, have a particularly good flavour and colour.

MAKES approximately 1 litre (1¾ pints)

2 tablespoons cooking oil	3 tablespoons tomato purée
1 onion, finely chopped	4 sprigs coriander
4 green chillies	2 chicken stock cubes
2 × 500 g (1¼ lb) cans peeled tomatoes and their juice	¼ teaspoon ground black pepper
	pinch of sugar

Heat the oil in a heavy-based frying pan and fry the onion and chillies for about 2 minutes. Squash the tomatoes in a food processor or with a potato masher, and add to the pan with the remaining ingredients. Simmer for about 20 minutes. The sauce is ready when the chillies are a dull green colour and soft, and the mixture has thickened. Discard the sprigs of coriander and chillies. If you wish this sauce to have more 'bite', chop up the chillies and return them to the sauce.

■

Salsa típica

Raw tomato sauce

Salsa Típica is used as a filling for *tacos*, a topping for *tostadas*, a garnish for *antojitos* or a side dish with any bean, rice or meat dish. Its preparation is very simple, and there is no cooking involved. The one shortcoming of this sauce is that it does not keep long after you have prepared it. So either use it all up, or, if you have a lot left over, fry it in a little oil to turn it into *Salsa para Enchiladas*, which you can then pour over *Huevos Rancheros* for breakfast!

SERVES 4 (makes approximately 300 ml/½ pint)

4 ripe, firm tomatoes   *juice of ½ lemon*
8 sprigs coriander   *½ teaspoon salt*
¼ onion, finely chopped   *¼ teaspoon pepper*
2 green chillies, finely
*   chopped*

Chop the tomatoes, discarding the dark circles at the top. Pull the leaves off the thick coriander stems. Discard the stems and finely chop the leaves. Mix all the ingredients together and allow to marinate for about 15 minutes before serving.

■

Salsa de jitomate asado

Grilled tomato sauce

This sauce, like *Salsa Típica*, is used for topping *tacos* and *antojitos*, for adding to *Frijoles Refritos*, or simply for filling soft warm tortillas. Grilling the tomatoes adds flavour; and because they are then either mashed or blended in a liquidizer, the texture of the sauce is smoother than *Salsa Típica*.

SERVES 4

4 ripe, firm tomatoes
2 green chillies
8 sprigs coriander
1/4 onion

juice of 1/2 lemon
1/2 teaspoon salt
1/4 teaspoon ground black
   pepper

Grill the tomatoes and chillies, turning frequently, until the skins are blistered. Peel off the blistered skin and remove stalks and seeds from the chillies. Put all ingredients in a blender and blend at high speed for 30 seconds. Keep refrigerated until required.

If you prefer not to use a blender, pound the tomatoes and chillies together with a pestle and mortar, finely chop the onion and coriander and add together with the other ingredients.

■

Salsa de chile chilpotle

Smoked jalapeño sauce

Smoked *jalapeños*, or *chilpotles* as they are called in Mexico, are a delicacy, and I make them into this sauce to use instead of gravy for meat and *tacos*. You can buy *chilpotles* loose or in tins—because they are dried their flavour is very smoky.

MAKES approximately 500 ml (18 fl oz)

4 chilpotle chillies or
   1 × 100 g (4 oz) can
   chilpotles
150 ml (1/4 pint) water

1 clove garlic
1 teaspoon cooking oil
1/2 quantity Salsa para
   Enchiladas

OPPOSITE: **1** bananas, **2** corn, **3** pumpkin, **4** coconut, **5** sweet potato, **6** pineapple, **7** plantain, **8** cho-cho, **9** dried corn husks, **10** dried chilli *mulato*, **11** dried chilli *ancho*, **12** dried chilli *pasilla*, **13** mild green chillies, **14** dried chillies, **15** strawberries, **16** dried corn kernels, **17** ripe mango, **18** lime, **19** hot green chillies, **20** courgettes, **21** cloves, **22** Scotch bonnets, **23** cinnamon sticks, **24** bay leaves, **25** beef tomatoes, **26** capsicum pepper, **27** red capsicum pepper, **28** fresh coriander, **29** shelled peanuts, **30** pumpkin seeds.

If you are using tinned *chilpotles*, blend the sauce with the contents of the tin and use it as suggested below.

If using loose *chilpotles*, heat them in a dry frying pan until supple, then remove the stalks and seeds. Bring the water to the boil, remove from the heat and soak the *chilpotles* in it for about 1 hour. Liquidize the garlic, *chilpotles* and their liquid at top speed for 1½ minutes. Heat the oil in a frying pan and fry the mixture for about 10 minutes. When cool, add it to the sauce and use as a sauce for meats, beans or vegetables.

■

Salsa borracha

Tipsy sauce

Salsa Borracha is always served with *Barbacoa* (see page 159) but it goes well with other *antojitos* in much the same manner as *Salsa Típica*. Its name is derived from the fact that, instead of water or stock, it is prepared with *pulque* (a milky alcoholic drink made from the *agave* plant). But when *pulque* is not available, beer or tequila will do. There are a number of different types of dried chilli you could use for this sauce, but I have specified *cascabel* chilli which hasn't been used elsewhere in this book, so that you could try out a new type of chilli. If you can only get some other variety, however, simply treat it in the same way.

MAKES about 300 ml (½ pint)

10 cascabel chillies
150 ml (¼ pint) beer
2 ripe tomatoes
1 clove garlic

½ teaspoon salt
pinch of sugar
1 tablespoon cooking oil

PREVIOUS PAGES: Tortillas produced on a home-made press. The corn tortillas in the basket were made from the *masa harina* (maize meal) in the bowl, after mixing with water and plain flour to make hand-patted balls of dough. In the pan is a cooked wheat tortilla.
OPPOSITE: Dried red kidney beans, black beans, pinto beans and (bottom) borlotti beans; re-fried pinto beans of spreading consistency (page 44); and, in the bowl, cooked borlotti beans (page 42).

Heat the chillies on a dry hot heavy-based pan until they soften and you can remove the stalks and seeds. Warm the beer (without boiling), remove from the heat, and soak the chillies in it for 1 hour. Grill the tomatoes and garlic until the tomato skins blister. Peel the tomatoes and place them together with the garlic, chillies, beer, salt and sugar in a blender. Blend at high speed for 1½ minutes. Heat the oil in a frying pan and fry the mixture in it for about 5 minutes, stirring occasionally. Serve at room temperature.

Salsa adobada

Dried chilli sauce

This is one of the many versions of sauce that can be used in making *tamales*. I have chosen it because it is relatively quick and simple as well as very tasty. It also makes a terrific barbecue sauce for spare ribs (see page 153) and a good base for *Chile con Carne* (see page 146).

MAKES enough sauce for 10 *tamales*, and a little extra to add before serving

3 cloves garlic
5 cm (2 inch) stick cinnamon
1 large onion, coarsely
chopped
2 tablespoons cooking oil
6 tablespoons tomato purée
1 litre (1¾ pt) chicken stock

2 chicken stock cubes
1 tablespoon cooking chocolate,
finely grated
6 tablespoons mole powder or
3 tablespoons chilli powder
½ teaspoon sugar

Put the garlic, cinnamon and onion in a blender and blend to a paste. Heat the oil in a large saucepan and pour in the onion paste. Cook, stirring constantly, for about 5 minutes or until it starts to look dry. Add the remaining ingredients and simmer until it thickens, about 20 minutes.

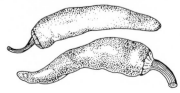

Sazón para carnes, aves y pescado

Meat, poultry and fish seasoning

This seasoning is more or less standard for any meat, poultry or fish you might be cooking. Marinating meat often improves the flavour of the finished dish, as well as tenderizing the meat. In the case of fish and shellfish, I always substitute lime juice for vinegar, and this also works for chicken.

MAKES enough for 450 g (1 lb) meat, poultry or fish

3 teaspoons malt vinegar (or lime juice)
¼ teaspoon salt
⅛ teaspoon ground black pepper

pinch of sugar
1 clove garlic
½ onion, roughly chopped

Mix together all the ingredients, crushing the garlic for a stronger flavour, or leave it whole. Pour the seasoning over the prepared meat or fish and leave to marinate for at least 1 hour. The meat or fish can now be roasted, simmered or barbecued and the stock or gravy will be well-flavoured.

■

Conserva de tomate verde y jalapeños

Tomatillo and jalapeño chillies relish

This relish can be used with meats in a similar way to mint sauce. It is very hot, but if you prefer it mild, substitute 2 green peppers for the green chillies. It bottles well but must be kept in the refrigerator.

MAKES 200 ml (7 fl oz)

200 g (7 oz) can tomatillos or 8 fresh tomatillos, loose skins removed
12 green chillies
1½ teaspoons cinnamon

75 g (3 oz) granulated sugar
65 ml (2½ fl oz) malt vinegar
1 onion, quartered
1 teaspoon salt

Put all the ingredients in a blender and blend at top speed for 40 seconds. Pour into a saucepan and simmer, stirring frequently, for about 20 minutes until it thickens. Allow to cool, then bottle, seal and store. Keeps for up to 1 month.

■

Jalapeños en vinagre

Jalapeño-style pickles

This is an appetizing, healthy-looking vinaigrette which is deceptively hot! However, you can control the amount of sting in it by reducing the number of chillies. It goes particularly well with *frijoles*, *tortas*, *empanadas*, *quesadillas* and with all *antojitos*. You can put it on the table for those who like really hot food, without making the non-chilli lovers feel bad, so it is a useful standby. I often add it in small amounts to cooked food. It will keep in or out of the fridge for weeks. Be sure to wear gloves when handling chillies and cut the chillies on absorbent kitchen paper.

MAKES 750 ml (1¼ pints)

4 tablespoons cooking oil
12 jalapeño chillies (or green chillies), sliced lengthwise
2 large carrots, cut into 2½ cm (1 inch) sticks
2 large onions, sliced
½ medium cauliflower, divided into florets
1 red pepper, sliced
¼ teaspoon dried oregano
¼ teaspoon dried marjoram

¼ teaspoon dried thyme
¼ teaspoon whole cumin
¼ teaspoon aniseed
1 tablespoon salt
1 teaspoon ground black pepper
2 bay leaves
½ teaspoon garlic powder
1 tablespoon granulated sugar
600 ml (1 pint) distilled vinegar

Heat the oil in a large saucepan and fry the chillies and vegetables for about 2 minutes, stirring. Remove to a mixing bowl. Add the remaining ingredients to the pan, bring to the boil, then pour immediately over the vegetables and allow to cool, uncovered. Bottle, seal and store. Refrigerate only after the jars have been opened. Keeps for up to 3 months.

Caldo

Stock

Soup is a must in Mexican meals—even when the midday sun is beating down! Creamed soups are popular, but this stock is used as the base for a wide range of soups, from consommé to pasta, vegetables, rice and finally meaty soups. Because so many Mexican dishes are made with boiled meats, the use of a lot of stocks is not surprising, since it kills two birds with one stone. The meat is used separately, thus providing another dish. At any rate, a good *caldo* is a must, and though it is easy to produce, the addition of seasoning and vegetables always improves it.

Whether or not you use meat like a whole chicken or a piece of beef, never throw away any bones from roasts. All the trimmings and leftover gravy and vegetables could be the reason behind your success as a cook!

MAKES about 1 litre (1¾ pints)

1½ kg (3½ lb) chicken and giblets or other meats with bones
2¼ litres (4 pints) water or vegetable stock
1 teaspoon salt
½ teaspoon ground black pepper
3 tablespoons malt vinegar

2 chicken stock cubes
4 sticks celery (including leaves), halved
2 carrots, unpeeled
4 cabbage leaves
2 turnips, unpeeled
3 cloves garlic
3 large onions

Wash the chicken well, removing any feathers, the parson's nose and any loose skin. Wash the giblets, removing any yellow parts, and check that the chicken liver has no green staining on it. If it does, discard the liver altogether.

Put the chicken and all the ingredients in a large saucepan, bring to the boil and skim off any foam that forms on the surface. Cover and boil for 1 hour, then test for readiness by pricking the drumstick with a fork. If only clear liquid oozes out and the drumstick is loose and moves easily, remove the chicken. Remove and discard the vegetables. Or, if they are to be eaten, peel and quarter them. Increase the heat and boil the stock rapidly, for 20 minutes, uncovered, to reduce it. Strain and cool. When the grease settles on the top, spoon it out. If time allows, refrigerate the stock overnight. In the morning the grease will have congealed on the top and so you can easily dispose of it. The stock is now ready to use in soups and sauces, and the meat can be used separately.

Botanas

Hors d'Oeuvres and Starters

Botanas have a special place in the Mexican way of life because they keep the guest going until the food arrives! This is because meals are served at no set time in Mexico. The fact that you are asked to arrive at certain times does not really mean you are actually expected then, or that you will be fed soon after. It just means you will be welcome, you can come when you are ready, and being late is quite acceptable. For this reason, *botanas* are very varied and do not necessarily have to be light—your appetite is unlikely to be spoiled, as you will have ample time to acquire another appetite before the meal is finally served!

With the exception of *Crepas de Cuitlacoche*, the cocktails and one or two others, all the dishes in this chapter can be eaten by hand. So be sure to have lots of paper napkins handy, as some *botanas* may prove a little large for the European 'good manners'. But fear not, they will not prove too large the second time round although you might have to start your guests off by showing them what to do.

In this chapter I have also included some of the famous *antojitos* which can be served with drinks before the meal or as a starter to the meal.

Nachos

Tortilla chips with cheese and chillies

Nachos are actually more of an American dish, but they still retain a Mexican identity. They are easy to make at home, with little last-minute preparation required—you just pop them into the oven as your guests arrive. Serve as an hors d'oeuvre.

SERVES 6

oil for deep frying
10 corn tortillas
100 g (4 oz) Cheddar cheese,
  coarsely grated
50 g (2 oz) Mozzarella
  cheese, coarsely grated

4 jalapeño chillies, cut into
  strips or 4 tablespoons
  Jalapeños en Vinagre,
  drained

Heat the oil in a deep fryer to 180°C, 350°F. Meanwhile, stack the tortillas and cut into quarters. Place half in the frying basket and carefully lower it into the hot oil, lifting it out for a moment if the bubbling becomes too fierce. Shaking the basket, fry the chips for about 2 minutes or until just golden brown and crisp. Remove and drain on absorbent kitchen paper. Repeat the process with the remaining half. Spread the chips over baking trays and sprinkle with the grated cheeses, chillies or pickles and bake in a preheated oven at 220°C, 425°F, Gas Mark 7 for 8 minutes or until the cheese melts. Serve immediately, as they do not keep for very long.

Totopos

Corn tortilla chips

Totopos are seldom sold commercially in Mexico, because it is a good way to use stale tortillas, and every home in Mexico has an adequate supply of these. They are ideal for dips. Stronger than potato crisps, cheaper than biscuits, they can be flavoured with salt, cayenne or Parmesan cheese—or all three. They are also the basic ingredient in *chilaquiles*, the garnish for *Frijoles Refritos* and the base of *Sopa de Tortilla*. *Totopos* can be made from wheat or corn tortillas, but the wheat ones are much more brittle, and I would not recommend using them for any other dish. Serve with drinks.

SERVES 4

oil for deep frying
10 tortillas
1½ teaspoons salt

2 tablespoons grated Parmesan
cheese (optional)
1 teaspoon cayenne (optional)

Heat the oil in a deep fryer to 180°C, 350°F. Meanwhile, stack the tortillas and cut into quarters. Cut the quarters in half, making 8 triangles. Place half in the frying basket and carefully lower it into the hot oil, lifting it out for a moment if the bubbling becomes too fierce. Shaking the basket, fry the chips for about 2 minutes, until golden brown and crisp. Remove and drain on absorbent kitchen paper. Repeat the process with the remaining half. While still hot, sprinkle with salt, cheese and/or cayenne. Serve cold.

To store, place the cold chips in an airtight container and keep for up to 1 week. If they lose their crispness, just place in a hot oven for 5 minutes.

VARIATION:

Mix a few *totopos* into a tossed salad just before serving: they add colour, flavour and texture.

Cacahuates enchilados

Peppered peanuts

Cacahuates are very popular in Mexico. They are sold in their shell, or salted, roasted, peppered and sugared, and they are also ground and used in sauces. They make an hors d'oeuvre with a difference!

SERVES 6

225 g (8 oz) salted roasted
  peanuts

½ teaspoon cayenne

Mix the salted roasted peanuts and cayenne thoroughly and offer in bowls with drinks.

Pepitas de calabaza

Pumpkin seeds

Pepitas are considered humble fare in Mexico, and you often see Indian women selling them in the markets for a few pennies, roasted and ready salted. Part of the fun of eating *Pepitas* is having to munch away to get at the seed inside the husk, which is then discarded. But they are also sold ready-salted and husked. In Britain, health food shops stock hulled pumpkin seeds, which you can roast and salt in the following way. They are a good alternative to roasted peanuts.

SERVES 4

1 teaspoon cooking oil   ½ teaspoon salt
100 g (4 oz) pumpkin seeds

Heat the oil in a frying pan, add the pumpkin seeds, cover tightly and cook for about 2 minutes over high heat, shaking the frying pan to prevent burning. Lower the heat, uncover and stir constantly for 1 minute. The seeds will bulge and start to pop. Scatter the seeds over absorbent kitchen paper and sprinkle with salt while still hot. Serve cold with drinks. Stored in an airtight container, they will keep for about 2 weeks.

■

Frijoles con queso

Bean dip

Beans are a good stand-by in the Mexican kitchen, and here they are made into an excellent snack, served with either corn or wheat tortilla *totopos*.

SERVES 6

225 g (8 oz) Frijoles Refritos   1 green chilli, finely chopped
100 g (4 oz) cream cheese   ¼ onion, finely chopped
25 ml (1 fl oz) double cream   1 teaspoon lemon juice
2 tomatoes, finely chopped   pinch of salt and ground black
1 tablespoon finely chopped   pepper
   coriander

The beans should be the consistency of thick porridge and still warm. Stir in all ingredients and mix well. Serve at room temperature with *totopos*.

■

Guacamole

Avocado dip

Guacamole is a popular and versatile way of serving avocado. It makes an excellent hors d'oeuvre served with *totopos* and drinks, an attractive garnish, a delicious filling for *tacos*, or a side dish for any other Mexican dish. This dish also has the virtue of making an avocado pear go a long way. The flavour of the fresh coriander is very distinctive and enhances the delicate flavour of the avocado, so if fresh coriander is unobtainable, it's best to do without rather than try to find a substitute.

The traditional way of making *Guacamole* is by chopping all the vegetables very fine and adding the avocado pulp which has been mashed with a fork, but for the sake of speed a food processor may be used to do the chopping.

SERVES 6 for hors d'oeuvres (makes approximately 600 ml/1 pint)

2 firm ripe tomatoes, finely chopped
4 sprigs fresh coriander, finely chopped
½ onion, finely chopped
2 green chillies, finely chopped

juice of ½ lime or lemon
¾ teaspoon salt
½ teaspoon ground black pepper
1 very large or 2 medium-size ripe avocados

Mix all the ingredients together, except the avocado(s), not more than 2 hours ahead of time. Cover with cling film until required. This will draw the juices from the onions and tomatoes and thus provide the liquid required to make the *Guacamole* creamy. About 30 minutes before required, cut the avocado(s) in half, reserve the stone(s), and spoon out the flesh, scraping the skin clean. Mash with a fork and add to the vegetable mixture. Put in a serving dish, placing the stone in the centre of the dish to prevent the avocado from going black. Cover with cling film until required.

Cocktail de espárragos y aguacate

Asparagus and avocado cocktail

Asparagus and avocado combine here to make a mouthwatering starter.

SERVES 4

2 tablespoons mayonnaise
1 tablespoon tomato ketchup
1/2 teaspoon Worcestershire
   sauce
1/4 teaspoon Tabasco
3 tablespoons single cream
1/4 teaspoon salt

1/4 teaspoon black pepper
2 avocados
350 g (12 oz) can asparagus
   tips
2 spring onions, finely chopped
1 lettuce, finely shredded

Mix together the mayonnaise, ketchup, Worcestershire sauce, Tabasco, cream, salt and pepper and leave for 20 minutes. Just before serving cut the avocados in half, discarding the stones. Cut the asparagus tips in four, arrange on the avocado halves, then pour the sauce over them and garnish with chopped spring onions. Serve on the shredded lettuce.

■

Cocktail de aguacate

Avocado cocktail

This makes an excellent vegetarian starter. The sauce can be made well in advance and stored in the refrigerator.

SERVES 4

8 tablespoons tomato
   ketchup
50 g (2 oz) cream cheese
juice of 1/2 lime or lemon
1/4 teaspoon Worcestershire
   sauce
1/4 teaspoon Tabasco

1/4 teaspoon ground black
   pepper
1/2 lettuce, finely shredded
2 ripe avocados
4 spring onions, finely chopped,
   to garnish

Mix together all the ingredients except the avocados, spring onions and lettuce. Cover and chill in the refrigerator for at least 1 hour. Just before serving, slice each avocado into eight, then remove the peel without breaking the slices (it is easier to work this way rather than peeling first). Divide the shredded lettuce between individual cups, lay the avocado slices on top and spoon the sauce over. Garnish with chopped spring onions.

■

Cocktail de ostiones

Oyster cocktail

This makes a sophisticated starter which is also suitable for prawns or lobster. You will need about 275 g (10 oz) shelled weight of either of these fish.

SERVES 4

*120 ml (4 fl oz) tomato
  ketchup
½ teaspoon Tabasco
1 teaspoon Worcestershire
  sauce*

*juice of 2 limes
24 fresh oysters, well chilled
85 ml (3 fl oz) dry white wine
½ lettuce, finely shredded*

Mix the sauces, lime juice and wine together and leave for 20 minutes. Crack open the oysters and scoop out with their juice. Arrange in individual cocktail dishes lined with shredded lettuce, and pour over the marinade. Serve cold with cheese biscuits.

■

Seviche

Fish marinated in lime juice

In this dish the fish is not cooked, but the action of the acidic lime juice marinade has the same effect. The fish has to be cut into small pieces so that the lime can penetrate it. Also, it is important to use lime and not lemon juice, which is slightly sweeter and not quite as effective. Red snapper is the fish most commonly served in this manner, but prawns, lobster tails, or any other mollusc, or a mixture, can be treated in the same way. Preparation starts the night before and it will keep for up to 4 hours after the final mixture is ready. It makes an excellent starter by itself, or a filling for avocados with cheese crackers as garnish.

SERVES 4

225 g (8 oz) cod or haddock fillets, skinned and boned
juice of 1 orange
juice of 3 limes
6 spring onions, thinly sliced
2 tablespoons olive oil
2 tablespoons tomato ketchup
½ teaspoon Worcestershire sauce
dash of Tabasco

¼ teaspoon dried oregano
¼ teaspoon salt
¼ teaspoon ground black pepper
2 ripe tomatoes, finely chopped
8 sprigs coriander
1 green chilli, very finely chopped
2 ripe avocados
cheese biscuits, to garnish

Remove any bones you can find, then cut the fish into very small, bite-size pieces and place in a non-metal container. Pour the juices over the fish and add the spring onions. Stir well, cover and refrigerate for at least 3 hours or overnight. The fish will change colour and become very white instead of translucent. One hour before serving, add all the remaining ingredients, except the avocados. Stir and leave to marinate until required. Just before serving, cut the avocados in half, remove stones and place on individual dishes. Fill them with the *Seviche* and garnish with cheese biscuits.

■

Quesadillas Mexicanas

Tortillas with melted cheese

In Mexico, you'll see everyone eating *quesadillas* in the open air. The street vendors make them in the traditional way, filling the tortillas when they are still raw and then shallow-frying them, creating an irresistible aroma. This recipe has been adjusted to using cooked tortillas, which are much more convenient, and can be eaten as a snack or even a light lunch or supper. *Quesadillas* also freeze well in a plastic container.

SERVES 4

8 cooked corn   100 g (4 oz) sliced cheese
  tortillas   (any type)

If the tortillas are cold, heat them in a dry hot frying pan for about 30 seconds, then remove. Place a slice of cheese on one half of the warm tortilla, fold over the other half to cover the cheese and secure with a cocktail stick. When all the tortillas have been filled, heat a heavy-based frying pan until a few drops of water sizzle on it. Cook the *quesadillas* on one side for about 45 seconds, turn them and cook for another 45 seconds. As soon as the cheese melts, they are ready to eat and should be served immediately.

VARIATION:

If you want a little variety, you can use cream cheese instead, with a little chopped onion and some chilli strips.

USING FROZEN QUESADILLAS:

Place the frozen *quesadillas* in a hot, heavy-based frying pan for 1½ minutes on each side. For larger numbers, place the *quesadillas* on a baking tray, cover tightly with kitchen foil and bake on the top shelf of a preheated oven at 190°C, 375°F, Gas Mark 5 for 15 minutes. Serve with *Guacamole* and *Salsa Típica*.

■

Quesadillas Sonorenses

Tortillas filled with cheese

This dish comes from *Sonora*, the Mexican state that borders with the U.S.A. It is from here that much of the Mexican food has crossed the *Rio Grande* into the United States. The recipe calls for wheat tortillas which are more common than corn tortillas in northern Mexico. To make these *quesadillas*, you only need half as many wheat tortillas as corn ones. When served with *Salsa Típica* and *Frijoles Refritos* they make an appetizing lunch or light supper.

SERVES 4

4 wheat tortillas
175 g (6 oz) Cheddar cheese,
  coarsely grated

about 4 green chillies, cut into
  strips
1/2 onion, sliced

Heat a dry frying pan, until a few drops of water will sizzle on it. Place a tortilla on the pan, and lower the heat to medium. Divide the cheese into 4 portions and place one portion on half of the tortilla, together with some onion rings and chilli strips. Fold the tortilla in half and cook for 1 minute. Turn it over and cook for about 45 seconds until the cheese melts.

For larger numbers, warm the tortillas in the same way, fill them and fold in half, securing with a cocktail stick. Place on an ungreased baking tray and cover tightly with kitchen foil. Bake in a preheated oven at 180°C, 350°F, Gas Mark 4 for about 15 minutes. Just before serving, remove the cocktail sticks.

■

Quesadillas de chorizo y papa

Tortillas filled with chorizo and potato

Another way to fill *quesadillas*, using either spicy sausage (see page 156) or cheese. An alternative filling is *cuitlacoche*.

SERVES 4

1 teaspoon cooking oil
1/2 onion, finely chopped
1 green chilli, chopped (optional)
100 g (4 oz) Chorizo, crumbled,
  or 150 g (6 oz) Cheddar cheese,
  coarsely grated

225 g (8 oz) potatoes, boiled
  and mashed
salt and ground black pepper
8 cooked corn tortillas

Heat the oil and fry the onion until golden and the chilli, if used. Add the *Chorizo* and fry, stirring until it has rendered some fat and is dark red. Add potatoes and season with salt and pepper. (If using cheese, remove the pan from the heat and stir in.) Fill and heat up the tortillas as for *Quesadillas Mexicanas* (see page 62).

Quesadillas de San Luis

Tortillas with chillies and cheese

Quesadillas de San Luis take their name from *San Luis Potosi*, a northern state of Mexico where they grind *ancho* chillies and mix them into the maize dough used for their *quesadillas* filled with cheese. This has the effect of flavouring the dough and colouring it a dark reddish brown. When served with traditional *quesadillas*, alternating the plain with the coloured, the dish looks most attractive. It makes a good hors d'oeuvre or starter garnished with radishes and shredded lettuce. Preparation must start two hours before required.

SERVES 4

2 ancho chillies
150 ml (¼ pint) boiling
   water
150 g (5 oz) masa harina
1 teaspoon baking powder
1 teaspoon salt
50 g (2 oz) plain flour
25 g (1 oz) lard

2 tablespoons double cream
100 g (4 oz) Cheddar cheese,
   grated
2 green chillies, sliced
   lengthwise (optional)
oil for shallow frying

Heat the *ancho* chillies in a dry heavy-based frying pan, turning them until they soften. Discard the seeds and stalks, then soak the chillies in the boiling water for 1 hour. Meanwhile, mix together the dry ingredients, rub in the lard and stir in the cream. Put the chillies and their liquid in a blender and liquidize to a fine paste for about 1 minute at high speed. Add to the *masa harina* mixture and knead to a soft dough consistency for about 5 minutes. Press into tortillas as instructed on page 38. When you take the first layer of waxed paper off each pressed tortilla, put the grated cheese and strips of green chilli (if used) on half the tortilla, leaving about 1 cm (½ inch) round the edges. Fold in half and seal the edges. Lower into a frying pan of hot oil, removing the paper, and fry for about 3 minutes until golden, turning once. Drain on absorbent kitchen paper and serve hot.

Tacos

American-style fried tortillas

The great American invention—*Taco* shells are sold everywhere in America. They are the fast-food industry's version of the cigar-shaped *taco*. It is all very well, but they have to be fried into shape, which requires both practice and patience. Home-made *taco* shells are not as perfect in shape as the bought ones but they are much more tasty. They can be fried several days in advance and kept in an airtight container ready for use. The filling can be practically anything you wish, but the most popular fillings are shredded lettuce with cooked chicken, *Guacamole* and soured cream as in this recipe; or shredded lettuce with *Picadillo*, soured cream, cheese and *Jalapeños en Vinagre*. They can be served as starters, or if you make them small, with drinks. Only corn tortillas are used, which may be fresh or frozen.

SERVES 6

oil for deep frying	*12 corn tortillas*

Filling

1 lettuce, finely shredded	*75 ml (3 fl oz) soured cream*
3 chicken breasts, cooked	*Jalapeños en Vinagre*
and finely shredded	(optional)
1 quantity Guacamole	

Heat the oil in a deep fryer to 180°C, 350°F. Fry the tortillas by holding 2 at a time with kitchen tongs, and pressing against the side of the pot to make a U-shape. Hold them in this position for about 1 minute, then separate the 2 tortillas and fry for about 3 minutes until golden brown. They should keep their shape but if they don't, then hold on to them a little longer with the tongs. Drain, upside down, on absorbent kitchen paper. Use immediately, or cool and store in an airtight container for up to 10 days.

To fill the *taco* shells, divide the lettuce generously between them. Add the chicken, then spoon some *Guacamole* over the top, followed by a little soured cream. If you are using other fillings always put the lettuce in first, then the meat and finally the toppings. Serve garnished with the pickles. Once filled, *taco* shells must be eaten within 30 minutes because the moisture from the filling softens them.

VARIATION:

To make miniature *taco* shells, use a biscuit cutter to cut the tortillas into 7 cm (3 inch) circles, then fry in the same way. The trimmings can be used for *totopos*.

■

Enfrijoladas

Tortillas with beans, cheese and sauce

Enfrijoladas is the name given to tortillas which have been shallow-fried then covered with beans. The toppings are as varied as the cooks who make them: for example, *Salsa para Enchiladas* with lettuce and cheese; *Chorizo* with crumbled cheese; or avocado and onions with *Salsa de Tomate Verde*; or just any leftover meat, fried and garnished with a sauce, raw onions and cheese. *Enfrijoladas* make a good starter, lunch dish or light supper served with a tossed green salad. Double this recipe if you are going to use it for a light meal.

SERVES 4

150 g (6 oz) shredded cooked meat, or crisp fried Chorizo Toluqueño (see page 156) or chopped crisp fried bacon
little chopped onion
oil for shallow frying

4 corn tortillas
225 g (8 oz) Frijoles Refritos
8 tablespoons Salsa para Enchiladas
50 g (2 oz) crumbly white cheese

To garnish

½ onion, thinly sliced

Jalapeños en Vinagre (optional)

If using leftover meat, fry it first with some chopped onion in a little oil for 5 minutes. Shallow fry the tortillas in the hot oil for 30 seconds on each side, drain on absorbent kitchen paper and keep warm. Heat the beans and the *Salsa para Enchiladas*. Cover the surface of each tortilla with the beans, then spoon 2 tablespoons of

67

sauce over it, followed by the shredded meat and crumbled cheese. Garnish with the onion rings and pickles and serve hot.

■

Chalupas

Boat-shaped tortillas

Chalupas, literally translated, means boats. They are named after the flat boats which were used in the canals of old *Tenochtitlán*, now Mexico City. In *Xochimilco* (the floating gardens in the south of the city), you can still see these beautiful flat boats which are filled with flowers, food and Mexican curios, with the vendors sitting amongst their wares.

Chalupas are cooked in a similar way to *Tortillas de Maíz*, but the edge is pinched into a ridge all the way round to hold the sauce. They must be eaten hot and make an excellent starter, though they are floppy and messy for hors d'oeuvres. The 'boats' may be prepared in advance and the filling and garnish added just before serving.

SERVES 4

¼ quantity corn tortilla dough
6 tablespoons cooking oil
1 quantity Salsa de Tomate Verde, Salsa para Enchiladas or Salsa Adobada

225 g (8 oz) white cheese (Wensleydale or white Cheshire), crumbled
1 small onion, finely chopped
1 small lettuce, finely shredded

Form the dough into 8 cigar shapes about 10 cm (4 inches) long, 2½ cm (1 inch) in diameter. Place on waxed paper squares, as for tortillas, but positioned diagonally. Cover with waxed paper and press lightly to the thickness of 3 mm (⅛ inch). If you do not have a tortilla press, roll with a rolling pin between 2 squares of waxed paper or press with the base of your hand. Grill on both sides as for tortillas and keep warm under a tea-towel. While they are all still hot, pinch the edge into a ridge all the way round, using thumb and forefinger. (If this is not done immediately after the *Chalupas* are cooked, it will be impossible to form a ridge.)

Heat the oil in a heavy-based frying pan and fry each *Chalupa*, ridge side up, basting with hot oil to seal. Fill each *Chalupa* with at least 2 tablespoons of sauce, crumbled cheese and chopped onion, and serve immediately, garnished with shredded lettuce.

■

Sopes

Maize dough shells with beans and chorizo filling

Sopes are one of several *antojitos* which are made of a thick maize dough, grilled like a tortilla and then fried in lard or oil. They are used as hors d'oeuvres or starters, and are very attractive and tasty, though filling! Garnishes for *Sopes* are as varied as the people who cook them, but I have included some ideas you can try. They have the added attraction that you can make them without any special equipment, by simply pressing them between two squares of waxed paper, with the base of your hand.

SERVES 6

For the sauce

3 tomatoes, grilled and
  skinned
1 clove garlic
3 cascabel or 3 green chillies
6 tablespoons cooking oil
4 tablespoons water

For the dough

175 g (6 oz) masa harina
40 g (1½ oz) plain flour
175 ml (6 fl oz) water
½ teaspoon salt

For the filling

¼ quantity Frijoles Refritos
225 g (8 oz) Chorizo, crumbled
  and fried
1 small lettuce, finely shredded
50 g (2 oz) grated Parmesan
  cheese
½ onion, finely chopped
Jalapeños en Vinagre
radish flowers, to garnish

Liquidize together the tomatoes, garlic and chillies. Heat 1 tablespoon of the oil in a heavy-based pan and fry the mixture for about 3 minutes, stirring frequently, then add the water and continue cooking. When the water has been absorbed, remove from the heat. Meanwhile, mix together the *masa harina*, flour, water and salt. Make the *Sopes* in a tortilla press, into 5 cm (2 inch) diameter circles, about 1 cm (½ inch) thick. Place each circle on a hot dry frying pan, cook for 1 minute, until brown spots appear, then turn over and pinch all around the edge to turn into small 'bowls'—be careful not to burn your fingers on the hot dough. When all the *Sopes* are cooked, dip them in the chilli sauce, one at a time, and fry in the remaining oil for about 2 minutes, basting with oil. Drain on absorbent kitchen paper, then spread with the hot beans, *Chorizo*, a little more sauce, lettuce, cheese, onion and finally a little of the *Jalapeños*. Garnish with radish flowers and serve immediately.

■

Rollo de frijol

Re-fried beans with sardines and avocados

Yet another way of eating beans, this dish is good served at room temperature, either on its own as a starter or with a green salad and *Jalapeños en Vinagre* for a light lunch.

SERVES 4

2 tablespoons oil
½ onion, finely chopped
225 g (8 oz) tomatoes,
  skinned, or tinned tomatoes
1 green chilli, finely chopped

1 teaspoon salt
400 g (14 oz) Frijoles
2 × 100 g (4 oz) cans sardines
  in tomato sauce

To garnish
50 g (2 oz) Parmesan cheese,
  grated
2 avocados

2 tortillas fried into Totopos
  (see page 56)
10 radish flowers

Heat the oil and fry the onion until soft, then sieve in the tomatoes and add the salt and chilli. Continue frying until the mixture reduces by half. Add the beans, mashing them as they fry. Split the sardines open lengthwise, discard the bones and mash the fish with the can liquid. Add to the beans and continue frying until the mixture is dry enough to toss. Toss onto a serving dish and garnish with cheese, *totopos* and avocado slices. Arrange the radishes around the edge. Serve hot or at room temperature.

Crepas de cuitlacoche

Pancakes filled with cuitlacoche

Cuitlacoche is a delicacy, similar to truffles, which has been popular since the days of the Aztec Emperors. It is a fungus which has developed on a type of corn, deforming the kernels by causing them to swell up and darken. It is similar to wild mushrooms in colour, texture and flavour. The Indians have always used it as a filling for *quesadillas* or *tacos*, and it is now a sign of refinement in Mexico City to serve it as a filling for pancakes (crêpes). *Cuitlacoche* is now available in cans.

This light and unusual dish makes an excellent starter, served with cream. The pancakes are prepared at least 2 hours in advance, and the filling can be made at the same time, then the dish assembled just before required.

SERVES 6

For the pancakes
125 ml (4 fl oz) warm water
200 ml (⅓ pint) milk
2 eggs

pinch of salt
100 g (4 oz) plain flour, sifted
2 tablespoons cooking oil

Cuitlacoche filling
butter for greasing
1 teaspoon cooking oil
½ onion, finely chopped
1 clove garlic, finely chopped
200 g (7 oz) can cuitlacoche
  or mushrooms

1 green chilli, finely chopped
3 leaves epazote or coriander,
  chopped (optional)
¼ teaspoon salt
150 ml (5 fl oz) soured cream
2 tablespoons milk

To make the pancakes, put the liquids, eggs, salt, flour and then the oil into a liquidizer. Blend at top speed for about 1 minute. Use a spatula to dislodge any unblended flour from the blades and blend again for about 5 seconds. Alternatively, make the batter by hand: place the flour in a mixing bowl, make a well in the centre and slowly blend the eggs into the flour. Gradually blend in the water and milk, followed by the oil. Cover and chill for at least 2 hours.

Grease with oil a heavy-based frying pan about 15 cm (6 inches) in diameter, until it just starts to smoke. Pour off any surplus oil.

71

Pour in about 2 tablespoons of batter, tilting the pan so that it covers the base thinly. Any surplus batter remaining in the pan can be poured straight back into the bowl. Fry for about 1 minute over medium heat, using a spatula to separate the pancake from the sides of the pan, and shaking the pan a little to prevent sticking. When the pancake is golden brown on the underside, turn it and cook for another 30 seconds, then slide it on to a plate and cover with another plate. Continue in this manner, cooking, stacking and covering the pancakes until the batter is finished.

To make the filling, heat the oil in a heavy-based frying pan and fry the onion and garlic until golden. Add the *cuitlacoche*, or mushrooms, chilli, *epazote* and salt and cook for about 5 minutes, stirring occasionally. Grease an ovenproof dish with butter, fill each pancake with 1 tablespoon of *cuitlacoche* mixture, roll up and place in the greased dish. When all the pancakes are filled, cover tightly with foil and bake in a preheated oven at 180°C, 350°F, Gas Mark 4 for 15–20 minutes. Meanwhile, mix the milk with the soured cream. Remove the pancakes from the oven, spoon over the soured cream and serve immediately.

Sopas

Soups

There are two types of soup in Mexican cooking. The first is *sopa aguada* (literally 'wet soup'), a dish acquired from colonial days, and, despite the heat in the middle of the day, no Mexican meal is complete without it. It is served hot throughout the year. A good *caldo* (stock) is of utmost importance, and beans, avocados, pumpkin blossoms, stale tortillas and fresh and dried chillies all provide a great diversity of flavours.

More unusual is the second soup, called *sopa seca* or literally 'dry soup'. This is actually pasta or rice which is served as a separate course after the *sopa aguada*. Pasta 'soups' like *Sopa Seca de Fideo* or *Sopa de Macarrón con Queso* are of Italian origin, while *arroz* (rice) was introduced by the Spaniards and has taken its own well-deserved place in the Mexican diet.

In this book, however, we are treating rice as a vegetable or side dish to be eaten as part of the main course. Therefore you will find rice recipes in the chapter on Vegetables and Salads, leaving this chapter entirely to soups and pasta.

Pozole Jalisciense

Pork and hominy soup

This is a meal in itself, a soup which is revitalizing, nourishing and delicious. In Mexico City the best *Pozole* is sold in the restaurants around *Plaza Garibaldi*, a small square with a lively market atmosphere. Here the *Mariachi* bands congregate in the hope of attracting customers to hire them by the song—or cheaper, by the hour. The bands consist of anywhere between three to thirteen musicians, all dressed in complete *Charro* attire with big *sombreros*, guitars and brass trumpets. There will also be caricaturists and street vendors persuading you to buy anything from chewing gum to hot corn on the cob, tempting *tostadas*, sweets and drinks. In my youth, ladies were not supposed to go to such places, so when I did go I had to keep it secret. It's a good idea to go with several friends! This is the place where people go after a party, and in the early hours of the morning, when the spirits flag, the restaurants in the square sell this succulent soup which would revive even the dead!

Pozole is traditionally made with the head of a pig, but I prefer to use hand of pork. Because dried *maíz cacahuazintle* is not available in England, I have not included it in the recipe. But, if you are able to obtain it, cook it as directed on page 41 and substitute it for the hominy or sweet corn.

SERVES 8

1 kg (2 lb) hand of pork, boned, bones reserved	½ teaspoon salt
1 beef marrow bone	¼ teaspoon ground black pepper
1 kg (2 lb) pork neck bones	2¾ litres (5 pints) cold water
2 onions	400 g (14 oz) can tomatoes, mashed
2 cloves garlic	400 g (14 oz) can hominy or sweet corn kernels
4 cabbage leaves	
2 carrots	1 teaspoon dried oregano
4 sticks celery	
1 tablespoon malt vinegar	

Garnishes

¼ quantity Salsa Adobada   1 ripe avocado, sliced

6 green chillies, finely
 chopped
1 small lettuce, shredded
1 bunch radishes, topped,
 tailed and sliced
6 spring onions, finely
 chopped

15 sprigs coriander, finely
 chopped (optional)
Totopos made from 16 tortillas
 (see page 56)
2 limes or lemons, cut into
 eight

Cut the meat into large pieces. Put all the ingredients (including bones), but not the tomatoes, corn and oregano, into a very large saucepan. Bring to the boil quickly and skim off any froth that appears. Simmer, partly covered, for about 2 hours or until the meat is tender. Remove the meat and cut into bite-size pieces. Strain the broth, discarding all bones and soggy vegetables. Return the meat to the broth, add the tomatoes and drained hominy or sweet corn and boil for 20 minutes. Allow to cool for about 2 hours, when the grease will float to the top. Skim carefully, then reheat the soup with the oregano. Serve very hot in a soup tureen surrounded by individual bowls of garnishes. Let each person help themselves by sprinkling a little of each garnish on to their soup and adding a squeeze of lime or lemon.

■

Sopa de albóndigas

Miniature meatball soup

This is an unusual soup which is hearty and very tasty.

SERVES 6

175 g (6 oz) best minced beef
1 teaspoon malt vinegar
pinch of salt
pinch of ground black pepper
1 egg, beaten
1 tablespoon chopped parsley
25 g (1 oz) breadcrumbs

2 tablespoons cooking oil
1 clove garlic
¼ onion, finely chopped
1 quantity hot Caldo or 1 litre
 (1¾ pints) boiling water and
 3 beef stock cubes
2 tablespoons tomato purée

Season the meat with the vinegar, salt and pepper. Mix in half the egg and half the parsley. Take ½ teaspoonfuls of mixture and form into small meatballs. Dip the meatballs in the remaining egg, then toss them in the breadcrumbs.

Heat the oil, fry the garlic until it turns black and discard it. Fry the meatballs in the flavoured oil for 5 minutes or until light brown all over. Drain on absorbent kitchen paper, reserving the oil. Heat ½ tablespoon of the reserved oil in a saucepan and fry the onion for 3 minutes, then add the *Caldo* or boiling water and stock cubes, and the tomato purée. Finally add the meatballs, simmer for 5 minutes and serve hot, sprinkled with the remaining parsley.

■

Caldo Tlalpeño

Chicken breasts in broth with avocado

This is a hearty soup, but not quite a meal in one.

SERVES 4

4 tortillas
oil for shallow frying
900 ml (1½ pints) Caldo
1 boneless chicken breast,
  cooked and shredded
2 avocados

1 tablespoon chopped coriander
2 green chillies, chopped
  (optional)
¼ teaspoon black pepper
1 lemon, quartered

Unless your tortillas are already stale, cut them into strips and leave uncovered overnight. Otherwise, break them into bite-size pieces. Heat the oil and fry the tortillas until golden. Drain on absorbent kitchen paper. Bring the *Caldo* to the boil, add the chicken meat and simmer for 5 minutes. Peel, stone and slice the avocados. Place the tortilla strips into 4 individual bowls and pour over the boiling *Caldo* and chicken meat. Serve garnished with the avocado slices, chillies, black pepper and coriander. Serve with lemon quarters.

Menudo

Tripe and chilli soup

Menudo is famous in the north of Mexico as a good remedy for hangovers—something you will appreciate if you ever suffer a tequila hangover! It is a good soup to prepare ahead of time for New Year's Day because of its 'special' powers, and it has the added advantage of being an all-in-one dish at a time when you do not feel like cooking. It should be served in large bowls accompanied by warm soft tortillas filled with *Guacamole*.

SERVES 8

450 g (1 lb) tripe, cut into small pieces
2¾ litres (5 pints) water
1 pig's trotter
2 bay leaves
6 peppercorns
4 sticks celery
5 cloves garlic
1 carrot
225 g (8 oz) potatoes, peeled and diced

400 g (14 oz) maíz cacahuazintle, cooked, or can hominy, drained
450 g (1 lb) fresh or canned tomatoes, sieved
2 leeks, sliced
2 chicken stock cubes
½ teaspoon ground black pepper

To garnish
jalapeño chillies, sliced
6 spring onions, chopped
4 tablespoons finely chopped coriander

2 lemons, quartered
2 avocados, cut into wedges

Wash the tripe carefully and place in a saucepan with the water, trotter, bay leaves, peppercorns, celery, garlic and carrot. Cover and simmer for about 4 hours or until the tripe is very tender. Skim off and discard the foam on the surface whenever necessary. Strain, discard the trotter, bay leaves and celery, remove the tripe and sieve the broth. Boil the broth until reduced by half, then add all the remaining ingredients except the tripe. Cover and simmer for about 20 minutes until the potatoes are tender. Replace the tripe and serve boiling hot, accompanied by small bowls of garnish.

Sopa de pescado

Fish, tomato and potato soup

You can start this delicious soup from scratch. I often use the leftovers from *Huachinango a la Veracruzana* to start me off, but trout, haddock and cod are all suitable.

SERVES 4

450 g (1 lb) fish heads, tails,
  bones and scraps
900 ml (1½ pints) water
1 onion
1 bay leaf
¼ teaspoon salt
¼ teaspoon ground black
  pepper
1 potato, peeled and cubed,
  (reserve the skin)

2 tablespoons chopped parsley
2 tablespoons tomato purée
100 g (4 oz) fish fillet, skinned
  and boned
1 chicken stock cube
25 g (1 oz) peas
10 stuffed olives
1 lemon, quartered

Boil the fish trimmings for 30 minutes with the water, onion, bay leaf, salt, pepper and potato skin. Strain into a saucepan and discard the trimmings, then add the remaining ingredients. Cover and simmer for 20 minutes. Serve hot, with lemon wedges.

■

Macarrón con queso

Spaghetti in tomato sauce with cheese

This qualifies as a 'dry soup' or starter. It also makes a nice snack on buttered toast. It can be prepared ahead of time and baked just before serving.

SERVES 4

1 litre (1¾ pints) water
½ onion
1 bay leaf
½ teaspoon salt
rind of 1 lemon

1 onion, chopped
4 tablespoons tomato purée
1 chicken stock cube
¼ teaspoon ground black
  pepper

225 g (8 oz) spaghetti
75 g (3 oz) butter
100 g (4 oz) button
  mushrooms, sliced

150 ml (¼ pint) double cream
1 canned pimento, sliced
175 g (6 oz) Cheddar cheese,
  grated

Bring the water to the boil with the ½ onion, bay leaf, salt and lemon rind. Add the spaghetti and cook for about 12 minutes or until it is tender. Drain, reserving the liquid, and rinse the spaghetti under cold water. Drain. Discard onion, bay leaf and rind.

In a large frying pan, heat the butter and fry the mushrooms and chopped onion for 5 minutes. Add the tomato purée, chicken stock cube and black pepper. Stir in 400 ml (14 fl oz) of the reserved liquid (topping up with milk if necessary). Simmer for 5 minutes, then add the spaghetti. Grease an ovenproof dish and make 2 layers each of the spaghetti, cream, pimento and cheese, finishing with cheese. Bake in a preheated oven at 180°C, 350°F, Gas Mark 4 for 20 minutes.

■

Sopa seca de fideo

Vermicelli soup

Sopa Seca is an alternative to rice and is eaten frequently in Mexican homes. It is unusual in its method of preparation, but quite tasty and quick to prepare. It makes a good starter instead of soup.

SERVES 4

6 tablespoons cooking oil
1 clove garlic
100 g (4 oz) vermicelli
½ onion, finely chopped
4 tablespoons tomato purée
1 litre (1¾ pints) boiling
  water

2 chicken stock cubes
4 sprigs parsley
1 green chilli
¼ teaspoon ground black
  pepper
25 g (1 oz) grated Parmesan
  cheese

In a large frying pan, heat the oil and fry the garlic until black. Discard the garlic and fry the vermicelli over low heat until golden brown, taking care not to let it burn. Drain the vermicelli on absorbent kitchen paper.

Discard all but 1 tablespoon of the oil then fry the onion for 3 minutes until soft. Add the tomato purée, water, chicken stock cubes, parsley, chilli and pepper. Simmer for about 3 minutes, add the vermicelli, cover and simmer over low heat for about 15 minutes, stirring occasionally. The mixture is ready when all the liquid is absorbed and the vermicelli has doubled in size and is quite easy to squash between two fingers. Discard the parsley and chilli, sprinkle with cheese and eat hot.

■

Sopa aguada de fideo

Vermicelli and tomato soup

Another hot soup with a *Caldo* base. I find this recipe good if I have any leftover vermicelli and just use it up. This is a light starter.

SERVES 4

1 quantity Caldo or
  2 chicken stock cubes
  dissolved in 1 litre
  (1¾ pints) water
3 tablespoons tomato purée
1 onion, finely chopped
50 g (2 oz) cooked vermicelli,
  spaghetti or other pasta

1 tablespoon finely chopped
  parsley
¼ teaspoon ground black
  pepper
½ lemon, quartered

Place all the ingredients, except the lemon, in a saucepan. Bring to the boil and simmer for 20 minutes. Serve hot with lemon wedges.

OPPOSITE: *Pozole Jalisciense* (pork and hominy soup, page 74) with accompaniments.
FOLLOWING PAGES: Barbecue suggestion—*Tacos al Carbón* (charcoal-grilled steak wrapped in tortillas, page 139); *Costillitas Adobadas* (spare ribs in chilli and cream sauce, page 153); *Cebollitas Asadas* (grilled spring onions, page 133); and *Elotes Asados* (roast corn on the cob, page 129).

Sopa de aguacate

Avocado soup

Serving this soup at room temperature brings out its delicate flavour beautifully.

SERVES 4

900 ml (1½ pints) Caldo
2 avocados
juice of ½ lemon
¼ teaspoon salt

¼ teaspoon black pepper
1 tablespoon chopped
   coriander, to garnish

Heat the *Caldo* to body temperature. Peel and stone the avocados, then place in a blender with the lemon juice, salt, pepper and *Caldo* and blend until smooth. Serve in individual bowls, garnished with chopped coriander.

Sopa de poro y papa

Leek and potato soup

Quick and easy, yet full of goodness, this soup is a great favourite in my family.

SERVES 4

½ tablespoon cooking oil
½ onion, finely chopped
900 ml (1½ pints) Caldo
2 potatoes, peeled and
   diced

2 fresh leeks, sliced
2 tablespoons chopped parsley
1 tablespoon tomato purée
1 chicken stock cube
¼ teaspoon black pepper

OPPOSITE: Vegetarian dishes—*Chiles Rellenos estilo Zacatlán* (peppers stuffed with fruit, page 114); the fan-shaped *Enchiladas Anita* (stuffed tortillas in a chilli sauce, page 91), garnished with crumbled cheese and chopped onions; *Arroz con Frijoles* (rice with beans, page 113); and *Cocktail de Aguacate* (avocado cocktail, page 60).

Heat the oil in a saucepan and fry the onion for 3 minutes. Add the remaining ingredients, cover and simmer for 15 minutes or until the potato is cooked. Serve hot.

VARIATION:

Crema de Poro y Papa—Cream of leek and potato soup
Cool the soup, then purée in a blender and add 150 ml (¼ pint) single cream. Garnish with chopped parsley and serve at room temperature.

Sopa de frijol

Bean soup

This soup is a great favourite, especially garnished with croûtons. It is hearty and will make a good luncheon dish or starter to a light meal. The type of beans you use is up to you.

SERVES 6

450 ml (¾ pint) Frijoles
½ onion, quartered
600 ml (1 pint) Caldo
4 tablespoons cooking oil
1 clove garlic
1½ tablespoons tomato
   purée
1 green chilli, chopped

4 tablespoons chopped
   coriander
¼ teaspoon salt
¼ teaspoon ground black
   pepper
pinch of sugar
1½ slices stale white bread cut
   into 1 cm (½ inch) squares

Place the beans, onion, and half the *Caldo* in a blender and blend at full speed until smooth. Heat 1 tablespoon of the oil in a saucepan and fry the garlic until black. Discard the garlic and sieve the bean mixture carefully into the pan. Add the remaining *Caldo* and the tomato purée, chilli, coriander, salt, pepper and sugar. Simmer, uncovered, for 20 minutes until it thickens.

To make the croûtons, put the bread squares on a baking tray and bake for 15 minutes in a preheated oven at 180°C, 350°F, Gas Mark 4 until golden. Alternatively, use the remaining 3 tablespoons of cooking oil and fry the bread, stirring constantly, until golden. Drain on absorbent kitchen paper and keep warm. Add to the soup just before serving.

■

Crema de verduras

Cream of vegetable soup

I use this recipe over and over with all sorts of different vegetables. It is particularly good with parsnips, corn, mushrooms, spinach or peas in their pods, or with carrot and cabbage combined. If you use root vegetables you may like to thin the soup a little with extra milk or water.

SERVES 4

600 ml (1 pint) milk
300 ml (½ pint) water
1 large onion
1 medium-size potato,
* peeled and quartered*
2 chicken stock cubes

450 g (1 lb) vegetable of your
* choice*
¼ teaspoon ground black
* pepper*
25 g (1 oz) butter
1 tablespoon chopped parsley

Place all the ingredients, except the parsley, in a saucepan and boil for 20 minutes until the potato is soft. Liquidize to a purée in batches. Sieve into a clean saucepan and reheat. Serve hot, garnished with parsley.

■

Sopa de ajo

Garlic soup

A good soup for garlic lovers and very easy too.

SERVES 4

½ tablespoon olive oil
12 cloves garlic
2 tablespoons tomato purée
900 ml (1½ pints) Caldo
pinch of sugar

½ chicken stock cube
¼ teaspoon ground black
* pepper*
croûtons (see page 82), *to*
* garnish*

Heat the oil in a saucepan until it smokes, then add the garlic and stir continually until it is black. Add the tomato purée, *Caldo*, sugar, chicken stock cube and pepper and simmer for about 10 minutes. Strain into individual bowls and garnish with croûtons.

■

Sopa de flor de calabaza

Courgette blossom soup

If you have had the patience to save the blossoms from your courgette or marrow plants (as described on page 123) and have a reasonable amount in the freezer, you can now surprise everyone with this lovely soup.

SERVES 4

900 ml (1½ pints) Caldo
100 g (4 oz) corn kernels,
  fresh or frozen
25 g (1 oz) butter
1 tablespoon chopped
  coriander
½ onion, finely chopped

1 clove garlic, crushed
50 g (2 oz) mushrooms, sliced
225 g (8 oz) courgette blossoms
  or 100 g (4 oz) spinach, chopped
25 g (1 oz) Cheddar cheese,
  grated

Bring the *Caldo* to the boil, add the corn and boil for 10 minutes. Heat the butter and fry the coriander, onion, garlic, mushrooms and blossoms or spinach for about 5 minutes. Add to the *Caldo* and serve hot, garnished with grated cheese.

■

Sopa de nuez

Walnut or almond soup

This is a soup from northern Mexico where nuts grow in abundance. Traditionally it is made with newly cropped green walnuts which can be skinned, but when this is not possible, use dried walnuts or almonds. The flavour is not altered so much as the appearance which would be white instead of light brown.

SERVES 4

900 ml (1½ pints) Caldo
100 g (4 oz) walnuts or
   almonds

50 g (2 oz) butter
2 sticks celery, chopped
3 tablespoons double cream

Put half the *Caldo* in a blender with the nuts and blend at top speed for 40 seconds. Heat the butter in a saucepan, add the celery and nut mixture and the remaining *Caldo* and simmer for 15 minutes. Stir in the cream and serve hot or cold.

Sopa de elote con rajas

Sweetcorn and pepper soup

This is a milky, tasty soup, for a light lunch or a starter for dinner.

SERVES 4

225 g (8 oz) corn
   kernels
1 green chilli, sliced
1 green pepper, sliced
2 chicken stock cubes
600 ml (1 pint) milk

300 ml (½ pint) water
25 g (1 oz) butter
¼ onion, finely chopped
1 tablespoon cornflour
pinch of cayenne, to garnish

Simmer the corn, chilli, pepper and chicken stock cubes in the milk and water for 5 minutes. Strain, reserving the liquid and vegetables. In a saucepan heat the butter and fry the onion for 4 minutes, then stir in the cornflour. Gradually add the milk, stirring continually. Add the vegetables and bring to the boil. Pour into individual soup bowls and garnish each with a little cayenne.

Sopa de tortilla

Tortilla soup

When tortillas are stale, they can be turned into soup and you can impress your guest with a brand new taste. If you are using fresh tortillas, preparation starts the night before.

SERVES 4

4 corn tortillas
900 ml (1½ pints) Caldo
1 pasilla chilli
2 tablespoons cooking oil

1 clove garlic
½ onion, finely chopped
1½ tablespoons tomato purée

If using fresh tortillas, cut them into 1 cm (½ inch) strips and leave uncovered overnight. If stale, break the tortillas into bite-size pieces. Soak the chilli in 150 ml (¼ pint) of boiling *Caldo* for 30 minutes. Drain, reserving the *Caldo*. Discard stem and seeds, and chop the chilli finely.

Heat the oil in a saucepan and fry the tortilla strips until golden, then drain on absorbent kitchen paper. Fry the garlic until black, then discard. Fry the onion for 3 minutes, add the tomato purée and *Caldo* and simmer for 15 minutes skimming off any foam that comes to the surface. Just before serving, place the tortilla strips in 4 individual bowls, bring the soup back to the boil and pour into the bowls. Garnish with chopped chilli.

Antojitos, Enchiladas y Tamales
Snacks

Antojitos—little whims or 'what you fancy'—are meant to attract your attention and make your mouth water—in other words, as their name indicates, to satisfy your appetite whether you are hungry or not!

In Mexico *antojitos* are cooked everywhere and sold on street corners, outside cinemas, at schools, on the roadside, in homes, in the markets, in parks and at bullfights!

The word *antojitos* covers a whole range of Mexican food, from fruit peeled and cut to look like a flower, then sprinkled with lime juice, salt and cayenne, to *tacos*, *tamales*, *enchiladas*, *tortas* and *quesadillas*. Eating in the street is quite common, and every now and again you will see groups of people drinking beer and eating *tacos*. There are a lot of outdoor restaurants and the atmosphere is always gay, with laughter and music filling the place.

Since mealtimes are not set in Mexico, *antojitos* are hard to resist when the main course is a long time appearing! In the Mexican markets you will see the women with their freshly made tortillas offering *Barbacoa* with a piquant sauce, next to the fellow who, armed with an orange squeezer, has put up a stall selling freshly squeezed orange juice by the pint. In the evening, after the theatre or cinema, you have to be very strong to go past the freshly made *quesadillas*, filled with pumpkin blossoms and a little cheese. Any of the following recipes can be classified as *antojitos* and served as starters if you make them small, or as main courses if you make them larger.

■

Enchiladas

Tortillas stuffed with cheese

Enchiladas are about the most popular of the tortilla dishes. It is a popularity which is well deserved, because they are an excellent combination of flavour, texture and colour. *Enchiladas* are more commonly prepared with corn tortillas, but wheat tortillas may also be used and are treated in exactly the same manner.

A good *salsa* (sauce) is as important as a good tortilla. Traditionally, *enchiladas* have no meat; they are filled with chopped raw onion and cheese, then rolled up, with generous amounts of boiling sauce poured over them, followed by more onions and cheese to garnish. Beans are an excellent companion to this dish, and they are usually garnished with very finely shredded lettuce.

The sauce may be of any type. Tomato-based ones make the most well-known *enchiladas*, but you will find you can make them with any type of sauce with equally delicious results. If you are making several *enchiladas*, your best bet is to shallow fry them, dip in sauce, fill and roll up, then keep them warm. When they have all been made and you are ready to eat, then add the boiling sauce and the final garnish. If you are entertaining a large group, *Budín Azteca* (see page 171) would be a better choice than *enchiladas*. It can be prepared ahead of time and, though different in appearance, it is equally delicious.

SERVES 4

oil for shallow frying
12 corn tortillas
1 quantity Salsa para
 Enchiladas
1 onion, finely chopped

225 g (8 oz) white Cheshire cheese
 or feta, crumbled
1 lettuce, finely shredded, to
 garnish

Heat the oil and shallow fry the tortillas for 30 seconds on each side then drain on absorbent kitchen paper. Heat the sauce in a saucepan and keep it hot. Now dip 1 tortilla in the sauce and place it on a hot dinner plate. Put about 1 teaspoon of onion and 1 teaspoon of crumbled cheese down the middle of the tortilla and roll it up. Repeat this procedure until you have 3 *enchiladas* on each plate. Spoon over the hot sauce, sprinkle with onions and crumbled cheese and serve immediately, garnished with shredded lettuce.

■

Enchiladas verdes

Tortillas stuffed with pork

Here's another traditional way of making *enchiladas*—but don't feel that you must restrict yourself to these precise recipes. Swapping meats and sauces from different recipes can produce excellent results. These *enchiladas* are made with *poblano* chillies, but if they are not available, green peppers can be used instead if you also include a couple of green chillies to make the sauce hot. Beans and rice are perfect accompaniments for a main meal.

SERVES 6

8 poblano chillies or 8 small green peppers and 2 green chillies
6 sprigs coriander
275 g (10 oz) can tomatillos and their liquid
1 chicken stock cube
150 ml (¼ pint) soured cream

75 g (3 oz) cream cheese
350 g (12 oz) cooked pork, shredded
2 small onions, finely chopped
¼ teaspoon ground black pepper
oil for shallow frying
18 corn tortillas

To garnish
50 g (2 oz) white cheese (Wensleydale, white Cheshire or feta), crumbled

1 lettuce, finely shredded
radish flowers

Grill the *poblano* chillies (or peppers and green chillies) under a hot grill until the skins blister, then place inside a polythene bag for 20 minutes. The steam cooks them further. Peel the chillies, discarding the seeds, stalks and veins. Place in a blender with the coriander, *tomatillos* and their liquid, chicken stock cube and soured cream, and blend to a paste. Mix the cream cheese and the pork with half the chopped onions and the black pepper.

Heat the oil in a frying pan and fry the tortillas for 30 seconds on each side, stacking them in layers of absorbent kitchen paper. Fry the *tomatillo* mixture in 1 tablespoon of oil and dip 1 tortilla at a time in the boiling sauce. Fill with the meat mixture, roll up and keep warm. When all the *enchiladas* have been rolled, pour more boiling sauce over them and garnish with the crumbled white cheese, shredded lettuce and radishes. Serve immediately.

■

Enchiladas Suizas

Tortillas stuffed with chicken and melted cheese

The name Swiss Enchiladas is given to this dish because of the melted cheese and cream, yet it is surprisingly Mexican in flavour! *Enchiladas* are quick to prepare, provided the tortillas are already made. Green *Enchiladas Suizas* are served as a speciality at a well-known restaurant in Mexico City called Sanborn's, which has made this dish famous. The tortillas, which are filled with cooked chicken and covered with generous quantities of tomato sauce, cheese and cream, are baked in a hot oven and served with *Frijoles Refritos* and salad. This could make a good informal dinner dish.

SERVES 4

8 tablespoons oil	*100 g (4 oz) mature Cheddar*
12 corn tortillas or 6 wheat	*cheese, grated*
tortillas, halved	*100 g (4 oz) Mozzarella cheese,*
½ cooked chicken, boned,	*grated*
skinned and in large pieces	*150 ml (¼ pint) double cream*
1 quantity Salsa de Tomate	*½ onion, finely chopped*
Verde or any basic sauce	

Heat the oil in a heavy-based frying pan and seal the tortillas by frying on each side for 30 seconds. Add more oil as required. Drain on absorbent kitchen paper, stacking them up with layers of the paper. This helps to keep them warm and drain the tortillas.

Fill each tortilla with cooked chicken pieces, roll up and place in an ovenproof dish. Use individual dishes with 3 tortillas per dish, or one 25 × 20 cm (10 × 8 inch) casserole. This can be done ahead of time. Cover tightly with foil, and bake in a preheated oven at 190°C, 375°F, Gas Mark 5 for 20 minutes. Meanwhile, bring the sauce to the boil and mix the cheeses together. Uncover the *enchiladas*, pour over the boiling sauce, then the cream and sprinkle with cheese and onion. Return to the oven for a few minutes until the cheese melts, then serve immediately.

■

Enchiladas Anita

Stuffed tortillas in a chilli sauce

These *enchiladas* were my grandmother's favourites and I can remember as a child it was always an occasion when Grandma, who was British, came for lunch and *enchiladas* were being prepared especially for her. My mother made them so well that she gained quite a reputation and had to offer them to guests upon special request! These *enchiladas* have the virtue of making a terrible mess of your cooker, but it is well worth it! Garnish them with salad and serve them with a roast meat and beans. Preparation should start 4 hours ahead of time.

SERVES 4

150 g (2 oz) ancho chillies *1 chicken stock cube*
300 ml (½ pint) single cream *1 teaspoon granulated sugar*
½ onion, coarsely chopped *8 corn tortillas*
1 clove garlic *oil for shallow frying*

To garnish
225 g (8 oz) Wensleydale *½ onion, finely chopped*
  cheese, crumbled

Wash the *ancho* chillies in hot water to soften them a little. Remove the stalks and the seeds, then soak them in the cream for at least 2 hours. Liquidize the chillies with the onion, garlic and chicken stock cube. Sieve the paste and stir in the sugar. Allow to cool.

Dip the tortillas in the *cold* sauce and shallow fry, one at a time, until the sauce dries up a little. Turn over and fry the other side, then place on a warm plate. Reserving a little cheese and onion to garnish, sprinkle the remainder over each tortilla. Fold each one in half and then in half again so it looks like a fan. Arrange on a heated serving dish, with sides touching. When all the *enchiladas* have been fried, place any sauce you have left in the pan, simmer for about 2 minutes and spoon over the folded tortillas. Sprinkle with the remaining cheese and onion before serving. Eat hot.

Tamales

Corn dumplings steamed in corn husks

Tamales are amongst the oldest of Mexican dishes—they were even served at Aztec banquets. They are so popular in Mexico today that there are shops which sell nothing but *tamales*, from dusk until midnight. They are steamed in corn husks or banana leaves, then filled with every conceivable vegetable, meat and sauce or just prepared on their own without flavouring to eat with a sauce, straight from the corn husks. When they are good, they are delicious and very filling! *Tamales* are also served in Mexico at breakfast parties to celebrate a seven-year-old's first Holy Communion. And they are a special feature of the evening parties known as *Tamalada*, where only *tamales* of different types will be served. The most usual types are the red *Tamales de Chile Colorado*, green *Tamales de Mole Verde* and sweet *Tamales de Dulce* which are coloured pink and have raisins and pineapple in them. In the south of Mexico they make *Tamal de Oaxaca*, which is altogether different (see recipe on page 95).

When I was a child, while *tamales* were being steamed, and we were all eagerly waiting to see how they turned out, no one was allowed to be sad or to quarrel. Happiness, according to tradition, is the magic ingredient that makes *tamales* fluffy and light! (Remember the Indians had no baking powder—they used a mixture of saltpetre and green *tomatillo* husks instead.) A couple of years ago, a Mexican cookery class that I was teaching suddenly exploded with laughter. My 80-year-old mother, on learning we were making *tamales* that day, had burst out singing and dancing to encourage the gods to assist us!

Since *tamales* are time-consuming to prepare, it is a good idea to make a large amount and freeze them in their husks. This recipe yields about 30, so you could make 10 red, 10 green and 10 sweet ones as indicated. It is easy to tell the difference between the red and green ones, because the red stains the husks while the green ones appear to stay clean. Freshly-made *tamales* can be kept in the refrigerator for up to 3 days and reheated by steaming for 10–15 minutes. Another popular way of heating them is by shallow-frying—but I warn you, your waist will suffer!

If you can't get corn husks, use 20 cm (8 inch) squares of kitchen foil with waxed paper squares placed on top. For the savoury filling you can use pork, beef, chicken, turkey or fish.

MAKES 30

60 or more dried corn husks

Tamal dough
750 g (1½ lb) masa harina
750 ml (1¼ pints) warm water
225 g (8 oz) lard, softened
600 ml (1 pint) warm meat stock

4 heaped teaspoons baking powder
1 teaspoon salt

Savoury filling for 10 red and 10 green *tamales*
750 g (1½ lb) cooked meat, shredded into large pieces
1½ quantity Salsa Adobada

1½ quantity Salsa de Tomate Verde

Filling for 10 sweet *tamales*
3 tablespoons granulated sugar
10 glacé cherries, chopped
4 slices crystallized pineapple, chopped

25 g (1 oz) raisins
2 drops cochineal

Soak the husks overnight to soften them. (Alternatively, cover completely with water, bring to the boil and drain.) In a large bowl mix together the *masa harina*, water and softened lard. Slowly add the warm stock, mixing all the time. Add the baking powder and beat until bubbles start to appear. To test the dough for readiness, drop a little in a glass of cold water—it should float and stick together. If it drops to the bottom and disintegrates, keep on mixing. You should have a warm sloppy dough similar to cake mix. Stir in the salt.

Place 2 husks overlapping in the palm of one hand and spoon in 1 tablespoon of sauce, 1 tablespoon of dough and a piece of the cooked meat and finally another tablespoon of sauce. Wrap the husks carefully to overlap, then fold the tail end towards the top, leaving it loose to allow room for expansion. If using waxed paper and kitchen foil, place the dough, sauce and meat in the centre, then wrap over, allowing for expansion, and pinch the ends of the foil to make it water-tight.

To make sweet *tamales* separate off about ⅓ of the dough before adding the salt, and stir in the sugar instead. Replace the meat and sauce filling with the mixed fruits. Dab the husks with a little cochineal to distinguish them from the savoury ones, then cook all the *tamales* together as described.

Arrange the *tamales* in the top half of a steamer and cover with greaseproof paper. Cover tightly and steam for 1½ hours, topping up with hot water when necessary.

To test if done, carefully open 1 or 2 *tamales* and pinch the dough between the fingers. It should be light and fluffy. If it feels sticky, cook for a little longer. Heat the leftover sauces separately and place them on the table for people to help themselves.

VARIATION:

Tamal de Cazuela—Mexican dumpling pie
This is a simplified version of the original *tamales*. I often use this method, described on page 97, for large parties, since there are no husks to remove and the dough, sauce and meat are evenly distributed.

Tamal de Oaxaca

Corn dumplings steamed in banana leaves

Tamal de Oaxaca comes from the south-west region of Mexico, where the climate is tropical and bananas grow abundantly. The banana leaves give the *tamal* a distinct texture and flavour, and it would be a shame to have to do without them. In Britain, there are a few high-class Indian restaurants which serve food steamed in banana leaves, and they may be willing to sell you some. If you cannot find them, the alternative is kitchen foil and greaseproof paper. The shape of these *tamales* is very different from that of conventional ones. These are flat and square, probably because the banana leaves could not be wrapped up in the same way as corn husks. The steaming is done in a similar manner to other *tamales*, but the leaves are plunged in boiling water to soften them. This recipe uses *mole negro*, made from a special variety of chilli called *chilhuacle*, which is burned to a cinder. This colours the dough and gives it a distinct flavour. If *mole negro* is unobtainable, double the amount of *mulato* chilli. Should all the Mexican chillies be unobtainable, substitute 10 teaspoons of ground chillies. These *tamales* can be prepared in advance: preparation time is about 4 hours.

MAKES about 18

4 ancho chillies
4 mulato chillies
1 litre (1¾ pints) hot stock
  from boiled chicken
4 cloves garlic
1 large onion, quartered
½ teaspoon dried oregano
2 chicken stock cubes
¼ teaspoon ground black
  pepper

1 tablespoon cooking oil
750 g (1¾ lb) can tomatoes,
  mashed
175 g (6 oz) mole negro de
  Oaxaca
about 40 banana leaves
1¾ kg (4 lb) chicken, boiled
  (see recipe on page 53)
1 quantity Tamales dough (see
  page 93)

Heat the chillies in a hot dry frying pan for 3 minutes. Remove and discard the stems and seeds, then soak in 300 ml (½ pint) of the stock for 30 minutes until soft. Liquidize the chillies and their liquid with the garlic, onion, oregano, chicken stock cubes and pepper to a smooth paste. Heat the oil in a large saucepan and sieve the mixture into it. Fry for 5 minutes, stirring, then add tomatoes, *mole negro* and remaining stock. Simmer for 20 minutes until the sauce thickens. If you have managed to obtain banana leaves, remove and discard the centre stalk. To soften the leaves, plunge into boiling water for 10 minutes. Drain and pat dry.

Skin, bone and shred the cooked chicken. Place 2 tablespoons of the dough in the centre of a 25 cm (10 inch) square of leaf (or kitchen foil lined with greaseproof paper). Press out to about 1 cm (½ inch) thickness. Follow with a piece of meat and enough sauce to cover the surface of the dough. Overlap the sides and ends of the dough to form square parcels. Secure with cotton string or a strip of banana leaf. Kitchen foil parcels will not need securing. Arrange the parcels in the top half of a steamer and cover with a few banana leaves or greaseproof paper. Cover tightly and steam for 1½ hours, topping up with hot water when necessary. These *tamales* can be refrigerated for 3 days or frozen in their leaves. Serve hot with *Frijoles*.

■

Tamales al horno

Baked tamales

This recipe turns *tamales* into yet another delicious dish in which you layer them with sauce, cream and green chillies. It will make an excellent main course with salad and black beans.

SERVES 6

6 cooked Tamales (see
   page 92), red or green or
   both
1 tablespoon cooking oil
1 quantity Salsa de Tomate
   Verde (see page 45)

2 jalapeño chillies, seeds
   removed, thinly sliced
3 tablespoons double cream

Cut the *tamales* lengthwise in half and lightly fry them in the hot oil. Drain on absorbent kitchen paper. Grease an ovenproof dish and place the *tamales* in it. Spoon the sauce over them, arrange the chilli strips on top, then pour over the cream. Bake in a preheated oven at 180°C, 350°F, Gas Mark 4 for about 30 minutes or until warmed through. Serve hot.

VARIATION:

Tamal de Cazuela—Mexican dumpling pie

When corn husks are not available, or you are in a hurry, this recipe is a good substitute for *tamales* at half the preparation time. Though not so authentic, the dish is just as flavourful. Use the recipe for *tamales*, but instead of wrapping the dough, filling and sauce in corn husks, assemble them in the following way.

Grease two 20 × 30 cm (8 × 12 inch) ovenproof dishes. Generously cover the bottom of the dish with sauce, then spoon some of the dough on to it to resemble small islands, leaving room for them to expand during cooking. Place large pieces of cooked meat on top, then cover with more sauce. Layer the rest of the dough, meat and sauce in the same way, reserving a little of the sauce. Cover very tightly with foil and cook in the centre of a preheated oven at 180°C, 350°F, Gas Mark 4 for about 1 hour. Prick the dough with a fork to test for readiness. Heat the reserved sauce and serve with the pie.

For cocktail parties, I make *Tamal de Cazuela*, cut it into 2½ cm (1 inch) squares, place it in paper cake cups and serve it hot.

■

Tamales de elote

Fresh corn tamales

Tamales de Elote are very popular and quick to make. They are excellent for breakfast, as they are light and sweet. The last time I had them was on a trip to Mexico City when staying with friends, and I managed to eat six for breakfast! The fresh green husks that are used look especially appetizing with the light yellow corn dough inside. It is a good recipe for using up corn on the cob which is past its prime and is too tough to eat boiled. You can tell this by pricking a kernel with your nail. If a milky liquid comes out, they are tender; if it does not, they are tough. This recipe has to be prepared quickly once the kernels are off the cob to prevent them from becoming bitter. If corn on the cob is not available, you may use frozen corn, thawed at room temperature for about 2 hours.

MAKES 12 small *tamales*

12 large cobs of corn or	*½ teaspoon salt*
1 kg (2 lb) frozen corn	*1 teaspoon brown sugar*
50 g (2 oz) masa harina	*1 tablespoon baking powder*
50 g (2 oz) butter, melted	*25 g (1 oz) raisins* (optional)

To remove the husks from the ears of corn, carefully peel them back towards the base, revealing the kernels. Insert a sharp knife at the base to pull the cob away without disturbing the husks any further; they tend to split lengthwise easily. Wash the leaves in hot water, and drain.

Cut the kernels from the cobs as near to the core as possible. (Each cob will yield about 100 g (4 oz) of kernels.) Grind them, in batches, into a rough textured purée in the liquidizer. Empty the mixture into a large bowl and mix in the remaining ingredients except the raisins. Working quickly, hold enough corn husks in the palm of your hand to cover it, place 1 heaped tablespoon of the mixture on them and add a few raisins. Arrange the leaves over the centre and neatly fold the tail up towards the top. Steam for about 40 minutes as described for *Tamales* (see page 94). Serve hot with *Chocolate Caliente* (see page 226) or *Café de Olla* (see page 227).

Tamales de elote Veracruzanos

Fresh corn tamales with meat and chilli sauce

This is a more complicated version of *Tamales de Elote* (see page 97) and is a meal in itself. Like other *tamales* the meat and sauce are inside the leaves but the texture is coarser than in traditional *tamales*. Once the kernels are off the cob, you have to work quickly or the mixture will turn bitter.

MAKES 12 medium-size *tamales*

3 ancho chillies	*12 cobs of corn or 1 kg (2 lb)*
150 ml (5 fl oz) hot stock	*frozen corn kernels, thawed*
400 g (14 oz) can peeled	*50 g (2 oz) masa harina*
tomatoes	*1 teaspoon salt*
2 green chillies	*1 tablespoon baking powder*

1 clove garlic
1 chicken stock cube
pinch of sugar
100 g (4 oz) lard, melted

225 g (8 oz) cooked pork,
  shredded
few leaves of epazote (optional)

Warm the chillies in a dry frying pan over medium heat for about 3 minutes until tender, then remove from the heat. Discard all seeds, veins and stems and soak in the hot stock for about 1 hour. Place the chillies and stock in a liquidizer together with the tomatoes, green chillies, garlic, chicken stock cube and sugar and blend to a purée. Heat 1 tablespoon of the measured lard in a saucepan, sieve in the purée and stir over medium heat for about 5 minutes, or until the mixture thickens.

Take the leaves off the cob as described in *Tamales de Elote* (see page 97), wash and drain them. Using a sharp knife, cut off the kernels from the ears of corn. Liquidize to a coarse purée, then add the remaining melted lard, *masa harina*, salt and baking powder. Hold 2 overlapping leaves of the corn in one hand and fill with 2 tablespoons of the dough, some shredded pork, sauce and if desired, a leaf of *epazote*. Arrange the leaves to cover the mixture, tucking up the tail end. Place in a steamer, cover with foil and steam for about 2 hours.

Tostadas compuestas

Fried tortillas with a salad topping

Tostadas are one of Mexico's most picturesque dishes, and they are nutritious too! If you want to add atmosphere to a party and help break the ice—that is, if the tequila cocktail hasn't done it for you—you can lay out all the ingredients and let your guests assemble their own *tostadas*.

The size of the *tostada* depends on the size of the tortilla you use. Small tortillas 7½ cm (3 inches) in diameter are less forbidding than larger ones. But if you don't mind making a mess, try 25 cm (10 inch) tortillas—for which you'll need not only a better appetite, but also plenty of courage. If you have some tortillas which are too large for your requirements, use an empty can to cut them down to size before frying, saving the left-over edges for *totopos* (see page

56). This recipe uses 15 cm (6 inch) tortillas, which make a good starter.

SERVES 6

oil for deep frying
6 corn tortillas 15 cm
  (6 inches) in diameter
200 g (7 oz) Frijoles Refritos,
  at room temperature
1 small crisp lettuce, finely
  shredded
¼ cooked chicken, boned, or
  175 g (6 oz) cooked
  shredded meat
12 slices tomato

12 onion rings
6 tablespoons soured cream,
  mixed with 2 tablespoons
  milk
50 g (2 oz) Cheddar or Edam
  cheese, grated
Jalapeños en Vinagre (optional)
1 quantity Guacamole or
  1 avocado, sliced
salt and ground black pepper

Deep fry the tortillas in very hot oil (180°C, 350°F) for 2–3 minutes or until they are golden brown. *Tostadas* need not be entirely flat, so don't worry if the tortillas curl slightly as you fry them; use a slotted spoon and a fork to flatten them. If they start to puff up, just flatten the bubble with the back of the spoon. Drain on absorbent kitchen paper.

When all the tortillas are done, spread each one with beans and top with lettuce, chicken, sliced tomato, onion rings, soured cream mixture, grated cheese, pickle and *Guacamole* or sliced avocados. Season lightly with salt and pepper. Eat within 20 minutes of preparation. The frying can be done up to 1 week in advance, provided the *tostadas* are cooled and kept in an airtight container.

■

Chilaquiles

Tortilla chips in a sauce

In Mexico, *chilaquiles* is a popular breakfast dish, as it's not too heavy but quite filling. With *Frijoles Refritos* and a little salad, it can be used for a light lunch or supper. Occasionally I use it to liven up dinner menus because of its texture and colour. It is quick and easy to prepare, provided that the tortillas are already made. If you want the tortillas to be crisp, it must be eaten as soon as it is made.

Otherwise, it can be prepared ahead of time—the flavour and texture are different, but it is still good.

SERVES 4

oil for deep frying
1 onion, finely chopped
2 tablespoons tomato purée
1 chicken stock cube
2 green chillies

¼ teaspoon ground black
  pepper
½ teaspoon sugar
300 ml (½ pint) water
6 corn tortillas, cut into eight

To garnish
½ onion, finely chopped
4 tablespoons soured cream
  (optional)

100 g (2 oz) Cheshire cheese,
  crumbled (optional)

Heat 1 tablespoon of the oil in a frying pan and fry the onions for 2 minutes, until golden. Add the tomato purée, chicken stock cube, chillies, black pepper and sugar. Stir well, add the water and simmer for 10 minutes over medium heat, until the sauce thickens and reduces by about half. Remove the chillies. Meanwhile, heat the oil for deep frying to 180°C, 350°F. Fry the tortillas in 2 batches for about 5 minutes each or until they just change colour. Drain on absorbent kitchen paper and keep warm.

Just before serving, toss the tortilla chips in the sauce, making sure they are well covered. Place on a serving dish and sprinkle with chopped onion. Soured cream and/or white crumbly cheese may also be sprinkled on top.

■

Burritos Chilangos

Tortillas with ham and cheese

This recipe is named after the inhabitants of Mexico City who are known as Chilangos in other South American countries. The *burritos* are a lot smaller than those popular in the north of Mexico (and in the United States, where they grow out of all proportion!). The city dwellers make their wheat tortillas about 20 cm (8 inches) in diameter and fill them with ham and cheese. It is really the equivalent of a toasted sandwich. Like many other *antojitos*, this dish is quick to prepare provided you already have the tortillas. It goes well with *Guacamole* and *Frijoles Refritos*.

SERVES 4

8 wheat tortillas
225 g (8 oz) Cheddar
  cheese, grated

4 slices cooked ham, cut into
  strips 1 cm (½ inch) wide
Jalapeños en Vinagre (optional)

Place 4 tortillas on an ungreased baking sheet, and fill each one with grated cheese, strips of ham and some *Jalapeños en Vinagre*. Lay another tortilla on top. Cover tightly with foil and bake in a preheated oven at 200°C, 400°F, Gas Mark 6 for 10–13 minutes until the cheese has melted. Serve immediately.

Burritos norteños

Tortillas with chilli con carne

In the north of Mexico, *burritos* are medium-sized wheat tortillas with a filling, which are rolled up in the shape of cigars. In the United States, however, *burritos* are much larger with more filling inside, and are wrapped up into neat parcels or left open. Similarly, corn tortillas with a filling, known as *tacos*, are cigar-shaped in Mexico while in the U.S. they are larger and partly left open. Whether you prefer to roll or fold them, *burritos* are a filling dish, especially when served with *Guacamole*, salad and *Frijoles Refritos*. A popular filling is *Chile con Carne*, but they can be filled with any cooked meat, beans, or cheese, or a combination of all three.

SERVES 6

6 wheat tortillas
¼ quantity Chile con
  Carne (see page 146)
100 g (4 oz) Cheddar
  cheese, coarsely grated

50 g (2 oz) Mozzarella cheese,
  coarsely grated
1 quantity Guacamole

To garnish
½ onion, thinly sliced

1 lettuce, finely shredded

Warm each tortilla in a dry hot frying pan for 40 seconds until pliable. Remove from the pan. Fold 2 sides into the centre, overlapping the edges slightly. Now fold the part nearest to you towards the centre, forming a pocket; secure with a cocktail stick. Fill the pocket with *Chile con Carne*, then place the *burrito* in a greased ovenproof dish. Continue until you have filled all the tortillas. Sprinkle over the cheese, cover tightly with foil and bake in a preheated oven at 180°C, 350°F, Gas Mark 4 for 30 minutes. Remove the cocktail sticks. Spoon on the *Guacamole*, garnish with onion slices and shredded lettuce and serve immediately.

■

Indios vestidos

Tortillas in batter and tomato or chilli sauce

The literal translation of this dish is 'dressed Indians', the dress being a coating of egg! In any case, it is a very good alternative to the traditional *peneques* which are extremely difficult to make and impossible to obtain outside Mexico. This dish could make a good starter or light lunch accompanied by *Frijoles Refritos*. If you cannot find the *ancho* chillies, try this dish with the *Salsa para Enchiladas* instead, omitting the first four and last four ingredients.

SERVES 4

2 ancho chillies
450 ml (¾ pint) chicken stock
1 clove garlic
¼ teaspoon cinnamon
6 corn tortillas
200 g (6 oz) Cheddar cheese, coarsely grated

2 eggs, separated
3 tablespoons cooking oil
2 tablespoons flour
1 onion, finely chopped
2 tablespoons tomato purée
½ teaspoon salt
¼ teaspoon sugar

Warm the *ancho* chillies in a hot dry heavy-based frying pan until they soften, about 2 minutes on each side. Remove and discard the stems, seeds and veins, cover with stock and leave to soak for 30 minutes. Blend the garlic, chillies, stock and cinnamon in a liquidizer until it is a thick paste. Set aside. Halve the tortillas, then warm through in a hot heavy-based pan for about 30 seconds on each side. Place some grated cheese on 1 tortilla half, then fold it in half to form a triangle, securing with cocktail sticks. Fill all the tortillas in this manner. Save a little cheese to garnish. Beat the egg yolks until pale and fluffy. In a separate bowl, whisk the whites until stiff and blend in the yolks.

Heat the oil in a frying pan. Dip each filled tortilla in flour, then in the egg and fry until light golden. Drain on absorbent kitchen paper. Use the remaining hot oil to fry the onion until soft, then add the tomato purée, salt and sugar. Sieve the chilli mixture into the pan and simmer for about 15 minutes. Remove the cocktail sticks from tortillas, place them in an ovenproof dish and cover with foil. Cook in a preheated oven at 180°C, 350°F, Gas Mark 4 for 20 minutes. Bring the sauce to the boil and pour over the tortillas before serving. Garnish with reserved cheese.

Huevos rancheros típicos

Ranch-style eggs with tomato sauce

Huevos Rancheros is more a brunch than an early morning breakfast; at my home we eat them for lunch or supper. They are colourful, and a delightful blend of textures and flavours. The tortillas are fried until crisp, but if you prefer soft tortillas, just shorten the frying time. The number of eggs per person can vary according to appetite, but remember that for this dish you need to have the tortillas made, the beans cooked and the sauce ready before frying the eggs. Serve with hunks of crusty white bread to soak up every bit of the delicious sauce.

SERVES 4

4 tablespoons cooking oil
8 corn tortillas
600 ml (1 pint) Salsa para
  Enchiladas

100 g (4 oz) Frijoles Refritos, of
  spreading texture
4 eggs

To serve
50 g (2 oz) Cheddar cheese,
  grated (optional)

1 ripe avocado, sliced
  (optional)

Heat the oil in a frying pan and fry the tortillas 2 at a time until golden brown and crisp. Drain on absorbent kitchen paper. Drain most of the oil from the frying pan, leaving about 2 tablespoons. Heat the sauce and the beans in separate saucepans. Spread the hot beans over each tortilla and place 2 tortillas slightly overlapping on a warm dinner plate for each person. Now fry the eggs in the pan and place on top of the beans and tortillas and cover generously with piping hot sauce. Some people like to add grated cheese and slices of avocado which makes it an even more colourful dish. Serve immediately.

■

Huevos con tortillas y perejil

Tortilla chip omelette

Definitely my favourite way to eat eggs, but for some reason I have only come across this dish in my own home in Mexico. One of my family's favourites and I hope it will be yours too. It makes a tasty breakfast accompanied by beans or a light lunch with Mexican rice.

SERVES 4

4 tablespoons oil
6 eggs, well beaten with
  1 tablespoon water
4 spring onions, finely
  chopped
4 sprigs parsley,
  finely chopped

2 green chillies (chopped
  if you prefer it hot)
4 corn tortillas fried into
  totopos (see page 56) *and cut*
  into bite-size pieces
pinch of ground black pepper
pinch of salt

To garnish
¼ quantity Salsa Típica or
  4 teaspoons tomato ketchup

sprigs of parsley

Heat the oil in an omelette pan over moderate heat. Add the remaining ingredients and stir with a wooden spatula, carefully tilting the frying pan to ensure all the egg cooks. Lower the heat and cover tightly for about 3 minutes, to ensure it is cooked through. Garnish with hot sauce or ketchup, and sprigs of parsley.

Huevos revueltos con chorizo

Scrambled eggs with chorizo and tomatoes

Another of my favourites which I love to eat on crusty warm French bread which has been buttered. Served with *Frijoles Refritos* and rice, this egg dish is perfect for an impromptu meal, provided you have the cooked beans and *Chorizo* on hand.

SERVES 4

2 tablespoons cooking oil
100 g (4 oz) Chorizo
  (sliced if bought)
2 ripe tomatoes, quartered
1/2 onion, finely chopped

1/4 teaspoon salt
1/8 teaspoon ground black
  pepper
1 green chilli, sliced
4 eggs, well beaten

Heat the oil in a frying pan and fry the *Chorizo* for about 3 minutes, stirring continually, then remove from the pan. Add the tomatoes, onions, salt and pepper to the pan and fry for about 3 minutes until the tomato is partially cooked. Add the chilli, *Chorizo* and beaten eggs and cook for a few minutes, stirring once to ensure the egg is cooked evenly. Slide the mixture onto a warm plate, divide into portions and serve immediately.

Frijoles con chorizo

Beans with spicy sausage

This is one of my favourite ways of eating *frijoles*. I like them on toast with a fried or scrambled egg on top. A very simple and tasty combination for a hearty breakfast if you already have the beans and either home-made or bought *Chorizo*.

SERVES 4

1/2 tablespoon cooking oil
75 g (3 oz) Chorizo
275 g (10 oz) Frijoles

1 onion, finely chopped, to
  garnish

Heat the oil in a frying pan and fry the *Chorizo* for about 7 minutes or until crisp. Add the beans and cook for 10 minutes, stirring occasionally. Serve hot, garnished with the chopped onion.

■

Moyetes

Crusty rolls with beans and cheese

This is a breakfast dish, often served with *Huevos Revueltos con Chorizo*. It is the Mexican version of an open sandwich and is suitable for a light lunch served with salad. It is a quick snack too, provided the beans are already cooked.

SERVES 4

4 crusty rolls, halved
25 g (1 oz) butter
225 g (8 oz) Frijoles Refritos
½ quantity Salsa Típica

1 avocado
salt and ground black pepper
50 g (2 oz) grated cheese

Remove some of the centre from the rolls. Butter the rolls liberally and spread with the beans. Bake in a preheated oven at 160°C, 325°F, Gas Mark 3 for 20 minutes. Spoon a tablespoon of sauce over each piece of bread. Peel the avocado, cut into 8 slices and arrange over the sauce. Sprinkle with salt, pepper and grated cheese and serve immediately.

■

Pambacitos compuestos

Crusty rolls in a chilli sauce

Pambacitos Compuestos are bread rolls with potato and *Chorizo* in a chilli sauce. *Pambazo* is the name of the particular type of bread used, but if it is not available, crusty rolls are a good substitute. This is a quickly put together snack—always provided you have some *Salsa Adobada* ready made. In Mexico it is often used for brunch but it makes a good supper or light lunch dish with a green salad and some beans.

SERVES 4

4 crusty rolls	pinch of salt and ground black
3 tablespoons oil	pepper
100 g (4 oz) Chorizo	½ lettuce, finely chopped
2 large potatoes, boiled	½ quantity Salsa Adobada
and cubed	

Cut the rolls in half and remove the centres. Heat 1 tablespoon of the oil in a frying pan and fry the *Chorizo* until crisp, about 7 minutes. Add the cooked potato, salt and pepper and stir for 4 minutes. Drain and keep.

Fill the bread bases with the potato mixture and some of the lettuce. Put the other piece of bread on top and secure with cocktail sticks. Heat the remaining oil in a frying pan, dip 1 roll at a time into the cold sauce then fry on each side for about 3 minutes. Remove from the heat and keep warm. Finish frying the other rolls. Heat any leftover sauce in the pan, spoon it over the rolls and serve immediately.

■

Tortas compuestas

Crusty rolls with a filling

Tortas Compuestas are crusty buns with a filling of any kind—it can be cooked meat such as ham, steak, roast beef, pork or roast chicken, or an egg, cheese or vegetarian filling. I have omitted the meat from this recipe, but do include it if you wish. It will make a light lunch or snack. In Mexico, these are a popular take-away which are sold at specialist shops called *torterias*.

SERVES 4

4 medium-size crusty buns	2 tomatoes, sliced
or 1 French stick, cut into 4	½ onion, finely sliced
½ quantity Frijoles Refritos	pinch of dried oregano
2 avocados, mashed	salt and ground black pepper
1 lettuce, finely shredded	Jalapeños en Vinagre
4 slices processed cheese	

Warm the bread in a preheated oven at 180°C, 350°F, Gas Mark 4 for about 15 minutes to make it nice and crusty. Cut each bun in half and spread the bottom half with warm beans, avocado, lettuce, one slice of cheese, 2 tomato slices, sliced onion, oregano, salt and pepper and pickles. Cover with the other half of the bread and serve immediately.

■

Pepitos

Beef and avocado sandwich

Pepitos (not to be confused with *pepitas*, which are pumpkin seeds), are a type of *torta*. Like *tacos*, *tortas* are snacks that people eat on their way to work or after any form of entertainment. *Pepito* is literally translated as 'little Joe'—which is not at all surprising because in Mexico all men are christened Joseph before any chosen name (and all women are christened Mary before their chosen name). So this is a steak and avocado sandwich with a proper name!

SERVES 4

1 French stick or 4 crusty buns	*4 slices roast beef*
	2 ripe avocados, mashed
French mustard	*salt and pepper*
225 g (8 oz) Frijoles Refritos	*Jalapeños en Vinagre*

Warm the bread in the oven for 10 minutes. Cut in half and spread mustard and beans on the bottom half. Top with roast beef, some mashed avocado, salt and pepper and a touch of pickles and cover again.

Arroz, Legumbres y Ensaladas
Rice, Vegetables and Salads

This chapter has been written with vegetarians in mind. It seems that in Mexico no vegetable is served just as it is; we always cook it with a little of this and a little of that! The results are not only ingenious, but also tasty and nutritious.

Mexico is a vegetarian's paradise, as practically any fruit or vegetable can be grown in the country at any time of the year. If you look hard enough, you can always find what you are after, even if it is out of season. Frozen foods are not popular because of the sheer variety of fresh fruits and vegetables constantly available.

Special attention has been given to peppers as there are so many interesting ways of stuffing them with fruits, beans, cheese, fish or meat; whether in a tomato sauce or a vinaigrette, they turn out to be the topic of conversation amongst my friends.

Plantains, the large cooking bananas, are featured because they add a new dimension to the Mexican table. Corn can be cooked in so many delicious ways; and sweet potatoes and cho-cho also contribute to the incredible variety of vegetables you can offer.

Dried beans occupy a very important place in the diet and are often used for soup, or for stuffing *poblano* chillies or simply by themselves; they all contain fibre and B vitamins and most of them also have calcium, phosphorus and iron in varying amounts. Chillies when they are dried are especially rich in vitamin A as well as having substantial amounts of calcium, vitamin B and other minerals.

Rice is served as a separate course (*sopa seca* or 'dry soup'), normally after *sopa aguada* or 'wet soup'. However, outside Mexico it is more often served as a side-dish, so it is included as such in this chapter. The rice is mixed with everything from beans, chillies, carrots, peas and corn to chicken, fish and shellfish to give it flavour and colour. Rice and beans feature in almost every menu, either separately or together. Because the rice has been fried before steaming, it lends itself to freezing and reheating without losing either flavour or texture. It also reheats well in microwave ovens.

Salads play an important part in the Mexican cuisine, being basically mixtures of raw or cold cooked vegetables. If they contain meat, chicken or fish, they are mostly used as light meals, otherwise they take the place of hot cooked vegetables. Often meals are started with a selection of fresh fruits, which gives a clean and fresh start to a meal. Though not an indispensable part of the Mexican meal, as for example tortillas or beans are, salad greens are included in a great many of the *antojitos* and are also used lavishly as garnishes for other dishes.

Basically any salad you wish to prepare will enhance a Mexican meal, especially if you use lemon or lime juice instead of vinegar and oil for a dressing. Sliced tomatoes and onions, as well as radishes cut in the shape of flowers, are a very Mexican touch, as are fresh coriander, very finely shredded lettuce and avocado slices. In this chapter I have concentrated on the vegetable salads. Meat, fish or chicken salads can be found in other chapters.

■

Arroz blanco

White rice, Mexican-style

Rice is a popular dish in Mexico. This is a practical way of cooking it because it keeps well and can be frozen, and also used as a basis for other dishes. Basically it is fried and then steamed which ensures fluffiness.

SERVES 4

2 tablespoons cooking oil	½ teaspoon salt or 1 chicken
1 clove garlic	stock cube
175 g (6 oz) long grain	2 sprigs parsley or coriander
white rice	½ onion, finely chopped
450 ml (¾ pint) boiling	1 green chilli
water	

Heat the oil in a heavy-based saucepan with a tight-fitting lid, and fry the garlic until it becomes black. Add the rice, and fry for about 4 minutes, stirring continually, until it loses its stickiness and becomes white instead of translucent. Discard the garlic and drain off any excess oil. Add the water and remaining ingredients and bring to the boil quickly. Reduce the heat, cover and simmer slowly for 15 minutes. When ready, there will be no water left in the bottom of the pan, and the rice will have doubled in volume and be light and fluffy. Discard the herbs and chilli. Serve hot or cold.

VARIATION:

Arroz con Verduras—Vegetable rice

SERVES 4–6

100 g (4 oz) corn kernels, 50 g (2 oz) peas, 50 g (2 oz) cubed carrots: when the rice has been fried and the oil drained, you can add all or any one of these vegetables before adding the water and simmering.

■

Arroz con rajas

Rice casserole with peppers, cream and cheese

In Mexico this rice and pepper casserole would contain *poblano* chillies but green peppers cut into strips are an acceptable substitute. This dish is perfect for a buffet as it is attractive and tasty, and it can be prepared hours ahead of time, then just baked before serving.

SERVES 8

120 ml (4 fl oz) soured cream
50 ml (2 fl oz) single cream
½ teaspoon salt
¼ teaspoon ground black
  pepper
75 g (3 oz) Cheddar cheese,
  grated

75 g (3 oz) Mozzarella cheese,
  grated
1 quantity Arroz Blanco (see
  page 111)
2 green peppers, sliced
1 red pepper, sliced

Lightly grease a 25 × 18 cm (10 × 7 inch) ovenproof dish. Mix the creams with the salt and pepper. Blend the cheeses together. Layer the cooked rice, sliced peppers, cream and cheese in the dish, finishing with cheese. Bake on the top shelf of a preheated oven at 180°C, 350°F, Gas Mark 4 for about 30 minutes. The cheese should be brown and the rice should look dry around the edges. Serve hot.

Arroz con frijoles

Rice with beans

This dish is a seaside speciality, popular throughout Latin America and the Caribbean, where it is eaten with fried egg on top and garnished with slices of ripe fried plantain. The combination of the pulse and the cereal seem to be beneficial for best absorption of nutrients.

SERVES 6

2 tablespoons corn oil
1 clove garlic
175 g (6 oz) long grain
  white rice
1 chicken stock cube
2 tablespoons chopped
  parsley

½ onion, finely chopped
1 green chilli
2 tablespoons tomato purée
150 g (6 oz) Frijoles, with their
  liquid
450 ml (¾ pint) boiling water

Heat the oil and fry the garlic until it turns black. Discard the garlic and add the rice, stirring occasionally, to achieve an even golden colour. Drain off as much oil as you can, then add the remaining ingredients. Stir for 1 minute and bring to the boil quickly. Lower the heat, cover and simmer for 20–25 minutes or until all the liquid has been absorbed.

Arroz con Jitomate—Tomato rice

SERVES 6

2 tablespoons tomato purée   ½ teaspoon salt

Fry the rice until it becomes pale golden, then drain the oil and add the tomato purée and salt. Continue as in the main recipe, simmering for 20 minutes. (See also *Arroz con Verduras*, page 112.)

Arroz con Pimentón—Rice with red peppers

SERVES 6

4 red peppers   ½ teaspoon salt
1 tablespoon tomato purée   12 stuffed olives

Fry the rice until pale golden and drain the oil. Blend 3 of the peppers in the liquidizer at high speed with some of the measured water. Add the sieved purée to the rice. Slice 1 pepper into fine strips and add it to the rice with the rest of the ingredients. Simmer for 25 minutes.

■

Chiles rellenos estilo Zacatlán

Peppers stuffed with fruit

These peppers are similar to the more traditional *Chiles Rellenos* recipes (see variations), except that they are filled with fruit. For this recipe I have omitted the minced pork which is traditionally added, in order to achieve an original and tasty vegetarian dish which will go well with *Frijoles Refritos* and rice, courgettes and corn. Should you wish to incorporate the meat, however, fry 50 g (2 oz) minced pork for about 10 minutes with the onions and when it browns, proceed as instructed.

SERVES 6

6 peppers 9–10 cm
  (3½–4 inches) long

For the stuffing

2 tablespoons cooking oil
1 small onion, finely chopped
2 tablespoons tomato purée
25 g (1 oz) monkey nuts,
  shelled
2 green chillies
¼ teaspoon salt
pinch of ground black pepper
pinch of dried thyme
pinch of dried oregano

1 teaspoon malt vinegar
1 fresh peach, peeled and
  stoned, or 2 tinned peach
  halves, cubed
1 pear, peeled, cored and cubed
2 slices pineapple, cubed
25 g (1 oz) desiccated coconut
25 g (1 oz) flaked almonds
25 g (1 oz) raisins

For frying

3 eggs, separated
vegetable oil
2 tablespoons flour

Salsa para Enchiladas,
  to finish

Place the peppers under a hot grill for about 4 minutes, turning regularly, so the skins scorch evenly. Place in a polythene bag and leave for about 20 minutes. This traps the steam inside the peppers, cooking them further. Remove the peppers from the bag, peel them, cut off the tops and discard the pith and seeds.

To make the stuffing, heat the oil and fry the onion until soft. Add the remaining ingredients (reserving a few nuts for garnish) and simmer gently for about 10 minutes until the mixture thickens. If you prefer a mild flavour, discard the chillies at this stage. If you like it hot, chop the chillies and put them back in the pan. Stuff the peeled peppers with the fruity mixture, securing with cocktail sticks.

Beat the egg yolks until pale and fluffy. In a separate bowl, whisk the whites until stiff, then blend in the yolks. Heat at least 5 cm (2 inches) of oil in a saucepan. Dip 1 pepper at a time in the flour, then in the egg batter and fry on all sides, keeping the heat quite low to prevent burning. When they are golden brown, drain on absorbent kitchen towels. Now remove the cocktail sticks (the egg coating will keep the filling in place). Bring the sauce to the boil, add the peppers and simmer for 5 minutes. Serve very hot, garnished with the remaining nuts.

This dish will keep in the refrigerator for 2 days, and it freezes well.

VARIATIONS:

To make *Chiles Rellenos de Queso*, substitute the fruit mixture with slices of Cheddar cheese, using 1 slice for each pepper.

To make *Chiles Rellenos de Picadillo*, substitute the fruit mixture with *picadillo* (see page 145), using 2 tablespoons for each pepper.

■

Chiles en nogada

Stuffed peppers in a nut and cream sauce

This patriotic dish is popular around the Mexican Independence festivities because it features the green, white and red of the Mexican flag. It is traditionally made with green walnuts which are easy to peel; but almonds, walnuts or hazelnuts can be used instead, and though the cream will not look so white the flavour will still be excellent. It helps to prepare the *picadillo* ahead of time. Serve at room temperature with *Arroz Blanco* and *Frijoles*.

SERVES 4

*4 medium-size green
  peppers
175 g (6 oz) Picadillo (see
  page 145)
1 small lettuce, shredded
25 g (1 oz) ground nuts
150 ml (¼ pint) soured
  cream*

*¼ teaspoon salt
seeds from 1 pomegranate
  kernel or 100 g (4 oz) canned
  pimentos, chopped, to
  garnish*

Place the peppers under a hot grill for about 4 minutes, turning them regularly so the skins will scorch evenly. Place in a polythene bag and leave for about 20 minutes to trap the steam inside the peppers. Remove and discard the stems and seeds. Stuff each pepper with 2 tablespoons of *Picadillo*. Place the lettuce on a serving dish and arrange the stuffed peppers on it. Mix together the ground nuts, cream and salt and spoon over the peppers. Garnish with pomegranate seeds or chopped pimentos.

■

Chiles en vinagreta

Peppers stuffed with beans in an onion vinaigrette

This is a good vegetarian dish for vinaigrette lovers! It is much better prepared two days ahead of time because it gives the vinegar time to evaporate. It is served cold so it would be a good summer dish, and it goes well with rice and avocado and tomato salad. You will require *Frijoles Refritos* which should be already prepared.

SERVES 4

120 ml (4 fl oz) salad oil
4 medium-size red or green
   peppers
2 large onions, thinly sliced
600 ml (1 pint) malt vinegar
1 tablespoon granulated
   sugar
1 green chilli, thinly sliced

1 teaspoon dried oregano
½ teaspoon dried thyme
½ teaspoon cumin
1 bay leaf
¼ teaspoon ground black
   pepper
½ teaspoon salt
400 g (14 oz) Frijoles Refritos

Heat the oil in a large heavy frying pan and fry the peppers whole for about 6 minutes, turning them frequently. Remove the peppers and fry the onion for about 4 minutes then remove from the pan. Add the remaining ingredients, except the beans, and simmer for about 15 minutes until the liquid is reduced by half.

Meanwhile, remove the stalks and seeds from the peppers and any blistered skin (it is not necessary to remove it all). Stuff each pepper with 1–2 tablespoons beans and secure the opening with cocktail sticks. Place the stuffed peppers and the onions on a heat-resistant dish and pour over the boiling vinegar mixture. Cool, and refrigerate uncovered for 2 days.

Chiles rellenos de queso crema

Peppers with cream cheese

This can be served as a vegetable with any roast meat, or as a main course with rice and beans.

SERVES 4

1 tablespoon cooking oil
¼ onion, finely chopped
225 g (8 oz) courgettes, quartered
225 g (8 oz) corn kernels
1 tablespoon chopped coriander or epazote
1 green chilli, finely chopped
½ teaspoon salt

¼ teaspoon ground black pepper
4 green peppers, grilled and peeled (see Chiles en Vinagreta on page 117)
225 g (8 oz) cream cheese
150 ml (¼ pint) soured cream
100 g (4 oz) Cheddar cheese, grated

Heat the oil and fry the onion, courgettes, corn, coriander and chilli for 3 minutes. Add salt and pepper, cover and simmer for 5 minutes. Remove from the heat and place in a well-greased ovenproof casserole. Stuff peppers with the cream cheese, secure with a cocktail stick and place on top of the courgette mixture. Cover with the soured cream, sprinkle with the grated cheese and bake for 15 minutes in a preheated oven at 200°C, 400°F, Gas Mark 6. Serve hot.

Chiles rellenos de frijol

Peppers stuffed with beans

There are many versions of the famous dish *Chiles Rellenos*. This particular one is a good, wholesome, tasty dish which is also suitable for vegetarians. *Chiles Rellenos* are traditionally made with *poblano* chillies, but peppers are an acceptable substitute. They go well with rice and *chilaquiles* (see page 100).

■

SERVES 4

4 medium-size green
  peppers
1 tablespoon cooking oil
½ onion, finely chopped
275 g (10 oz) Frijoles
  Refritos
3 tomatoes, grilled and
  peeled
2 green chillies, sliced

¼ teaspoon dried oregano
2 tablespoons chopped
  coriander
¾ teaspoon salt
85 ml (3 fl oz) soured cream
50 ml (2 fl oz) single cream
1 small lettuce, shredded
6 radish flowers,
  to garnish

Grill and peel the peppers (see *Chiles en Nogada*). Heat the oil and
fry the onion for 3 minutes, add the beans, tomatoes, chillies,
oregano, coriander and salt. Simmer, mashing the mixture for
about 5 minutes. Stuff the peeled peppers with the bean mixture
and place on a serving dish with a bed of lettuce. Mix the creams
together and pour over the peppers. Garnish with radish flowers
and serve cold.

■

Rajas de chile poblano

Peppers and onions in tomato sauce

There are a variety of dishes known as *rajas*, each using a different
type of chilli. The most popular version is this recipe, using
poblano chillies, but you can substitute green peppers. This dish
makes a very good filling for *tacos* or can be served as accompaniment to meats, *empanadas* and *frijoles*.

SERVES 4

1 tablespoon cooking oil
1 large onion, finely sliced
2 large peppers, finely sliced
2 green chillies, sliced
¼ teaspoon salt
¼ teaspoon ground black
  pepper

¼ teaspoon sugar
1 tablespoon chopped coriander
  or epazote
1 chicken stock cube, crumbled
2 tablespoons tomato purée
85 ml (3 fl oz) water

Heat the oil in a heavy-based frying pan and fry the onion, peppers and chillies, stirring, until they are just starting to change colour. Add the remaining ingredients. Stir, then cover tightly and cook for 2 minutes.

VARIATION:

Sprinkle with 50 g (2 oz) grated mature Cheddar cheese and spoon 4 tablespoons of soured cream over the top, then bake for 15 minutes at 180°C, 350°F, Gas Mark 4 or until the cheese is melted.

■

Chile con queso

Chillies and pepper with melted cheese

This dish can be served as a vegetable with any of the meats or as an appetizer to fill warm soft tortillas. The cheeses suitable for this dish are Cheddar and Mozzarella to substitute *Queso de Chihuahua* and *Queso Asadero*. I have much enjoyed this dish served in small amounts as it is a type of rich fondue.

SERVES 4

1 tablespoon cooking oil
½ medium onion, thinly sliced
2 green chillies, sliced into strips
1 green pepper, sliced
1 tomato, grilled, peeled and mashed

85 ml (3 fl oz) milk
100 g (4 oz) mild Cheddar cheese, grated
50 g (2 oz) Mozzarella cheese, grated

Heat the oil in a heavy-based saucepan and fry the onions, chillies and pepper for 4 minutes. Sieve in the tomato and fry for 4 minutes, then add the milk, cover and simmer for 5 minutes. Add the cheese and cook, stirring constantly, for about 1 minute until it melts. Remove from the heat before it starts to bubble. Serve immediately.

Plátano macho al horno

Baked plantain

This is a popular way of eating plantain in the south of Mexico, where they grow in abundance. The plantains have to be very ripe but still firm. Though they are sweet, they go well with rice, pork and lamb.

SERVES 4

2 ripe plantains
50 g (2 oz) butter

2 teaspoons granulated sugar
½ teaspoon ground cinnamon

Grease an ovenproof dish and arrange the plantains in it. Slit each plantain lengthwise, making sure you do not cut right through, and insert the butter, sugar and cinnamon in them. Cover and bake in a preheated oven at 160°C, 325°F, Gas Mark 3 for about 30 minutes. Remove the skin and cut in half crosswise just before serving. Serve hot.

■

Budín Bonampak

Plantain casserole

Located southeast of Mexico City, Bonampak is rich in vegetation and is responsible for a lot of banana and plantain dishes from that area. This casserole, also known as *Budín Tabasqueño*, has a sweet flavour similar to parsnips and makes a good vegetable side dish for pork, lamb and hot chilli dishes.

SERVES 4

2 very ripe plantains,
   unpeeled and quartered
600 ml (1 pint) water
150 g (5 oz) butter

1½ teaspoons baking powder
1 tablespoon caster sugar
85 ml (3 fl oz) single cream
½ teaspoon cinnamon

Boil the quartered plantains in the water for about 20 minutes until completely soft. Drain, peel and remove the centre vein. Mash to a pulp with the remaining ingredients, reserving a little of the cinnamon for garnish. Grease a 20 cm (8 inch) ovenproof dish, arrange the plantain in it and bake in a preheated oven at 180°C, 350°F, Gas Mark 4 for 30 minutes. Sprinkle over the remaining cinnamon and serve hot.

■

Plátano macho frito
Fried plantain

Although the flavour of plantain is similar to the ordinary banana, it is much larger in size and has to be cooked before being eaten. Cooked plantain does not keep well so must be fried just before you require it. Serve with rice and any meat.

SERVES 4

2 very ripe firm plantains   *75 g (2 oz) butter*

Skin the plantains, then cut in half. Slice each half lengthwise into four. Heat the butter in a frying pan and fry the plantain slices for about 4 minutes on each side until golden. Serve hot.

■

Lentejas adobadas con plátano macho
Lentils and plantain in hot chilli sauce

Lentils are full of goodness and this nutritious dish can be considered a meal in itself as it also includes meat. It goes well with rice and soft warm tortillas. It is a versatile dish—you can omit the *ancho* chillies, or turn it into a vegetarian dish by omitting the meat and still have a very tasty result.

SERVES 6

225 g (8 oz) red lentils   *1 chicken stock cube*
225 g (8 oz) stewing pork,   *1.2 litres (2 pints) water*
  cubed (optional)   *1 bay leaf*
1 teaspoon malt vinegar   *2 ancho chillies*
½ teaspoon salt   *1 tablespoon tomato purée*

1 teaspoon ground black
  pepper
1 ripe plantain, unpeeled
  and cut into 2 cm
  (1 inch) rounds
1 onion, chopped
½ teaspoon dried oregano

½ teaspoon ground cloves
¼ teaspoon cinnamon
1 clove garlic
2 tablespoons cooking oil
1 pineapple slice, coarsely
  chopped

Rinse the lentils then place in a saucepan with the meat, vinegar, salt, half the pepper, plantain, onion, chicken stock cube, water and bay leaf. Cover and simmer for 45 minutes until the meat is tender and the lentils and plantain are soft. Remove the plantain and peel off the skin.

Heat the chillies in a dry frying pan until supple. Discard the stems and seeds, and soak the chillies in 150 ml (¼ pint) of the liquid from the lentils. Put the chillies and their liquid in a blender with the tomato purée, oregano, cloves, remaining black pepper, cinnamon and garlic and work to a smooth paste. Heat the oil and fry the mixture for 5 minutes, then add the lentils, meat, plantain and chopped pineapple. Cover and simmer for 30 minutes. Serve hot.

Quesadillas de flor de calabaza

Pumpkin blossom quesadillas

Pumpkin or squash blossoms are frequently used in Mexican dishes, usually as a filling for warm tortillas or *quesadillas*, then served as starters or snacks. In the market, the bright pumpkin blossoms are a most attractive sight. When pumpkin blossoms are not for sale commercially, it is easy to grow your own—I keep an eye on my courgette plants and as soon as the courgette starts forming from the fertilized blossom, I carefully remove the blossom from the vegetable and save it in a plastic bag in the freezer. When I have enough of them I surprise guests and family alike with pumpkin blossom *quesadillas*! Boiled potato peelings also make an unusual alternative; they taste much better than you may think and are, of course, very nutritious. Marrow blossoms may also be used.

SERVES 4

Filling

350 g (12 oz) pumpkin blossoms or potato peelings	1/4 chicken stock cube
1 tablespoon cooking oil	1 tablespoon water or potato cooking water
1/2 onion, finely chopped	pinch of ground black pepper
1 green chilli, finely chopped	50 g (2 oz) Cheddar cheese, coarsely grated
1 tablespoon tomato purée	1 tablespoon chopped epazote or coriander

Dough

150 g (5 oz) masa harina	15 g (1/2 oz) lard
1 teaspoon baking powder	2 tablespoons double cream
1 teaspoon salt	150 ml (5 fl oz) warm water
50 g (2 oz) plain flour	175 g (6 oz) lard for frying

To prepare the filling, wash the pumpkin blossoms then trim off and discard the stems and 'whiskers'. (If using potato peelings, boil them in salted water until soft, then drain, reserving the liquid.) Heat the oil in a frying pan and fry the onion. Add the chopped blossoms or cooked potato skins together with the remaining ingredients and fry, stirring for about 5 minutes. Allow to cool.

To prepare the dough, mix together the dry ingredients. Rub in the lard, then stir in the cream and water. Knead for about 5 minutes to a soft dough consistency. Press into tortillas as instructed on page 38. When you take the first layer of waxed paper off the pressed tortilla, cover half the tortilla with a tablespoon of the filling, leaving about 1 cm (1/2 inch) round the edges. Fold the tortilla in half, leaving on the remaining piece of waxed paper. Press the edges to seal.

Heat the lard in a frying pan. Peel off half the waxed paper, and very carefully lower the filled tortilla into the pan, keeping the waxed paper on top and removing it as soon as possible. (The process is similar to that of cooking tortillas, but care must be taken when dealing with hot fat.) Fry the *quesadillas*, one at a time, over moderate heat until golden on one side, then turn over. When golden, remove from the heat, drain on absorbent kitchen towels and keep in a warm place until all the *quesadillas* are ready.

Calabacitas rellenas

Courgettes stuffed with parsley

Courgettes cooked like this look unusual and elegant and taste very good. Serve as a starter or as a vegetable accompaniment to meat.

SERVES 4

4 courgettes (about
  2.5 cm/1 inch in
  diameter), trimmed
2 teaspoons salt
300 ml (½ pint) water
25 g (1 oz) butter
½ onion, finely chopped
4 tablespoons finely
  chopped parsley

1 chicken stock cube
¼ teaspoon ground black
  pepper
pinch of nutmeg
2 tablespoons cornflour
4 tablespoons single cream
2 tablespoons grated Cheddar
  cheese

Boil the courgettes in the salted water for about 15 minutes, until tender but not soggy. Drain, and allow to cool. Cut the courgettes in half lengthwise and scoop out the centres with a teaspoon, reserving the pulp and leaving about ½ cm (⅓ inch) of flesh behind. Place the shells in a buttered ovenproof casserole.

Heat the butter and lightly fry the onions for 3 minutes, then add the parsley, chicken stock cube, courgette pulp, pepper and nutmeg. Mix the cornflour with the cream and add to the mixture, stirring constantly. Simmer for 2 minutes, then fill the empty courgette shells with this mixture. Sprinkle with the cheese, cover with kitchen foil and bake for 20 minutes in a preheated oven at 160°C, 325°F, Gas Mark 3. Serve hot.

VARIATION:

For a buffet dinner party you can use a large marrow for the shell. Cut the marrow in half while still raw, scoop out the centre and discard. Parboil 450 g (1 lb) courgettes for 15 minutes then mash them to a pulp. Mix the pulp with double the amount of ingredients in the above recipe and use to fill the marrow. Cook for 45 minutes and serve garnished with sprigs of parsley.

Calabacitas con rajas y elote

Courgettes with peppers and corn

Courgettes make an excellent addition to a Mexican meal. Mild in flavour, they add colour and help to minimize the 'hotness'. In Mexico you can buy them in different shapes as well, some being round, others long. *Calabacitas* can be served in a variety of ways: simply boiled and served with butter, cooked in an onion and tomato sauce, creamed with peppers, stuffed, or sliced in a sauce—the possibilities are endless. The ingredients in this recipe make a good combination and the dish is easy to prepare.

SERVES 4

*2 cobs of corn or 100 g
  (4 oz) frozen corn kernels
½ onion, finely chopped
½ green chilli, finely
  chopped* (optional)
*50 g (2 oz) butter
1 tablespoon tomato purée*

*150 ml (5 fl oz) water
450 g (1 lb) courgettes
1 poblano chilli or green
  pepper, grilled, peeled and
  cut into strips
½ chicken stock cube
pinch of ground black pepper*

If using corn on the cob, cut across with a sharp knife into 2 cm (1 inch) rounds. Fry the onion and chilli in the butter until soft, then add the remaining ingredients. Cover and simmer for 5 minutes, then uncover and simmer for a further 5 minutes. Serve hot.

■

Budín de flor de calabaza

Courgette blossom casserole

I love eating flowers—and courgette and marrow blossoms are so attractive and appetizing that they can also be used to decorate the dish. This casserole is similar to *Budín Azteca* but includes courgette blossoms and egg instead of chicken, so you can surprise your vegetarian friends with yet another unusual dish. It is suitable for a buffet or a luncheon dish accompanied by *Frijoles Refritos* and a tossed salad.

SERVES 4

oil for shallow frying
8 corn tortillas
25 g (1 oz) butter
½ onion, chopped
1 green chilli, finely chopped
4 epazote or coriander leaves,
    finely chopped
2 tomatoes, grilled, peeled
    and squashed
450 g (1 lb) courgette
    blossoms or 275 g (10 oz)
    cooked spinach, chopped

salt
¼ teaspoon ground black
    pepper
85 ml (3 fl oz) single cream
150 ml (¼ pint) soured cream
75 g (3 oz) Cheddar cheese,
    grated
75 g (3 oz) Mozzarella cheese,
    grated
2 eggs, well beaten
courgette blossoms or sprigs of
    parsley, to garnish

Heat the oil and shallow fry the tortillas for 30 seconds on each side. Drain on absorbent kitchen paper and keep warm. Heat the butter and fry the onion, chilli, epazote, tomato and chopped flowers or spinach for 3 minutes. Add ¼ teaspoon salt, the pepper and single cream and simmer for 5 minutes.

Grease a round 20 cm (8 inch) ovenproof dish and place 4 tortillas in it, overlapping slightly. Place half the flower mixture on top, then spoon a quarter of the soured cream over it, followed by half the grated cheese. Repeat with a second layer, finishing with cheese, and reserving the rest of the soured cream for a garnish. Pour over the beaten eggs, ensuring it goes down the sides. Bake in a preheated oven at 180°C, 350°F, Gas Mark 4 for about 30 minutes. Spoon the remainder of the soured cream over the top. Sprinkle with salt and garnish with more blossoms or parsley sprigs.

Esquites

Fried corn with courgettes

Fresh or frozen corn kernels may be used for this tasty side dish. The flavouring traditionally comes from *epazote*, but if this is not available, fresh coriander is a good substitute.

SERVES 4

2 tablespoons cooking oil
½ onion, finely chopped
1 red pepper, sliced
4 tablespoons finely
   chopped coriander
1 green chilli, thinly sliced

350 g (12 oz) fresh or frozen
   corn kernels
2 courgettes, sliced
1 chicken stock cube, crumbled
¼ teaspoon ground black
   pepper

Heat the oil in a frying pan and fry the onion, pepper, coriander and chilli for 3 minutes. Stir in the corn kernels, courgettes and chicken stock cube. Cover and simmer over medium heat for 5 minutes. Uncover and cook for 5 minutes, stirring occasionally, until the courgettes are soft. Serve hot, sprinkled with black pepper.

Elote con crema

Sweetcorn in white sauce

This delicious way of eating corn is a good side dish for a lunch or dinner.

SERVES 4

25 g (1 oz) butter
¼ onion, finely chopped
1 teaspoon cornflour
¼ teaspoon salt
¼ teaspoon granulated
   sugar

150 ml (¼ pint) milk
150 g (6 oz) sweetcorn, fresh or
   frozen

Melt the butter in a frying pan and fry the onion for about 5 minutes until golden. Mix the cornflour, salt and granulated sugar with the milk and add to the onion. Add the corn and bring to the boil, stirring constantly. Simmer for about 5 minutes and serve hot.

VARIATION:

Reduce the amount of corn by 50 g (2 oz), add a sliced red or green pepper and fry it with the onion.

Elotes asados

Roast corn on the cob

Another easy way to eat corn on the cob. In Mexico, where they are grown all the year round, the cobs are cooked still in their green leaf wrapping. Elsewhere, the cobs are sometimes sold without the leaves, but in either case the method of cooking is the same.

SERVES 4

4 cobs of corn (if frozen,	*2 lemons*
thaw completely)	*salt*
50 g (2 oz) butter, melted	*cayenne*

Insert a skewer into each end of the cobs. Brush with melted butter and cook on a barbecue for 10–15 minutes, turning frequently, and allowing them to burn slightly. Peel back the leaves, if present, squeeze half a lemon over each cob, sprinkle with salt and cayenne and eat hot.

Coliflor capeada

Cauliflower fritters in tomato sauce

Capeada means 'coated in egg and fried'. This is a most tasty way of eating cauliflower, ideal with any of the meat dishes or as a vegetarian main course with rice and beans.

SERVES 4

1 small cauliflower,	*2 eggs, separated*
quartered	*50 g (2 oz) flour*
¼ teaspoon salt	*½ quantity Salsa para*
150 ml (¼ pint) water	*Enchiladas*
100 g (4 oz) Cheddar cheese,	*2 tablespoons grated Cheddar*
cut into wedges	*cheese, to garnish*
oil for deep frying	

Parboil the cauliflower for 10 minutes in the salted water. Drain and allow to cool slightly. Using a sharp knife, make an incision about 5 cm (2 inches) deep half way down each quarter, without cutting all the way through. Insert the cheese in the slits and secure with cocktail sticks.

Heat the oil in a deep fryer to 180°C, 350°F. Beat the egg yolks until they change colour and beat the egg whites until they form peaks. Carefully blend together. Dip the cauliflower first into the flour, then into the egg batter and fry in the hot oil on both sides until golden, about 4 minutes. Remove the cocktail sticks, drain on absorbent paper and place in an ovenproof dish. Bring the sauce to the boil, pour it over the cauliflower, sprinkle with the grated cheese and bake in a preheated oven at 180°C, 350°F, Gas Mark 4 for 30 minutes. Serve hot.

VARIATION:

You can cook parboiled marrow in the same way by cutting the marrow in 2 cm (1 inch) rounds, securing the 2 rounds and the cheese with cocktail sticks and continuing as for cauliflower.

■

Chayotes rellenos

Cho-cho (christophenes) stuffed with ham and cream

A type of courgette which grows up fences and walls, *chayotes* are common in Mexico. They are heart-shaped and about the size of a fist, and can be light or dark green. The best kind is the dark green and very prickly *chayote*. The less prickly, lighter-coloured type is sold in West Indian shops in this country and it makes a good substitute. The *chayote* is always cooked in its leathery skin and then either peeled and served with lashings of butter, salt and black pepper, or left unpeeled and then stuffed. The single seed, often 4 cm (1½ inches) long, is edible and comparable to celery heart—it often goes to the cook! The root of this plant, called *chinchayote*, is a tuber similar to a West Indian yam; brown-skinned and about 10 cm (4 inches) in diameter. It has a delicate flavour and is good just boiled in its skin and served peeled with butter, salt and black pepper.

SERVES 4

2 chayotes
900 ml (1½ pints) water
½ teaspoon salt
½ teaspoon sugar
75 g (3 oz) butter
100 g (4 oz) cooked ham,
  chopped

2 tablespoons finely chopped
  parsley
1 chicken stock cube
¼ teaspoon ground black
  pepper
100 ml (3½ fl oz) double cream

Boil the *chayotes* in the water, salt and sugar for about 20 minutes, until tender. Drain and allow to cool. Cut in half lengthways, following the seam at the top. Carefully remove the pip and reserve. Scoop out the flesh carefully to avoid tearing the skin, and mash to a pulp.

Heat the butter in a saucepan and fry the ham, parsley and *chayote* pulp. Stir in the chicken stock cube, pepper and cream. Fill the *chayote* shells with the mixture, garnish each with half the pip and place in a well-greased ovenproof dish. Cover with kitchen foil and bake for 20 minutes in a preheated oven at 180°C, 350°F, Gas Mark 4. Serve hot.

Budín de camote

Sweet potato purée

Camote (sweet potato) is a root vegetable, either white or yellow inside with a purple or ochre skin. Its texture is similar to that of the potato but it is sweet. It must always be boiled first in its skin, then peeled and mashed or fried. Alternatively it can be baked as a potato in its 'jacket' by just piercing the skin. In the U.S. it is customary to eat sweet potato for Thanksgiving dinner. In Mexico it is popular as a vegetable or as a sweet, when sugar would be added to it. It is found in the U.K. at West Indian and Indian shops. This recipe is for a side dish to a main course.

SERVES 4

450 g (1 lb) sweet potato
600 ml (1 pint) water
1 teaspoon baking powder

75 g (3 oz) butter
150 ml (¼ pint) double cream
1 tablespoon breadcrumbs

Boil the sweet potato in the water for 35 minutes or until tender. Peel off the skin and while still hot, mash to a purée. Stir in the baking powder, butter and cream. Turn into a well-greased ovenproof dish and bake in a preheated oven at 180°C, 350°F, Gas Mark 4 for 20 minutes. Spread the breadcrumbs on the top and bake for another 10 minutes. Serve hot.

■

Budín de espinaca

Spinach and potato casserole

Spinach is not the most popular of vegetables, despite its nutritional value. This is a fancy way of presenting it and well worth the extra effort. I found this recipe in my grandmother's recipe book and I hope you will enjoy it.

SERVES 4

oil for greasing
2 tablespoons fine
  breadcrumbs
450 g (1 lb) potatoes, cooked
  and mashed
3 tablespoons grated Edam
  or Cheddar cheese
75 g (3 oz) butter
salt and ground black
  pepper

1 egg yolk, well beaten
450 g (1 lb) fresh spinach
2 teaspoons cooking oil
½ onion, finely chopped
1 tablespoon tomato purée
1 green chilli finely chopped
  (optional)
½ chicken stock cube
1 egg white, stiffly whisked
pinch of nutmeg

Grease an ovenproof dish and sprinkle in the breadcrumbs to cover the base and sides. Mix the mashed potatoes with the grated cheese, butter, salt, pepper and egg yolk, then cover the breadcrumbs with this mixture. Wash the spinach thoroughly, removing any tough stalks, place in a saucepan, with very little water, cover and simmer for 10 minutes. Drain the spinach, squeezing it in your hands to get rid of surplus water, then chop it finely. Heat the cooking oil and fry the onion until soft. Add the tomato purée, chopped spinach, green chilli and crumbled chicken stock cube, and simmer gently for 5 minutes. Allow to cool, then blend in the whisked egg white and nutmeg. Pour this mixture over the mashed potatoes and bake for 20 minutes in a preheated oven at 180°C, 350°F, Gas Mark 4. Serve hot.

Cebollitas asadas

Grilled spring onions

The most simple recipe of all, but none the less tasty. *Cebollitas Asadas* go well with any barbecued meat.

SERVES 4

8 spring onions, cleaned
½ lime or lemon

salt and ground black pepper

If you are barbecuing meat, place the spring onions on the same grill 3 minutes before the meat is ready, turning them to achieve an even brown colour. Sprinkle with lime or lemon juice, salt and pepper and eat hot.

Ensalada de col

Cabbage and pineapple salad

This is an excellent salad to serve with cold meat, especially turkey.

SERVES 6

450 g (1 lb) white cabbage
2 eating apples
2 slices fresh pineapple,
  cubed, or 200 g (7 oz) can
  pineapple chunks
3 tablespoons mayonnaise
100 g (4 oz) pecan nuts or
  walnuts, chopped

150 ml (¼ pint) soured cream
½ teaspoon salt
¼ teaspoon ground black
  pepper
pinch of cayenne

Shred the cabbage very finely. Halve, core and slice the apples. Drain off the pineapple juice (if using canned). Mix the cabbage, apples and pineapple with the remaining ingredients. Refrigerate until needed. Add a sprinkling of cayenne just before serving.

■

Ensalada de nopalitos

Nopal cactus salad

Nopales, or *nopalitos* (little *nopales*) as they are often called because they are chopped up, are one of the most original vegetables in the Mexican culinary collection. They are the oval, fleshy paddles of the prickly pear cactus plant. *Nopales* can be bought in the Mexican markets with the sharp thorns already cut off, and indeed, when prepared they are a most attractive dish. The young, thin pale-coloured leaves are more tender than the darker thicker ones, and once the thorns are cut off there is no need to remove the rest of the outer skin. Canned *nopales al natural* can occasionally be found in speciality shops in Britain, but French beans may be used as a substitute. A good side dish or filling for soft warm corn tortillas. Preparation starts 3 hours in advance.

SERVES 4

275 g (10 oz) fresh nopales
1 litre (1¾ pints) water
2 tablespoons salt
pinch of bicarbonate of soda
4 tablespoons chopped
*   coriander*
2 green chillies, sliced
3 tablespoons lime or lemon
*   juice*

1 tablespoon olive oil
½ teaspoon dried oregano
½ teaspoon salt
½ teaspoon ground black
*   pepper*
2 large ripe tomatoes, sliced
1 onion, thinly sliced
25 g (1 oz) white crumbly
*   cheese, finely crumbled*

Cut the *nopales* into 1 cm (½ inch) squares. Soak them in half the water and all the salt for about 3 hours, until all the slimy substance is released. Drain and wash under running water. Place the *nopales* in a saucepan with the remaining water and bicarbonate of soda. Simmer for about 20 minutes until tender, skimming frequently. Drain and place in a salad bowl. Add the coriander, chillies, lime or lemon juice, olive oil, oregano, salt and pepper and mix well. Top with the tomato slices, onion rings and crumbled cheese. Serve cold.

VARIATION:

If you are using French beans, boil in salted water for 5 minutes, drain and season as above.

Ensalada Navideña

Mexican Christmas salad

This is an unusual salad both in colour and in the combination and texture of its ingredients. The *jícama* is especially exotic to British palates. It is a tuber, shaped like a giant turnip, with a stringy brown skin and very white and juicy flesh, and is sometimes available in Britain from speciality shops. The salad is usually prepared for Christmas Eve, when it adds a special touch of colour to the meal.

SERVES 4

½ Webbs lettuce, very finely chopped
4 small cooked beetroot, thinly sliced
1 large orange, peeled and thinly sliced
1 eating apple, thinly sliced
2 ripe bananas, sliced
1 jícama, peeled, sliced and cut into bite-size pieces, or 10 cauliflower florets

50 g (2 oz) monkey nuts, shelled
15 g (½ oz) pine kernels or flaked almonds
juice of 1 lemon
150 ml (¼ pint) sweet sherry
½ teaspoon salt
pinch of cayenne

Arrange a bed of lettuce on a flat serving dish, then arrange all the vegetables and fruit in circles of colour. Just before serving, garnish with the monkey nuts and pine kernels or flaked almonds. Mix the lemon with the sherry and salt and spoon it over the salad. Garnish with a sprinkling of cayenne.

Ensalada de papa

Potato and herb salad

This salad is served with cold meats for light meals.

SERVES 4

4 medium-size potatoes, peeled, cooked and sliced	1 tablespoon olive oil
¼ teaspoon dried oregano	2 tablespoons malt vinegar
¼ teaspoon dried marjoram	½ teaspoon salt
¼ teaspoon dried thyme	¼ teaspoon ground black pepper

To garnish
8 stuffed olives, halved   4 spring onions, thickly sliced

Place the sliced potatoes in a salad bowl. Mix together the remaining ingredients and pour over the potato slices. Garnish with the spring onions and olives. Serve cold.

VARIATION:

Ensalada de coliflor—Cauliflower salad
Substitute 1 small cauliflower, cooked and cut into small pieces, for the potato.

Ensalada Tenango

Avocado salad

Avocados feature strongly in the Mexican kitchen. This is a tasty way of eating them.

SERVES 4

2 ripe avocados, sliced	½ onion, finely sliced
2 large ripe tomatoes, sliced	juice of 1 lemon
2 corn tortillas, fried into Totopos (see page 56)	½ teaspoon salt
1 tablespoon chopped coriander	¼ teaspoon ground black pepper
	pinch of dried oregano

136

Place alternating slices of avocado and tomato with the *totopos* in a salad bowl. Top with the coriander and onion rings. Make a dressing with the lemon, salt, pepper and oregano and pour over the salad. Allow to stand for 10 minutes, then serve.

Pico de gallo

Fruit and vegetable salad

This traditional way of eating cucumber, *jícama* (a large root vegetable resembling a giant turnip), radishes, orange, carrots, peppers and fresh pineapple is now favoured at social occasions because it can be offered with drinks and is low in calories.

SERVES 8

½ cucumber
2 peeled carrots
1 orange
1 green pepper
½ pineapple

10 radish flowers
juice of 1 lemon
salt
pinch of cayenne

Cut the cucumber and carrots into 5 cm (2 inch) sticks. Peel and slice the orange. Discard the stem and seeds of the pepper and cut into thick wedges. Peel the pineapple and cut into chunks. Arrange all the vegetables and fruits in a serving dish. Just before serving, sprinkle over the lemon juice, salt and cayenne. Serve immediately.

Carnes
Meat

Traditionally, Mexican cuisine is not based around meat or fish as a European meal would be. *Antojitos*, such as *enchiladas*, *tacos* and *tamales*, could well act as a main course. However, it is important to remember that in Mexico European-style cooking has become an intrinsic part of the cuisine, and nowadays a chicken or pork roast or fricassée is as at home on a Mexican table as it would be in Europe. It is the special ingredient, or the careful choice of a combination of unusual ingredients that can turn ordinary roast pork into a Mexican dish—for example, by the addition of a chilli-based seasoning and a little orange juice to the gravy. Don't be shy to mix and match cuisines—plain roast pork will be as delicious with *frijoles*, *Calabacitas Rellenas* and *Arroz Blanco* as it is with mashed potatoes, carrots and runner beans.

Pork plays a leading rôle in the Mexican kitchen, perhaps because the Aztecs were already used to cooking wild pigs before the conquest. Lamb is popular mostly as *Barbacoa* (barbecue), while goat is mostly roasted over open fires. In this chapter you will find a recipe for *Barbacoa* which is cooked in the oven and does not vary tremendously from roast lamb, except for the garnishes and accompaniments of chillies, *Guacamole* and soft warm tortillas.

Beef is also popular, and the best cuts found in restaurants are usually cooked in the international manner. However, they are often accompanied by hot *salsas* and warm tortillas, which lend a totally different flavour to the dish.

Meats are not often roasted in Mexico—they are generally grilled or boiled and shredded instead. The meat is lean, and fat is not included in the joints, though it is added in frying. The custom of shredding the meats or serving them in the small pieces they fall into after long cooking, is probably due to the fact that they are often used as a filling for *tacos* so that carving is not necessary. Meat is often used sparingly in Mexican cooking; all the garnishes, beans, rice and tortillas help to disguise in a skilful and delicious manner the small amount of meat that people are actually eating.

Before buying your meat, make sure to read the recipe as it is important that some meats are cut in a special way. A good example would be the loin of pork which is cut off the chop rib bone and must not be confused with pork fillet.

Finally, do remember that Mexican cuisine has no rigid rules for anything. For example, try interchanging the sauces or meats in the recipes, and discover new flavours. You will still be serving just as authentic a Mexican meal.

Tacos al carbón

Charcoal-grilled steak wrapped in tortillas

In Mexico City, *taquerías* (shops selling nothing but *tacos*) are numerous, and the range of different varieties of *taco* they sell is remarkable. Virtually every kind of meat and vegetable and every imaginable combination of sauces are used, as well as melted cheese. The *tacos* in this recipe are particularly good for an outdoor barbecue. The meat I use is beef skirt, which is easily available if you order it in advance, but it is important to marinate and to slice it against the grain quite thinly, otherwise it could be quite tough. Serve with either *Guacamole, Salsa Típica* or *Salsa de Tomate Verde* and/or soured cream as well as *Jalapeños en Vinagre*. Preparation starts the day before.

SERVES 6

1 kg (2 lb) skirt of beef   *about 20 corn tortillas*

Marinade

2 tablespoons cooking oil   *2 cloves garlic, crushed*
2 tablespoons malt vinegar   *½ teaspoon salt*
1 tablespoon lemon juice   *½ onion, sliced*
½ teaspoon dried oregano   *¼ teaspoon ground black*
¼ teaspoon granulated   *pepper*
  sugar

Mix together the marinade ingredients. Put the meat in a non-metal container and sprinkle the marinade over it, making sure all the meat is covered. Cover and leave to marinate overnight, or longer if possible. Remove the meat from the marinade and cook on the barbecue for 15–20 minutes. Carve the meat into thin strips, cutting against the grain. Place strips of meat in the middle of the soft warm corn tortillas, bathe with sauce, soured cream and pickles. Roll up and eat immediately.

■

Cuete mechado

Studded beef pot roast

Beef is as expensive in Mexico as it is in Europe. What is more, because they do not hang it, the meat is often tough and stringy, needing a lot of cooking to tenderize it. This cut looks magnificent as it resembles fillet of beef, and it has the added benefit of being a great deal less expensive. You will have to ask your butcher to prepare it especially for you—it is taken from the side of the blade and is commonly known as eye of beef or Pope's eye. Good for a hearty meal, it can be eaten hot or cold, served with new potatoes and green vegetables.

SERVES 8

1 kg (2 lb) eye of beef, in one   *4 tablespoons cooking oil*
  piece   *2 cloves garlic*
75 g (3 oz) gammon, cubed   *2 onions, sliced*

1 carrot, peeled and cut into
   2 cm (³/₄ inch) strips
10 stuffed green olives
10 blanched almonds
1 pepper, diced, or 2 green
   chillies, halved, if you
   prefer it hot
2 tablespoons malt vinegar
½ teaspoon salt
¼ teaspoon ground black
   pepper

600 ml (1 pint) water
¼ teaspoon cinnamon
pinch of ground cloves
pinch of sugar
4 sprigs parsley, chopped
1 tablespoon tomato purée
1 tablespoon cornflour
2 tablespoons water

Make small deep cuts all over meat. Insert the cubed gammon, strips of carrot, olives, almonds and diced pepper as deeply as you can in the cuts. Pour over the vinegar and sprinkle with salt and black pepper.

Heat the oil in a heavy-based pan and fry the garlic until dark brown, then add the meat and fry on all sides until golden brown, taking care not to dislodge the ham and vegetables. Remove the meat and discard the garlic. In the remaining oil, fry the onion until golden then add the water, cinnamon, cloves, sugar, parsley and tomato purée. Return the meat to the pan and spoon the liquid over it. Cover and simmer for at least 2 hours until the meat is tender, turning it occasionally.

Mix the cornflour with the water, and slowly add it to the liquid, stirring constantly. Simmer until thickened to a gravy. Serve hot or cold, with the meat sliced thinly and the sauce poured over it, accompanied with mustard.

■

Carne frita

Crispy fried shredded meat

Carne frita refers to any type of meat or chicken which has been previously boiled or roasted, then shredded and fried with chopped onions until it becomes crisp. The meat is used as a filling for *burritos* or soft warm wheat or corn tortillas, accompanied by *Salsa Típica* or *Guacamole*, garnished with lettuce. It is a good way of using up leftover meat.

SERVES 4

2 tablespoons cooking oil
½ onion, finely chopped
450 g (1 lb) cooked meat,
 finely shredded
1 green chilli, finely sliced

½ teaspoon salt
¼ teaspoon ground black
 pepper

Heat the oil and fry the onions for about 4 minutes until golden. Add the shredded cooked meat, chilli, salt and pepper. Fry for 15 minutes, tossing it, until the meat becomes dry and very crisp. Serve hot.

■

Carne deshebrada

Shredded beef salad

Carne Deshebrada is served throughout Mexico usually as a main course with soft warm tortillas, *Ensalada de Nopalitos* and *Guacamole*. The meat traditionally used is beef skirt, but stewing steak is also very good. I prefer to use a food processor to shred the meat; however, if you do it by hand, make sure you cook the meat until it is falling apart.

SERVES 4

450 g (1 lb) beef skirt or
 stewing steak
1 litre (1¾ pints) water
1 beef stock cube
1 clove garlic
1 bay leaf
1 tablespoon vinegar
2 tomatoes, finely chopped
½ onion, finely chopped

2 tablespoons finely chopped
 coriander
2 green chillies, finely chopped
juice of 1 lime or lemon
½ teaspoon salt
½ teaspoon ground black
 pepper
½ lettuce, finely shredded
2 ripe avocados

To garnish

2 ripe avocados

8 radish flowers

Put the beef in a saucepan with the water, beef stock cube, garlic, bay leaf and vinegar. Bring to the boil, cover and simmer for 1½ hours or until the meat is very tender and falls apart. Allow to cool in the stock. Drain and use the stock for soup. Use a food processor to shred the meat, or cut it finely across the grain then shred it by hand very finely. Add the tomatoes, onion, coriander and chillies and place on a serving dish. Mix the lemon or lime juice with the salt and pepper and pour it over the meat. Arrange the shredded lettuce around the dish. Just before serving, peel and slice the avocados and use to garnish the meat with the radish flowers.

■

Chivichangas

Crispy fried wheat tortillas with a meat or vegetable filling

Although the name sounds terribly Mexican, I am not sure that it is not another American invention. Be that as it may, it is still the best way of eating wheat tortillas. A *chivichanga* is in fact a *burrito* which has been shallow fried. The filling can be either vegetables or meat or both! Serve with *Frijoles Refritos* or rice and fresh salad.

SERVES 4

4 wheat tortillas
½ quantity Chile con Carne
  (see page 146) *or Rajas de*
  Chile Poblano (see page 119)
1 small lettuce, thinly sliced

4 spring onions, finely chopped
50 g (2 oz) Cheddar cheese,
  grated
6 tablespoons corn oil

To garnish

8 tablespoons Guacamole or
  1 avocado, sliced

4 teaspoons soured cream

Heat a heavy-based frying pan until drops of water will sizzle on it. Warm a tortilla in the pan, then fill it with 2 tablespoons of *Chile con Carne*, some sliced lettuce, spring onions and cheese and fold it like a small parcel, securing the ends with cocktail sticks. Repeat until all the tortillas are filled.
    Heat the oil in the pan and fry 2 *chivichangas* at a time, for 3

minutes on each side. Drain on absorbent kitchen paper and remove the cocktail sticks, then keep warm until the remaining 2 are fried. Garnish with *Guacamole* or avocado slices and soured cream. Eat hot.

■

Albóndigas con chilpotle

Meatballs in smoked jalapeño sauce

Meatballs are very popular in Mexico. They are usually eaten in a spicy tomato or chilli sauce, accompanied by rice and green vegetables like *chayotes* and courgettes, and soft warm tortillas.

SERVES 4

225 g (8 oz) minced pork
225 g (8 oz) finely minced
beef
1 slice bread, soaked in
water, drained
1 tablespoon malt vinegar
½ teaspoon salt
¼ teaspoon ground black
pepper

pinch of sugar
oil for shallow frying
1 quantity Salsa de Chile
Chilpotle
25g (1 oz) flaked almonds, to
garnish

Mix the meats, bread, vinegar, salt, pepper and sugar together and leave for 1 hour. Drain off any juices, then shape the mixture into chestnut-size meatballs. Heat the oil in a frying pan and fry the meatballs over low heat for 5 minutes covered. Uncover, turn the meatballs and continue frying until brown all over. Remove and drain on absorbent kitchen paper. Place the meatballs in a heated casserole, pour over the hot sauce, cover and cook in a preheated

OPPOSITE: Fish menu—*Empanada de Bacalao* (salted cod and tomato turnover, page 184), garnished with parsley; *Rosca de Camarones en Escabeche* (prawns and rice ring with red chilli sauce, page 190); and *Jaibas en su Concha* (savoury baked crab, page 189).

oven at 160°C, 325°F, Gas Mark 3 for 20 minutes. Serve hot, garnished with flaked almonds.

VARIATION:

Albóndiguitas—Baby meatballs

Make the meatballs even smaller and serve on cocktail sticks to go with drinks.

■

Picadillo

Minced meat with olives and raisins in tomato sauce

Picadillo is the most popular way of cooking minced meat and is often used as a filling for *Chiles Rellenos* and *empanadas* (see *Empanadas de Bacalao*). It can also be served with rice and *Rajas de Chile Poblano* for a nice supper or light lunch.

SERVES 4. Makes 6 empanadas

100 g (¼ lb) minced beef
100 g (¼ lb) minced pork
2 teaspoons wine vinegar
¼ teaspoon salt
¼ teaspoon ground black pepper
¼ teaspoon sugar
1 tablespoon cooking oil
½ onion, finely chopped
1 clove garlic, crushed
1 green chilli, chopped

1 red pepper, sliced
3 sticks celery, finely chopped
1 chicken stock cube, crumbled
1 small potato, cooked and cubed
9 stuffed olives, sliced
1 teaspoon flaked almonds
1 tablespoon raisins
400 g (14 oz) can peeled tomatoes
1 tablespoon tomato purée

PREVIOUS PAGES: Dinner party idea—*Seviche* (fish marinated in lime juice, page 61) with avocado to start; *Pierna de Carnero Adobada* (leg of lamb with chilli sauce, page 158); *Calabacitas con Rajas y Elote* (courgettes with peppers and corn, page 126); *Chilaquiles* (tortilla chips in a sauce, page 100); *Crema de Mango* (mango cream with almonds, page 197) for dessert; and *Café de Olla* (page 227).
OPPOSITE: *Taquitos de Pollo* (tortillas filled with chicken, page 172); *Chalupas* (boat-shaped tortillas, page 68); *Sopes* (maize dough shells with beans and *chorizo* filling, page 69); and *Quesadillas de Flor de Calabaza* (pumpkin blossom *quesadillas*, page 123).

Mix the minced meats together and season with the vinegar, salt, pepper and sugar. Heat the oil and fry the onion, garlic, chilli, pepper and celery for 3 minutes. Add the meat and stir over high heat for about 10 minutes or until it starts to brown. This can sometimes take longer than you would expect if the vegetables have a high water content, so just continue frying until the liquid is absorbed. Discard any surplus oil, taking care to retain the meat juices. Add the remaining ingredients and simmer for 15 minutes until it starts to dry out, stirring occasionally. Serve hot. (If using as a filling for *empanadas* allow to cool.)

■

Chile con carne

Beef or pork in a spicy chilli bean sauce

Chile con Carne is an American interpretation of Mexican food. I was 25 and living abroad when a Canadian neighbour prepared a party dish in my honour. All I could think of to say when he proudly displayed it was, 'What is it?' Well, apparently it was 'Mexican' *Chile con Carne*! I never came across the dish again until Harrods, the famous London department store, who sell my tortillas, asked me if I would make *Chile con Carne* for them as well! I said I didn't know how to make it and preferred to stick to authentic dishes only. So they suggested to me I should make a *Chile con Carne* for them in the 'Mexican way'—and it has been selling well now for several years!

The *Chile con Carne* I have chosen for this book is a main course dish, good for a party of 10 to 12, but you could halve or quarter the amounts for smaller numbers; it is also a good filling for *Burritos Norteños*. Serve with any of the rice recipes and a mixed salad.

SERVES 10–12

1 kg (2 lb) boned shoulder
   of pork or stewing steak,
   cubed
2 tablespoons malt vinegar
3/4 teaspoon salt

6 sprigs coriander
1/2 teaspoon dried oregano
1/2 teaspoon dried marjoram
1/2 teaspoon dried thyme
5 cm (2 inch) cinnamon stick

½ teaspoon ground black
  pepper
¼ teaspoon sugar
6 tablespoons cooking oil
2 bay leaves
750 ml (1¼ pints) water
2 cloves garlic
1 large onion
4 tablespoons mole powder
  or 2 tablespoons chilli
  powder

12 cloves
½ teaspoon cumin seeds or
  ¼ teaspoon ground cumin
½ teaspoon aniseed
1 tablespoon cayenne
1 teaspoon sesame seeds
750 g (1½ lb) can tomatoes
  with their juice, well mashed
150 g (5 oz) tomato purée
2 chicken stock cubes
1 quantity Frijoles

Season the meat with the vinegar, salt, pepper and sugar. Cover and marinate overnight in the refrigerator. (If you have not yet cooked your beans, soak them overnight.)

In a large casserole, heat the oil and fry the meat until golden brown. Drain off the oil and reserve it. Add the bay leaves and the water, cover and simmer for about 1 hour or until tender. (Or cook in a preheated oven at 160°C, 325°F, Gas Mark 3.) Drain and reserve the stock, and discard the bay leaves. Put 150 ml (¼ pint) of the stock in a liquidizer and add the garlic, onion, mole or chilli powder, herbs, spices and sesame seeds and liquidize to a smooth paste.

Heat the reserved oil and fry the paste for about 4 minutes, stirring continually, until it dries a little. Add the mashed tomatoes, tomato purée, chicken stock cubes and the stock from the meat. Simmer for 20 minutes, then add the cooked beans and their liquid and simmer for 15 minutes. Add the meat and continue simmering very gently for 30 minutes.

■

Carnitas

Marinated roast pork

Carnitas is a popular feature of the Mexican outdoor life, but it is equally suitable for a dinner party, accompanied by *Chiles Rellenos de Queso*, rice and beans. In Mexico, Sundays often include away-for-the-day family outings, and restaurants selling *carnitas* are full of people, music and the delicious aroma of meat, fresh coriander and newly baked corn tortillas. You can also buy warm *carnitas* and take them home to eat at leisure, often in the garden or by the side of the pool. Preparation starts the night before. Use the bone from the meat to flavour the sauce.

SERVES 4

1 onion	¼ teaspoon granulated sugar
3 cloves garlic	1½ kg (3 lb) shoulder of pork,
3 tablespoons malt vinegar	boned, in large cubes
1 teaspoon salt	600 ml (1 pint) water
½ teaspoon ground black	225 g (8 oz) lard, cubed
pepper	

Liquidize together the onion, garlic, vinegar, salt, pepper and sugar to a paste. Rub well over the meat, then marinate overnight in the refrigerator. Put the meat and the marinade in a casserole dish and add the pork bone, water and lard. Cover and cook in a preheated oven at 160°C, 325°F, Gas Mark 3 for about 2 hours, basting and turning occasionally. Remove the meat from the casserole and put it in a roasting tin, then return it to the oven for 30 minutes or until golden brown. Arrange the meat on a warm serving dish, and keep warm. Meanwhile, skim off all the fat from the liquid in the casserole and discard the bone. Reduce the juices by boiling briskly, until about 85 ml (3 fl oz) is left. Pour over the meat and serve immediately.

■

Cazuela Tabasqueña

Casserole of beans, shredded beef and plantain

This casserole is traditionally made with shredded beef or pork and black beans, but any other type of beans will be a good substitute so long as they are cooked as instructed on page 43, or you can use canned red kidney or pinto beans as described on the same page.

SERVES 8

2 very ripe plantains	2 sticks celery
600 ml (1 pint) water	1 clove garlic

100 g (4 oz) butter
450 g (1 lb) beef skirt or
  pork shoulder, cubed
2 cabbage leaves
1 carrot

1 bay leaf
1 tablespoon wine vinegar
½ teaspoon salt
¼ teaspoon ground black
  pepper

To finish

1 tablespoon cooking oil
1 onion, finely chopped
2 green chillies, finely
  chopped

2 tablespoons tomato purée
1 beef stock cube
½ quantity Frijoles Refritos

Quarter the plantains, leaving the skin on, and boil them in the water for 15 minutes or until soft. Drain, reserving the water. Peel the plantains and remove the centre vein, then mash to a pulp with half the butter. Put the meat in a saucepan with the reserved water, add the vegetables, garlic, bay leaf, vinegar, salt and pepper, then cover and simmer for about 40 minutes until tender. Drain, reserving the liquid, and shred the meat finely. Heat the oil in a frying pan and fry the onion and chillies for 5 minutes. Add the shredded meat and fry for 5 minutes, stirring occasionally. Add the tomato purée, reserved liquid and beef stock cube and simmer, uncovered, for 15 minutes or until the sauce thickens.

Grease an ovenproof dish liberally. Put the beans in the bottom, then the meat and sauce and finally the plantain purée. Dot with the remaining butter and bake in a preheated oven at 180°C, 350°F, Gas Mark 4 for 30 minutes.

■

Verdolagas

Purslane and pork in tomato sauce

Verdolagas (purslane) is the name of a succulent weed which grows in the rainy season, and it gives a special flavour to pork stew. I have not found it in Britain yet, but you can substitute spinach or even the outer leaves of a lettuce, very finely chopped. This is a main course meal and can be served with rice, beans and sweetcorn, and warm soft tortillas.

SERVES 4

300 g (12 oz) stewing pork,
  cubed
¼ teaspoon salt
¼ teaspoon ground black
  pepper
2 teaspoons wine vinegar
1 bay leaf
900 ml (1½ pints) water

1 tablespoon cooking oil
½ onion, finely chopped
1 tablespoon tomato purée
1 chicken stock cube
2 green chillies, finely chopped
  (optional)
450 g (1 lb) spinach, finely
  chopped

Place the meat in a saucepan with the salt, pepper, vinegar, bay leaf and water. Cover and simmer for 45 minutes until tender. Strain and reserve the stock. Heat the oil in a saucepan and fry the onion for 4 minutes, add the reserved stock, tomato purée, chicken stock cube, chillies and spinach. Simmer for 20 minutes, uncovered, then stir in the meat. This dish should have nice runny tomato gravy. Serve hot.

Rollo de carne

Minced pork and beef loaf

Easy, economical and different. This will make a good supper dish, accompanied by *Esquites* and green vegetables if served hot, or by *Guacamole* and salad if served cold.

SERVES 4

125 g (5 oz) minced loin
  of pork
125 g (5 oz) minced beef
¼ teaspoon salt
¼ teaspoon black pepper
1½ teaspoons malt
  vinegar
1 egg

1 tablespoon cooking oil
50 g (2 oz) Chorizo, crumbled,
  or bacon, chopped
1 green chilli, finely chopped
2 medium-sized potatoes, cut
  into thin strips
1 green pepper, thinly sliced
pinch of dried thyme

Mix together the meats, salt, pepper, vinegar and egg. Cut a piece of kitchen foil and a piece of greaseproof paper, each 30 cm

(12 inches) square, and grease the paper generously with oil. Lay the greaseproof paper over the foil.

Heat the oil in a frying pan and fry the chilli and *Chorizo* or bacon until it is crisp. Remove and drain on absorbent kitchen paper. Fry the potato strips and the pepper until soft, and drain. Place half the pepper strips and half the potato strips in the middle of the greased greaseproof paper, then lay the minced meat on top, roughly forming a rectangle. Top with the remaining potato and pepper together with the *Chorizo* and sprinkle over the thyme. Form the mixture into a roll, then seal the foil securely. Place on a baking sheet and cook for 1 hour in a preheated oven at 160°C, 325°F, Gas Mark 3. Uncover and return to the oven for 30 minutes to brown.

■

Carne de puerco con col

Pork loin with cabbage in a tomato sauce

This is a fricassée-type dish, the two main ingredients lending each other lots of flavour. It's good for a main course with mashed potatoes, courgettes with corn and *Conserva de Tomate Verde y Jalapeños*. You will need to ask your butcher to take the rind off the pork loin, leaving no fat around the loin, and to make incisions at the base of the chops so that they can be cooked in one large piece but easily sliced.

SERVES 6

1½ kg (2½ lb) loin chop, rind and fat removed
5 teaspoons malt vinegar
1 teaspoon salt
½ teaspoon ground black pepper
pinch of sugar
2 cloves garlic, crushed

2 tablespoons cooking oil
450 ml (¾ pint) water
2 large onions, quartered
1 medium-size cabbage, cut into 6
4 green chillies
2 tablespoons chopped parsley
2 tablespoons tomato purée

Season the meat with the vinegar, salt, pepper and sugar, and rub the garlic all over it. Heat the oil in a large saucepan with a tight-fitting lid and fry the meat on all sides until golden. Drain off all the oil, then add 150 ml (¼ pint) of the measured water together with the onions. Cover and simmer for about 1 hour, or until the meat is tender, adding more water if it has been absorbed, and turning the meat regularly.

Discard the onions and add the cabbage, chillies and parsley. Simmer until the cabbage is just tender, then add the tomato purée and baste the meat and the cabbage with the gravy, continuing to cook for another 5 minutes. Serve hot.

■

Patitas de puerco a la Mexicana

Pig's trotters in tomato sauce

Pig's trotters are not exactly the most elegant dish to serve, but they can be one of the most tasty, especially prepared in this manner. Rice, boiled carrots and beans go well with this dish. Preparation should start a day before.

SERVES 4

1 lemon	2 tablespoons cooking oil
3 pig's trotters	1 onion, finely chopped
225 g (8 oz) stewing pork, cubed	3 tablespoons tomato purée
	½ teaspoon salt
2 bay leaves	8 peppercorns
4 cloves	3 green chillies
600 ml (1 pint) water	4 tablespoons chopped parsley

Peel the rind from the lemon and reserve. Cut the lemons in half. Wash and pat dry the pig's trotters, then clean them by rubbing all over with the lemons, squeezing some of the juice as you go along. Put the trotters in a saucepan with the pork, lemon rind, bay leaves, cloves and water. Cover and simmer for 2½ hours or until completely tender; the meat should be falling off the bone. Strain off the liquid, allow to cool then refrigerate. Carefully pick out all the bones from the trotters without breaking them up too much, and refrigerate with the pork overnight.

Heat the oil and fry the onions for 3 minutes. Add the tomato purée, salt, peppercorns, chillies, parsley and reserved stock. Simmer, uncovered, for 15 minutes until reduced by one third. Add the trotters and the meat. Reheat gently and serve hot.

VARIATION:

Pancita—Tripe in tomato sauce

Substitute 750 g (1½ lb) tripe for pig's trotters and stewing pork and cook and serve in the same manner.

■

Costillitas adobadas

Spare ribs in chilli and cream sauce

Ideal for an outdoor barbecue party, spare ribs are very tasty with *ancho* chilli sauce spread on them. You need to use the long-boned spare ribs, not the more meaty spare rib chops. Serve with beans, rice, salad, warm tortillas, *Elotes Asados* and *Cebollitas Asadas*. Preparation should start 2 hours in advance.

SERVES 4

3 ancho chillies
150 ml (¼ pint) single
   cream
2 tomatoes, grilled and
   skinned
½ teaspoon sugar
1 clove garlic

1 chicken stock cube
¼ onion, finely chopped
1½ kg (3 lb) pork spare ribs
3 tablespoons malt vinegar
½ teaspoon salt
¼ teaspoon ground black
   pepper

Wash the chillies in very hot water to soften them. Remove the stalks and seeds and soak them in the cream for at least 2 hours. Put in a blender with tomatoes, sugar, garlic, chicken stock cube and onion and blend to a paste. Sieve and set aside. Remove any spare fat from the meat. Sprinkle with the vinegar, salt and pepper and marinate for 2 hours.

    When the flames start dying out in the barbecue, grill the ribs for about 10 minutes on each side, turning them so they cook evenly.

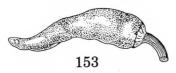

Brush liberally with the chilli sauce and continue cooking on both sides for 4–5 minutes. Serve hot.

■

Carne de puerco en mole verde

Pork in green tomatillo sauce

This is my favourite recipe using *Salsa de Tomate Verde*. It makes a good dinner dish with *Arroz Poblano, Frijoles Refritos* and any of the *calabacitas* recipes. Chicken portions may be used instead of the pork for a change.

SERVES 4

450 g (1 lb) stewing pork,
  cubed
1 tablespoon malt vinegar
¼ teaspoon salt
¼ teaspoon ground black
  pepper
pinch of sugar
1 tablespoon cooking oil

600 ml (1 pint) water
1 large onion, halved
1 clove garlic
1 bay leaf
1 quantity Salsa de Tomate
  Verde or 3 × 275 g (10 oz)
  cans tomatillos

Season the meat with the vinegar, salt, pepper and sugar. Leave to marinate for 1 hour. Heat the oil in a saucepan and fry the meat until golden. Drain off all the oil and add the water, onion, garlic and bay leaf. Cover and simmer for about 1 hour until very tender. Remove the meat, bring the liquid to the boil and boil for 15 minutes until reduced by half. Stir in the sauce and the meat and simmer for 20 minutes. Serve hot.

■

Frijoles borrachos

Tipsy beans

This is a meal in one dish, a hearty supper or a good side dish for buffet dinners. It goes well with a green salad and soft warm tortillas.

SERVES 6

225 g (8 oz) dried beans
  (any type)
1 knuckle of pork
225 g (8 oz) boned shoulder
  of pork, in 1 piece
1 clove garlic
1 teaspoon salt
1 teaspoon sugar
2 tablespoons cooking oil

100 g (4 oz) bacon, chopped
100 g (4 oz) Chorizo, sliced
½ onion, finely chopped
2 green chillies
4 tomatoes, chopped
4 tablespoons chopped
  coriander
350 ml (12 fl oz) beer

Remove any small stones in the beans. Place the beans in a sieve and wash under running water, until the water runs clear. Place in a large pan and soak overnight in cold water, allowing 10 cm (5 inches) of water to cover the surface of the beans. (If you have forgotten to soak the beans overnight, bring to the boil in the water and boil rapidly for 15 minutes, cover, remove from the heat and leave to soak for 1 hour.) Add the meat and garlic, cover and simmer for up to 3 hours until the meat and beans are tender. Add the salt and sugar. Top up with boiling water, if necessary.

Remove and discard the knuckle bone and skin, returning any meat to the pan. Cut the pork shoulder into bite-size pieces and add to the pan. Heat the oil and fry the bacon and the Chorizo until crisp, then add all the remaining ingredients except the beer. Fry for 5 minutes, then add to the beans with the beer. Simmer, uncovered, until the beans have absorbed the extra liquid. The finished dish should not be too dry.

■

Lomo Poblano

Pork loin with peppers in tomato sauce

Mexican recipes feature a lot of pork, probably because it goes so well with tomatoes and chillies! However, chicken is sometimes used as an alternative and most recipes adapt very well to it. This dish is normally cooked with *poblano* chillies, but green peppers are a good substitute.

SERVES 4

1 kg (2 lb) loin of pork
2 tablespoons malt vinegar
½ teaspoon salt
½ teaspoon ground black
  pepper
pinch of sugar
3 tablespoons cooking oil
100 g (4 oz) Chorizo
  Toluqueño (see below)

2 cloves garlic
1 chicken stock cube
300 ml (½ pint) water
1 large onion, chopped
2 green peppers, sliced
400 g (14 oz) can tomatoes,
  mashed

Season the meat with the vinegar, salt, pepper and sugar. Heat the oil and fry the *Chorizo* and garlic for 4 minutes, stirring continually. Remove the *Chorizo*, then fry the meat until golden on all sides. Remove the meat, discard the garlic, and reserve the oil. Place the meat on a wire rack over a roasting tin. Dissolve the stock cube in the water and pour into the roasting tin. Roast in a preheated oven at 180°C, 350°F, Gas Mark 4 for about 1½ hours, basting frequently, and turning the meat so that it browns evenly.

Meanwhile, heat 1 tablespoon of the reserved oil and fry the onion and peppers for 5 minutes. Add the mashed tomatoes and reserved *Chorizo*, cover and simmer for 5 minutes. Drain the juices from the cooked meat on to the onion mixture. Slice the meat and arrange it on a warm serving dish, pour over the sauce and serve hot.

Chorizo Toluqueño

Spicy sausage

Chorizo is another example of a Spanish dish which has been totally integrated into the Mexican cuisine. In Britain it can be obtained from delicatessens, the best make being San Rafael which is imported from Spain. You can make your own *Chorizo* and ask your butcher to put it into casings for you. Alternatively, keep it refrigerated, turning and stirring daily for 2 weeks.

MAKES about 500 g (1¼ lb)

450 g (1 lb) pork meat, finely
  minced
175 g (6 oz) pork fat, finely
  minced
75 ml (3 fl oz) malt vinegar
1 teaspoon salt
1 teaspoon ground black
  pepper
4 cloves garlic, crushed

1 tablespoon cayenne
2 tablespoons paprika
1 teaspoon coriander seeds
13 cm (5 inch) stick cinnamon
1 teaspoon dried oregano
1 teaspoon dried marjoram
½ teaspoon nutmeg
½ teaspoon ground cloves

Mix the meat and fat with the vinegar, salt and pepper. Mix the remaining ingredients together and blend into the meat, mixing thoroughly. Turn into a non-metal bowl and refrigerate, uncovered, for 4 days, stirring daily and draining any juices twice daily. Stuff the mixture into sausage casings, tying with string every 13 cm (5 inches). Hang in a very cold place and use as required. Alternatively, keep the loose mixture for up to 2 weeks in the refrigerator. To cook, crumble the desired amount into hot oil, fry for 6–7 minutes until crisp, then use as required.

■

Chorizo picante

Spicy pork sausage with ancho chillies

Here is another version of home-made *chorizo*, which is spicier than *Chorizo Toluqueño*. If *ancho* chillies are unobtainable, use 2 tablespoons ground chillies instead. It needs to marinate for 24 hours in the refrigerator before use.

MAKES 450 g (1 lb)

8 ancho chillies
300 ml (½ pint) boiling
  water
2 cloves garlic
¼ teaspoon cumin
½ teaspoon dried oregano
1 tablespoon tomato purée

pinch of sugar
¼ teaspoon cayenne
¼ teaspoon ground black
  pepper
½ teaspoon salt
85 ml (3 fl oz) malt vinegar
450 g (1 lb) minced pork

Heat the chillies in a dry frying pan for about 3 minutes until soft, turning frequently. Discard the stems and seeds. Soak the chillies in the boiling water for 1 hour. Drain, then work to a paste in a blender with the remaining ingredients, except the pork. Mix the paste into the meat thoroughly. Store for at least 24 hours in a covered plastic container in the refrigerator, draining off any liquid 2–3 times a day. The *Chorizo* will keep for several days in the refrigerator. To eat, fry tablespoons of the mixture in a little hot oil until crisp and use as a garnish for beans or *antojitos*.

Pierna de carnero adobada

Leg of lamb or pork with chilli sauce

This recipe is suitable for a dinner party, accompanied by rice and beans and a good helping of *Rajas de Chile Poblano*, as well as warm soft corn or wheat tortillas. It is also very good cold as a filling for *tacos* or *tortas*. If you are using leg of pork, ask your butcher to remove the skin.

SERVES 8

2 kg (4½ lb) leg of lamb
  or pork
4 tablespoons malt vinegar
½ teaspoon salt
¼ teaspoon ground black
  pepper
¼ teaspoon granulated
  sugar
50 g (2 oz) raisins
75 g (3 oz) flaked almonds
2 ancho chillies

1 mulato chilli
4 cloves garlic
4 tablespoons tomato purée
4 cloves
½ teaspoon cinnamon
½ teaspoon dried thyme
2 tablespoons cooking oil
4 small onions, coarsely
  chopped
1 bay leaf

Trim any surplus fat off the meat. Sprinkle with vinegar, salt, pepper and sugar. Make incisions in the meat about 5 cm (2 inches) deep with the point of a knife and insert the raisins and almonds. Place on a metal rack in a baking tray and leave for at least 2 hours.

Meanwhile, cook the chillies in a dry, heavy-based frying pan over moderate heat for 3 minutes, turning often, until soft and pliable. Wearing rubber gloves, or using a knife and fork, remove the stalks, shake all the seeds out and discard the veins. Place in a liquidizer and cover with very hot water. Leave to soak for about 1 hour, then add all the remaining ingredients, except the oil, onions and bay leaf, and liquidize to a smooth paste. Sieve, adding a little water if necessary to wash off any paste left in the sieve.

In a heavy-based saucepan, heat the oil until it sizzles. Remove from the heat and add the chilli paste, onions and bay leaf. Simmer slowly for 15–20 minutes until thickened. Remove from heat and allow to cool for 15 minutes. Pour about half the sauce over the meat to cover it, and reserve the rest.

Add 600 ml (1 pint) water to the baking tray under the meat. Loosely cover the meat with foil, and cook in a preheated oven at 160°C, 325°F, Gas Mark 3 for about 2 hours or until tender. Baste occasionally and add more water if necessary. Add the juices from the baking tray to the remaining sauce, bring to the boil and simmer for 5 minutes, then pour it over the meat and serve.

■

Barbacoa

Roast lamb in beer marinade

In Mexico the average number of guests for a *barbacoa* is about 50. Its name comes from *barba-cola* which means 'from head to tail'—in other words, the whole animal is steamed in a hole in the ground where red-hot stones have been placed. This is, in fact, where the modern word 'barbecue' comes from. The animal, which is usually a sheep, is wrapped in *agave* leaves and cooked for about 15 hours. Its flavour is due mainly to the *agave* and the extremely slow cooking time, and I can assure you the end result is well worth the wait. However, as I do not imagine you wish to dig up your garden, I have simplified the method of cooking by adapting a recipe I learned from a Mexican chef in London! It is not as good as the real thing, but in countries where *agave* is not available, *Barbacoa* cannot taste the same anyway. In this version, the meat is steam-roasted for about 3 hours. Preparation should start the night before.

Barbacoa is ideal for a summer buffet outdoors (although it would be cooked indoors), accompanied by other *taco* fillings such as *Guacamole*, *Salsa Borracha*, *Arroz Blanco*, *Frijoles*, *Quesadillas de Flor Calabaza* and *Cuitlacoche*, all of which are included in this book. Everyone can help themselves to the different sorts of *tacos* and eat it all as finger food. Beer is the best accompaniment, as the meat is cooked in beer.

SERVES 4

1 kg (2 lb) shoulder of lamb
2 tablespoons malt vinegar
½ teaspoon salt
¼ teaspoon ground black
  pepper
¼ teaspoon sugar

2 × 350 ml (12 fl oz) cans beer
  (Mexican XX or English lager)
2 cloves garlic, crushed
1 bay leaf
1 large onion, quartered
2 mulato chillies

To finish

bunch of radishes, sliced
½ onion, finely sliced

corn tortillas

Put the meat in a non-metal dish and season it with the vinegar, salt, pepper and sugar. Pour in the beer and add the garlic, bay leaf, onion and chillies. Cover and leave to marinate for 8 hours or overnight, basting once or twice.

Put the marinade in a baking tin, place the meat on a rack on top and roast in a preheated oven at 160°C, 325°F, Gas Mark 3 for 2–3 hours, basting occasionally. The meat is ready when it falls away from the bone. Remove the meat from the bone and cut into bite-size pieces, place on a serving dish and keep warm. Boil the marinade for 10 minutes, until reduced by half. Allow to cool for 15 minutes, then remove all but 1 tablespoon fat from the top. Discard the bay leaf.

Blend the marinade to a smooth paste in a blender. Heat the reserved fat in a saucepan and stir in the paste. Simmer for 5 minutes until thickened, then adjust the seasoning and spoon over the meat. Serve hot with sliced radishes and onions and warm soft corn tortillas. Use these to make *tacos*, placing meat, sauce, radishes and onions in a warm soft tortilla, then rolling it up.

Ternera al horno

Roast veal with orange and tomato sauce

Veal is often used in the Mexican menu and it is particularly nice in this combination of orange and tomato. Serve with rice or potato purée, carrots and *Rajas de Chile Poblano* for a main course.

SERVES 6

1½ kg (3 lb) loin of veal on
  the bone
3 tablespoons malt vinegar
¼ teaspoon salt
¼ teaspoon ground black
  pepper
pinch of granulated sugar

1 tablespoon cooking oil
300 ml (½ pint) water
3 cloves garlic
2 onions, quartered
1 tablespoon tomato purée
1 chicken stock cube
juice of 2 oranges

Season the meat with the vinegar, salt, pepper and sugar. Brush it with the oil, then place on a roasting rack in a roasting tin containing the water, garlic and onions. Roast in a preheated oven at 180°C, 350°F, Gas Mark 3 for 1½ hours until tender, basting frequently and turning the meat to achieve even browning. Sieve the contents of the roasting tin into a saucepan. Stir in the tomato purée, chicken stock cube and orange juice and cook for 5 minutes. Reheat the sauce and pour over the meat. Serve hot.

Cola de res

Oxtail in tomato sauce

Although oxtail is very good, it seldom seems to feature on the dinner table, and I often wonder if it is because it is not sophisticated enough. Well, we shall soon put that right! Try this delicious oxtail dish for dinner accompanied by rice and corn. Preparation starts the day before.

SERVES 4

1¼ kg (2½–3 lb) oxtail
  in pieces
2 cloves garlic, crushed
¾ teaspoon salt
½ teaspoon ground
  black pepper
2 bay leaves
1.2 litres (2 pints) water
2 tablespoons oil

1 large onion, finely chopped
1 green pepper, sliced
3 tablespoons tomato purée
1 beef stock cube, crumbled
2 green chillies, sliced
3 tablespoons chopped parsley
6 peppercorns

Place the oxtail in a large heavy pan with the garlic, salt, pepper, bay leaves and water. Cover and simmer for about 3 hours or until very soft. Remove the oxtail from the stock and cut off any unwanted fat. Strain the stock and refrigerate overnight. Remove and discard the fat from the surface of the stock, and sieve the stock.

Heat the oil in a saucepan and fry the onion and pepper for 4 minutes. Add the oxtail and fry for a few minutes, then add the tomato purée, beef stock cube, chillies, parsley and peppercorns. Add the sieved stock and simmer, uncovered, for about 30 minutes or until the gravy is thick and covers the meat well. Serve hot.

■

Hígados encebollados

Liver and onion rings

Liver is not one of my favourite foods—which is why I find this particular recipe appealing, as it actually makes liver taste delicious. It is best eaten with rice of any type and green vegetables and served as a supper dish. If ox liver is used, make sure to ask your butcher to peel off the membrane which causes liver to shrink and makes the edges tough. If using calves' liver, cut the cooking time by half.

SERVES 4

450 g (1 lb) liver, thinly
  sliced
3 teaspoons malt vinegar
½ teaspoon salt
¼ teaspoon ground black
  pepper

1 clove garlic, crushed
2 green chillies, finely chopped
3 tablespoons cooking oil
1 large onion, finely sliced

Place the liver in a dish with the vinegar, salt, pepper, garlic and chillies and leave to marinate for 20 minutes. Heat the oil in a heavy-based frying pan and fry the liver over moderate heat for 4 minutes. Turn and fry the other side for 4 minutes. Transfer to a heated serving dish and keep warm. Add the onion to the pan, sprinkle with salt and pepper and fry for about 3 minutes, stirring. Garnish the liver with the onion and serve immediately.

Aves

Poultry

Turkey was already a domesticated bird in the Aztecs' time. They also ate wild duck and pheasant. Of the three, turkey remains popular in Mexico today, probably because it was domesticated. The price of turkey has unfortunately remained high and so it is still considered a luxury for special occasions, rather than everyday fare. It is popularly cooked in *mole*, or roasted and the stock made from the carcass often served as a light soup at the beginning of the meal.

Chicken is as popular in Mexico as it is in Britain, and it is often used instead of pork in various recipes. Some restaurants specialize in roasting chicken slowly over a wood fire, which attracts customers just by the enticing smell and atmosphere it creates. Roast chicken is also sold as a take-away, accompanied by potato crisps made by the restaurant; the Mexican touch comes from the *jalapeño* chillies which add a distinctive flavour to the dish. Chicken is also often boiled, the stock being used for *Caldo* and the giblets to flavour rice, and the meat becomes a filling for *tacos* or *Budín Azteca*. Chicken roasted in the traditional way is equally good to fill soft warm tortillas accompanied by a *salsa* and *Guacamole*.

Pollo al pibil

Roast chicken with annatto

This dish is traditionally cooked in the Mayan oven known as a *pib*. As for a *barbacoa*, a hole is dug in the ground and filled with red-hot stones, followed by the meat covered in banana leaves. Fortunately, however, the dish can also be prepared in your own oven simply by wrapping the meat in well-greased greaseproof paper inside a square of kitchen foil. Preparation starts the day before so that you can marinate the chicken. Pork can also be used for this dish and it is equally delicious. The basic seasoning is *achiote*, also known as annatto seeds, which are not at all hot. They can be found in Indian shops, and their tandoori mixture is quite similar and therefore makes a good substitute.

Serve with soft warm tortillas, black beans and raw purple onion slices. If you can't find purple onions but want the dish to look authentic, slice ordinary onions thickly and soak them in the vinegar from pickled beetroot for 24 hours. Drain, sprinkle with salt and use as a garnish.

SERVES 4

4 chicken quarters

Marinade

½ teaspoon salt	*2 cloves garlic, crushed*
½ teaspoon ground black pepper	*½ teaspoon dried oregano*
	½ teaspoon ground cumin
pinch of sugar	*4 tablespoons achiote or tandoori mixture*
juice of 1 Seville orange or juice of ½ sweet orange plus juice of 1 lemon	*1 large purple onion, sliced, to garnish*

Mix the marinade ingredients together to a smooth paste. Rub generously over the chicken, cover and marinate for 24 hours, turning occasionally. Wrap each chicken portion in well-oiled greaseproof paper, then in kitchen foil and place in a baking dish. Bake in a preheated oven at 160°C, 325°F, Gas Mark 3 for 2½ hours or until the chicken is extremely tender and falling off the bone. Unwrap just before serving, arrange on a warm dish and garnish with the onion rings. Serve hot.

Pollo en salsa de chilpotle

Chicken in smoked jalapeño sauce

Chilpotle is the name which was given by the Aztecs to smoked *jalapeño* chillies. They are very popular throughout Mexico and their flavour is delightful. If *chilpotles* are not available, however, you could try any of the other Mexican dried chillies, or as a last resort, you could substitute 4 tablespoons of paprika plus a tablespoon of cayenne. Serve with rice and beans and a vegetable. Preparation should start 3 hours in advance.

SERVES 4

4 chilpotle chillies
450 ml (¾ pint) boiling
  water
4 chicken portions
2 tablespoons malt vinegar
½ teaspoon salt
¼ teaspoon ground black
  pepper

50 g (2 oz) butter
100 g (4 oz) mushrooms
2 chicken stock cubes
½ onion
2 cloves garlic
150 ml (¼ pint) soured cream

Heat the *chilpotles* (or chillies) in a dry frying pan until pliable. Remove the stalks and seeds, and soak the chillies in the boiling water for 1 hour. Season the chicken with the vinegar, salt and pepper and leave to marinate for 30 minutes. Heat the butter in a heavy-based frying pan and fry the chicken until golden on all sides. Remove from the pan and place in an ovenproof casserole.

Place half the mushrooms, and all the stock cubes, onion, garlic, *chilpotles* and their water in a blender and blend to a fine paste. Rub through a sieve into the casserole with the chicken and add the reserved mushrooms, sliced finely. Cover and cook in a preheated oven at 180°C, 350°F, Gas Mark 4 for about 1½ hours or until the chicken is very tender. Place the chicken on a warm serving dish and keep warm. Drain all the juices into a saucepan. Leave for 15 minutes, then remove any grease that floats to the top. Just before serving heat the sauce and add the cream, stirring all the time, being careful not to let it boil. Pour the cream sauce over the chicken and serve hot.

Arroz con pollo

Rice with chicken and vegetables

An all-in-one meal which can be prepared ahead of time as it reheats very well. Similar to Spanish *paella*, it is economical, tasty and colourful. If you prefer, you could substitute fresh fish, tinned tuna, fresh mussels or any combination of fish or meats for the chicken. Serve with a tossed green salad and avocado pear slices or *Guacamole*.

SERVES 8

4 chicken portions	*2 chicken stock cubes*
juice of 1 lemon	*4 green chillies*
½ teaspoon salt	*4 sprigs parsley*
¼ teaspoon ground black pepper	*3 tablespoons tomato purée*
4 tablespoons cooking oil	*50 g (2 oz) corn kernels*
2 cloves garlic	*50 g (2 oz) carrots, cubed*
150 ml (¼ pint) water	*50 g (2 oz) green peas*
2 onions, quartered	*50 g (2 oz) cabbage, shredded*
175 g (6 oz) long grain rice	*50 g (2 oz) runner beans, shredded*
450 ml (¾ pint) boiling water	*2 potatoes, peeled and cubed*
	1 red pepper, cut into strips

Season the chicken portions with the lemon, salt and pepper. Heat the oil and fry the whole garlic cloves until they are black, then discard. Fry the chicken on all sides in the flavoured oil until golden. Drain off all the oil and reserve. Add the water and quartered onions. Cover and simmer slowly for about 30 minutes until the chicken is just tender. Remove and discard the skin and bones, and leave the chicken meat in large chunks. Sieve any pan juices left, and reserve.

Heat the reserved oil in a large heavy-based frying pan with a tight-fitting lid. Fry the rice until pale golden, then drain off excess oil. Now add the chicken meat with all the remaining ingredients. Measure the reserved chicken juices and top up with boiling water to make 450 ml (¾ pint). Add to the rice mixture, stir, and bring to the boil quickly. Lower the heat, cover and simmer for 25–30 minutes until all the water has been absorbed. Rice must never boil briskly or it will stick. Discard the parsley, chillies and onions and serve hot.

VARIATION:

Arroz con camarón seco—Rice with dried fish

To make this flavourful variation, which will serve 6 rather than 8, substitute 75 g (3 oz) dried shrimps (available from Oriental shops) and 1 × 200 g (7 oz) can of tuna, drained, for the chicken. Wash the shrimps in a sieve under the tap, place them in 450 ml (¾ pint) water and simmer for 5 minutes. Drain and reserve all the liquid. Check that all the shrimps have been peeled and remove any skins, heads or whiskers. Fry the rice and instead of adding cooked chicken, add the boiled dried shrimps and the drained tuna along with all the other ingredients. Use the reserved shrimp water to boil the rice in, covering and simmering for 20–25 minutes.

■

Mancha manteles

Chicken in dark chilli sauce with pineapple, pears and plantain

Mancha Manteles means literally 'tablecloth stainer', a name that is well deserved as the chilli used in this recipe does produce very stubborn stains. So make sure that you have protected your clothing as well as your tablecloth. This is a main course dish and it goes well with beans and rice, accompanied by soft warm tortillas. Preparation should start 3 hours ahead of time.

SERVES 4

4 mulato chillies	*400 g (14 oz) can tomatoes*
600 ml (1 pint) boiling	*1 chicken stock cube*
water	*5 cm (2 inch) stick cinnamon*
4 chicken breasts	*2 cloves garlic*
½ teaspoon salt	*½ onion, quartered*
¼ teaspoon ground black	*1 ripe plantain or 2 green*
pepper	*bananas, sliced*

2 tablespoons malt vinegar
1 tablespoon cooking oil
1 tablespoon sesame seeds
25 g (1 oz) blanched
* almonds*

2 pears, peeled and quartered
2 pineapple slices
2 tablespoons granulated sugar

Warm the chillies in a dry frying pan for about 3 minutes until soft, turning frequently. Discard the stems and seeds, cover with 300 ml (½ pint) of the boiling water and soak for 1 hour. Season the chicken with the salt, pepper and vinegar and marinate for 1 hour. Heat the oil in a frying pan and fry the chicken until golden all over. Remove from the pan and keep warm, reserving 1 tablespoon of the oil.

Blend the soaked chillies and their water with the sesame seeds, almonds, tomatoes, chicken stock cube, cinnamon, garlic and onion together in a blender. Press through a sieve into the frying pan and fry for 3–4 minutes, stirring continually. Add the chicken breasts, plantain or green bananas and remaining water and simmer, uncovered, for about 40 minutes until the chicken is tender, stirring occasionally. (This can also be done in the oven in a covered casserole.) Add the fruit and sugar and simmer for 5 minutes. Serve hot. This dish improves if refrigerated overnight and then reheated.

Mole verde de pepita

Tomatillo and pumpkin seed sauce for chicken or pork

This dish, which is often called *Pipián*, can be red or green. Traditionally the red *pipián*, or *pipián rojo*, is made from *Salsa Adobada* thickened with ground sesame seed. *Pipián Verde* is made of *Salsa de Tomate Verde* thickened with ground pumpkin seeds. The meats used are chicken or pork, though these vary from region to region and occasionally duck or pheasant is used. The sauce is very rich and the dish makes a good main course, accompanied by white rice, beans, salad and soft warm tortillas.

SERVES 4

4 chicken portions or 450 g
    (1 lb) shoulder of pork,
    cubed
½ teaspoon salt
1 tablespoon malt vinegar
¼ teaspoon ground black
    pepper
2 tablespoons cooking oil
900 ml (1½ pints) water
1 bay leaf
50 g (2 oz) pumpkin seeds,
    shelled
1 teaspoon sesame seeds

2 green peppers, stalks and
    seeds removed
4 lettuce leaves
2 tablespoons chopped fresh
    coriander
2 green chillies, stalks removed
1 clove garlic
2 cloves
2 peppercorns
¼ teaspoon cinnamon
12 tomatillos, skinned, or
    2 × 275 g (10 oz) cans peeled
    tomatillos and their juice

Season the chicken portions with the salt, vinegar and pepper. Heat the oil in a frying pan and fry the chicken until golden on all sides. Remove the chicken and reserve the oil. Put the water in a saucepan with the bay leaf and chicken, cover and simmer for 45 minutes until the chicken is very tender. Reserve the stock.

Cook the pumpkin seeds in a dry frying pan over medium heat for 4 minutes, reserve. Cook the sesame seeds in the same way, then work to a paste in a blender for about 1½ minutes, with the remaining ingredients except the pumpkin seeds. Add about 150 ml (¼ pint) chicken stock if necessary.

Heat 1 tablespoon of the reserved oil in a saucepan and fry the paste for 3 minutes. Add 600 ml (1 pint) of the chicken stock and simmer for about 30 minutes or until the liquid is reduced by half. Add the chicken quarters and simmer for 15 minutes. Just before serving, blend the pumpkin seeds with a little stock to a soft paste and stir into the sauce. Serve immediately.

■

Rosca de aguacate Doña Margarita

Avocado and chicken ring

This is a very attractive dish suitable for a cold buffet, starter or light lunch. It is such a surprise to taste the delicious avocado and chicken mixture under the chopped nuts. This recipe was given to me by a very dear friend called Margarita and that is the reason for the name. Mexican recipes often bear the name of the dedicated ladies who passed them on, until they become a legend. I hope this will be the case in this instance.

SERVES 10

500 g (1¼ lb) cooked chicken meat (approximately 5 small chicken breasts), cubed
200 g (7 oz) cream cheese
300 ml (½ pint) single cream
½ teaspoon salt
½ teaspoon ground black pepper
4 medium-size ripe avocados

3 ripe tomatoes, skinned and seeded
2 green chillies
½ onion
3 tablespoons olive oil
juice of 1 lemon
1 tablespoon mayonnaise
25 g (1 oz) chopped pecan nuts or flaked almonds

Lightly butter a 25 cm (10 inch) ring mould. In a bowl mix the cubed chicken with the cheese, cream and half the salt and pepper. Cut 2 of the avocados in half, and remove the skins and stones. Purée the flesh in a blender with the tomatoes, chillies, onion, olive oil and half the lemon juice. Put half the chicken mixture in the ring mould, pressing firmly with the back of a spoon. Spoon on the avocado and tomato mixture, then the remaining chicken mixture. Cover with cling film and refrigerate for about 2 hours.

Run a knife around the edges of the ring, then invert the mould onto a serving dish. Halve the remaining avocados and mash them to a pulp. Add the mayonnaise, remaining lemon juice, salt and pepper and spread it over the chicken ring. Sprinkle over the chopped nuts and serve immediately.

■

Budín Azteca

Tortilla and chicken pie

This dish is ideal for entertaining, as it can be prepared ahead of time and baked before serving. It is a simplified version of *enchiladas*, without all the last-minute attention they require. Serve with *Frijoles Refritos*, tossed salad and *Guacamole*.

SERVES 8

oil for shallow frying
12 corn tortillas
100 g (4 oz) Cheddar cheese,
  grated
100 g (4 oz) Mozzarella
  cheese, grated
150 ml (¼ pint) soured cream

150 ml (¼ pint) single cream
1 quantity Salsa para
  Enchiladas
3 chicken breasts, poached,
  skinned and boned
1 green chilli, sliced
1 green pepper, sliced

Heat the oil in a frying pan and fry the tortillas for 30 seconds on each side; drain on absorbent kitchen paper and keep warm. Mix the cheeses together, then mix the creams together. Grease a medium-sized casserole.

Bring the sauce to the boil and spoon 4 tablespoons into the casserole. Dip 4 tortillas, one at a time, in the remaining sauce, then place them in the casserole. Cut the chicken into bite-size pieces and place a third on top of the tortillas. Then add a third of the sliced chillies and peppers, next a third of the cheese and finally a third of the cream. Continue layering in the same way finishing with cheese and cream. Bake in the centre of a preheated oven at 180°C, 350°F, Gas Mark 4 for 40 minutes. Serve hot.

■

Taquitos de pollo

Corn tortillas filled with chicken

Taquitos de Pollo must surely be the parent of the *taco* shell, the American fast-food way of eating *tacos* (see page 66). *Taquitos de Pollo* and *Taquitos de Carne* are tortillas rolled round cooked chicken or beef. They can be made in advance and secured with a cocktail stick, then shallow-fried just before serving. *Taquitos* are so popular that I do a whole batch of tortillas and cook enough chicken to fill them all, then freeze them to use at a later date. The amount of meat you put in each *taco* depends entirely on your own preferences.

Taquitos de Pollo are served with a good helping of *Guacamole* or any of the sauces and they go well with *Arroz con Jitomate* and *Frijoles Refritos*. They are ideally suited to an informal dinner and should be eaten by holding in the hand.

SERVES 6

18 corn tortillas
1½ kg (3½ lb) cooked
   chicken
6 tablespoons oil

1 quantity Guacamole (see
   page 59)
chopped lettuce, to garnish

Warm the tortillas in a hot dry heavy-based frying pan until they become pliable, about 30 seconds. Place a piece of cooked chicken on each tortilla and roll it up. Secure each *taco* with a cocktail stick.

Heat the oil in a medium-size frying pan and fry about a third of the *tacos*. They fry very fast and can burn easily; turn them carefully and remove from the heat when just turning colour and still a little soft. Drain on absorbent kitchen paper and keep warm until you finish frying. Now remove the cocktail sticks and spoon 1 tablespoon of *Guacamole* inside each and along the tortilla flap. Serve immediately, garnished with chopped lettuce.

■

Budín Xochitl

Tortilla casserole with chicken and tomatillo sauce

Tortilla casseroles are easy to make, provided you already have the tortillas. Generally they are used for a main course, together with *Frijoles Refritos*. This recipe calls for *Salsa de Tomate Verde*, but any other sauce may be used instead. Serve with a good tossed salad.

SERVES 4

8 corn tortillas, cut into 1 cm
   (½ inch) strips
4 tablespoons cooking oil
2 chicken breasts, poached
   and shredded

1 quantity Salsa de Tomate
   Verde
135 ml (4½ fl oz) soured cream
25 g (1 oz) grated Parmesan
   cheese

In a heavy-based frying pan, fry the tortilla strips in the oil until they just start changing colour. Remove from the heat and drain on absorbent kitchen paper. Fry the chicken and when it starts to brown add the sauce. Grease an ovenproof dish and make layers of tortilla strips, chicken mixture, cream and cheese, repeating until you finish with cheese.

Bake in a preheated oven at 180°C, 350°F, Gas Mark 4 for about 30 minutes or until it starts to brown around the edges. Serve hot.

■

Pavo al horno

Roast turkey with almond and raisin stuffing

Pavo is another word for *guajolote* which means turkey! At Christmas time *Pavo al Horno* is served in Mexican homes, very much in the same style as it is in Britain. The stuffing is made from a special type of white bread which is called *bolillo*, but French bread is a good substitute. This roast turkey can be accompanied by *Ensalada Navideña*, *Papas con Chorizo*, *Calabacitas con Elote* and a good helping of *Guacamole*. It is also suitable for a buffet or sit down formal dinner. The bread must be stale. Preparation should start the night before.

SERVES 8

2¼ kg (5 lb) turkey
5 tablespoons malt vinegar
1½ teaspoons salt
1 teaspoon ground black
   pepper

3 cloves garlic
2 onions, halved
600 ml (1 pint) water

Stuffing

225 g (8 oz) stale white bread
225 g (8 oz) butter
2 onions, finely chopped
8 sticks celery, sliced
3 tablespoons tomato purée
1 tablespoon Worcestershire
   sauce

1 chicken stock cube
25 g (1 oz) raisins
25 g (1 oz) flaked almonds
2 eggs, hard-boiled, sliced
1 tablespoon cornflour
1 tablespoon cooking oil
4 tablespoons water

Wash and trim the turkey, including giblets and neck. Make sure there is no trace of yellow skin in the giblets or green in the liver. Sprinkle the vinegar all over the inside and outside of the turkey, then sprinkle on the salt and pepper. Rub half the garlic inside the turkey and put the remainder in a roasting tin. Place the turkey on top and leave to marinate in a cool place overnight. Meanwhile, simmer the neck, giblets and 1 of the onions in the water for about 40 minutes. Strain and discard the meat and onions. Soak the stale bread in the hot stock overnight.

To make the stuffing, strain the bread, pressing to extract as much liquid as possible. Reserve the liquid. Heat the butter in a large frying pan and fry the onion for about 5 minutes until golden. Add the celery and fry for 2 minutes, then add the tomato purée, Worcestershire sauce, chicken stock cube and drained bread. Fry for about 15 minutes, stirring occasionally, until it dries. Add the raisins and almonds. Use to stuff the turkey, or place in a serving dish and just before serving garnish with sliced hard-boiled egg. Serve at room temperature.

Place the turkey on a wire rack over the roasting tin filled with the reserved water from the soaked bread, remaining onion and garlic cloves. Brush the turkey with the oil and roast in a preheated oven, at 160°C, 325°F, Gas Mark 3 for 2 hours (unstuffed) or 2½ hours (stuffed), basting frequently. If the breast browns too quickly, cover it loosely with kitchen foil and uncover 15 minutes before cooking is completed. Remove the turkey to a serving dish. Pour the contents of the pan into a bowl and leave to rest for 15 minutes. Discard any fat that floats to the surface. Sieve into a saucepan, crushing the onions and garlic through. Mix the cornflour with the water. Bring the gravy to the boil, stir in the cornflour and bring to the boil, stirring. Serve hot.

■

Enchiladas de mole sencillo

Chicken-stuffed tortillas in chilli sauce

Mexican cooking uses innumerable different sauces, and just about any of them can be used for *enchiladas*. This particular one also calls for some chocolate which is quite usual. However, don't expect it to turn out sweet; in fact the little sugar in the chocolate heightens the flavour of the chillies. Serve as a main course with *Arroz con Rajas*.

SERVES 4

2 pasilla chillies
4 ancho chillies
4 mulato chillies
275 g (10 oz) can tomatillos
and their juice, or
1 quantity Salsa para
Enchiladas
50 g (2 oz) ground almonds
25 g (1 oz) plain chocolate,
grated

1 chicken stock cube
½ onion, finely chopped
2 cloves garlic, crushed
2 tablespoons cooking oil
25 g (1 oz) sesame seeds
oil for shallow frying
12 corn tortillas
2 chicken breasts, poached and
shredded
1 lettuce, shredded, to garnish

Heat the chillies on a dry griddle or heavy-based frying pan until they soften. Discard the stalks, seeds and veins. Drain the *tomatillos*, putting the juice in a saucepan, or if you are using the made-up sauce, place it in a saucepan. Bring to the boil, pour over the chillies and leave to soak for about 1 hour. Liquidize the chillies and sauce to a smooth paste with the *tomatillos*, almonds, chocolate, chicken stock cube, onion and garlic. Heat the oil in a deep saucepan and fry the mixture for about 10 minutes until it thickens. Meanwhile, cook the sesame seeds by stirring them in a dry frying pan over medium heat for 3 minutes or until they start popping.

Heat the rest of the oil for shallow frying and immerse 1 tortilla at a time in it for 30 seconds on each side; drain on absorbent kitchen paper. Now bring the sauce to the boil and quickly dip each tortilla in it. Place 3 tortillas on a warm dinner plate, fill them with

OPPOSITE: For a light lunch—*Arroz con Pollo* (rice with chicken and vegetables, page 167); and *Ensalada Tenango* (avocado salad, page 136). FOLLOWING PAGES: For a cocktail party—*Tacos* (page 66); *Nachos* (tortilla chip quarters with cheese and chillies, page 56); *Pepitas de Calabaza* (roasted pumpkin seeds, page 58); *Frijoles con Queso* (bean dip, page 58) with *Totopos* (corn tortilla chips, page 56); and *Guacamole* (avocado dip, page 59); with *Limonada* (fresh lemonade, page 223) and Tequila Sunrise cocktail (page 221).

the shredded chicken, roll up, spoon over more sauce and sprinkle with the sesame seeds. Garnish with shredded lettuce. They should really be eaten straight away, which of course causes problems if you would like everyone to eat at once. In this case, dip, fill and roll all the tortillas and keep them warm. Just before serving, pour over the boiling hot sauce and garnish.

■

Mole Poblano

Turkey in rich chilli, nut and spice sauce

The Spanish word *mole*, meaning sauce, derives from *molli* in Nahuatl, the Aztec Indians' language. This has become Mexico's national dish and there are umpteen versions of it, each area claiming to have the best. However, it was in the State of Puebla that the dish was originated by nuns, hence its name *Mole Poblano*. It is also known as 'turkey in chocolate sauce' which is deceptive because it only takes 25 g (1 oz) of chocolate. The dark red colour is obtained from the dried chillies used in its preparation, not the chocolate which is used to darken the dish a little and to sweeten it slightly.

Mole Poblano is the celebration dish of the country and turkey is the most commonly used meat in it. However, pork and chicken are equally good. The usual accompaniments are white rice and beans with soft warm tortillas. It improves overnight when the flavours have had time to blend. It also freezes very well and any leftovers may be used for either *tamales* or as a filling for *tacos*. For an easier version of the sauce, use *Salsa Adobada*.

OPPOSITE: Breakfast selection—*Tamales* (corn dumplings steamed in corn husks, page 92); *Pan de Muerto* (Halloween bread, page 211); *Huevos Rancheros Típicos* (ranch-style eggs with tomato sauce served on fried tortillas and with beans, page 104); and *Chocolate Caliente* (hot chocolate, page 226).

SERVES 10

2¾ kg (6 lb) turkey, divided
  into portions
6 tablespoons malt vinegar
1½ teaspoons salt
1 teaspoon ground black
  pepper
1 teaspoon sugar
6 cloves garlic, crushed
100 g (4 oz) mulato chillies
100 g (4 oz) ancho chillies
50 g (2 oz) pasilla chillies
2 chilpotle chillies
1½ litres (2½ pints) water
50 g (2 oz) sesame seeds
50 g (2 oz) almonds

50 g (2 oz) monkey nuts,
  shelled
2 corn tortillas
100 g (4 oz) raisins
2 chicken stock cubes
4 tablespoons tomato purée
6 peppercorns
12 cloves
½ teaspoon aniseed
13 cm (5 inch) stick cinnamon
3 onions, quartered
25 g (1 oz) plain chocolate,
  grated
8 tablespoons oil

Wash and trim the turkey pieces and sprinkle with the vinegar, salt, pepper, sugar and half the garlic. Leave to marinate for about 1 hour.

Meanwhile, heat the chillies in a heavy-based frying pan for about 3 minutes, turning frequently, until pliable. Remove and discard the stems and seeds (unless you wish to have an extremely hot dish, in which case the seeds may be included.) Soak the chillies in 900 ml (1½ pints) of the boiling water for about 1 hour. Roast the sesame seeds, almonds and monkey nuts in a dry frying pan by tossing over moderate heat for about 5 minutes. Place the tortillas in the pan for 4 minutes, turning occasionally, until they become dry and brittle. Liquidize them with the soaked chillies and their liquid in 3 batches with the reserved garlic and remaining ingredients, except the oil, reserving some roasted nuts to garnish.

Heat the oil in a casserole and fry the marinated turkey pieces until light golden. Remove the turkey and set aside. Drain off most of the oil, leaving 4 tablespoons. Sieve the chilli mixture into the hot oil and fry, stirring continually, for 5 minutes. Add the turkey pieces and simmer gently, uncovered, for about 1½ hours until the turkey is tender. Alternatively, cover and cook in a preheated oven at 180°C, 350°F, Gas Mark 4 for about 1¾ hours, stirring occasionally. Garnish with the roasted nuts.

Pescados y Mariscos
Fish and Shellfish

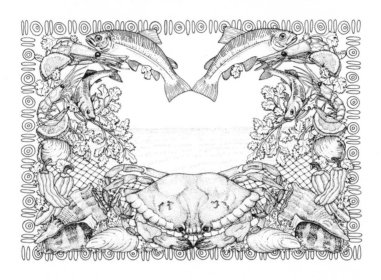

The 6,300 miles of coastline which surrounds Mexico provides a great abundance of fish and seafood offering unsurpassed opportunities for a varied fish menu, the Gulf of Mexico, Caribbean Sea, Gulf of Cortés and Pacific Ocean all contributing to its variety. There are a number of freshwater fish which are also popular.

Snapper, red snapper, flounder, mackerel, bass, tuna, albacore and sole are all common fish. In the San Juan Market in Mexico City, a banner proudly advertises 'the fish that you buy here today slept in the sea last night'! There are rainbow trout, perch and many other varieties in the lakes and rivers, and of course turtle, squid, clams, abalone, conch, oysters, mussels, crayfish, lobster, prawns, crabs and king crabs are all to be found as well.

Two of the most popular dishes in the Mexican repertoire are *Huachinango a la Veracruzana* and *Seviche*. Both are traditionally made with red snapper, but cod or haddock make a good substitute. Although fresh fish is abundant in Mexico, there are a number of popular recipes originally introduced by the Spaniards which call for dried fish, such as *Bacalao a la Vizcaina*.

Mexicans grill and fry their fish in much the same way as you would find in Europe. Lime or lemon juice is always used to season the fish and also as garnish, and sometimes a dash of Worcestershire sauce is added! In Yucatán, where fish is abundant, it is often steamed in banana leaves in very much the same manner as *Pollo Pibil*.

■

Corona de pescado

Haddock ring with olives

This is a good dish for a light lunch accompanied by *Ensalada de Aguacate con Jitomate* and *Arroz Blanco*.

SERVES 4

450 g (1 lb) haddock fillets, skinned
½ lime or lemon
½ onion
300 ml (½ pint) water
2 eggs, hard-boiled, chopped
¼ teaspoon salt
1 red pepper, seeded and finely chopped
50 g (2 oz) butter, cubed

50 g (2 oz) breadcrumbs, or cheese biscuit crumbs
50 g (2 oz) stuffed olives, sliced
dash of Worcestershire sauce
2 tablespoons chopped parsley
1 egg, well beaten
extra chopped parsley, to garnish

Place the fish in a saucepan with the lime or lemon, onion and water. Bring to the boil and simmer for 15 minutes. Drain, discard the lemon and onion, and flake the fish discarding any bones. Add the chopped eggs, salt, red pepper, butter, all but 2 tablespoons of the breadcrumbs, sliced olives, Worcestershire sauce and chopped parsley. Fold the beaten egg into the mixture then pour it into a well-greased ovenproof ring-mould. Sprinkle with the reserved breadcrumbs and bake in a preheated oven at 220°C, 425°F, Gas Mark 7 for 30 minutes. Invert the mould onto a serving plate and garnish with parsley. Serve hot.

Pescado al arriero

Cod fillets in white sauce with peppers

This dish is very quick to prepare and makes a good main course
with potatoes, boiled peas and corn.

SERVES 4

4 fillets cod or haddock
½ lemon
¼ teaspoon salt
¼ teaspoon ground
*   black pepper*
2 tablespoons flour
50 g (2 oz) butter
½ onion, sliced
1 pepper, finely sliced

275 ml (9 fl oz) milk
½ chicken stock cube,
*   crumbled*
2 bay leaves
2 green chillies
pinch of nutmeg
dash of Worcestershire sauce
sprigs of parsley, to garnish

Dry the fish with absorbent kitchen paper and rub with the lemon
half, squeezing any remaining juice over the fillets. Sprinkle with
salt and pepper and pat them with the flour. In a heavy-based
frying pan, heat the butter and fry the onion and pepper for 3
minutes more, then add the remaining ingredients except the fish.
Simmer for a few minutes more, then add the fish, spooning the
liquid over it. Cover and simmer over low heat for 20 minutes,
stirring occasionally to prevent sticking. Alternatively, bake for
30 minutes in a covered casserole in a preheated oven at 180°C,
350°F, Gas Mark 4. Garnish with parsley sprigs.

■

Huachinango o robalo en salsa de pimientos morrones

Haddock fillets in pimento and cream sauce

This is a pretty sauce that can be eaten hot or cold. It goes
particularly well with white fish, prawns or lobster. The fish is first
cooked in milk, and the flavouring is added towards the end just

before serving. I prefer to use tinned pimentos rather than fresh peppers because they have a more concentrated flavour. Cod may be used in place of haddock.

SERVES 4

4 haddock fillets	*½ onion*
½ lemon	*1 bay leaf*
¼ teaspoon ground	*200 g (7 oz) can pimentos*
* black pepper*	*½ chicken stock cube*
2 tablespoons flour	*150 ml (¼ pint) double cream*
150 ml (¼ pint) milk	

Grease an ovenproof dish. Dry the fish with absorbent kitchen paper and rub with the lemon half, squeezing any remaining juice over the fillets. Sprinkle with pepper, dust with flour and place in the dish with the milk, onion and bay leaf. Cover with foil and bake in a preheated oven at 180°C, 350°F, Gas Mark 4 for about 20 minutes. Discard the bay leaf and onion.

Drain the pimentos. Cut 8 strips of pimento for garnish. Place the remaining pimentos in a blender with the chicken stock cube and cream and blend to a purée. Drain as much milk as you can from the fish, and strain the purée over the fish. Cover and bake for 10 minutes. Garnish with the strips of pimento, and serve hot or cold.

■

Huachinango a la Veracruzana

Cod in tomato sauce with capers, olives and orange

This is by far the most popular way of eating fish in Mexico, and its popularity has spread to the U.S. and Europe. In Mexico it is made with red snapper, which is cooked and served whole in special dishes shaped like a fish. I have used cod in this recipe, but haddock or any white fish will do. Although whole fish is more authentic you may prefer to use fillets which contain fewer bones, as bones are hard to spot once the sauce is covering the fish.

This dish makes an excellent main course or, if you use half the recipe, a good starter. Crusty French bread goes well with it, together with mashed potatoes or rice, and green vegetables.

SERVES 4

4 cod fillets (about
   450 g/1 lb), or 1 whole fish
   of the same weight
½ lemon
¼ teaspoon salt
¼ teaspoon ground black
   pepper
450 ml (¾ pint) Salsa para
   Enchiladas
juice of 1 orange
1 red pepper, sliced

1 onion, finely sliced
18 capers
16 stuffed green olives
¼ teaspoon Worcestershire
   sauce
pinch of dried oregano
1 bay leaf
2 green chillies
2 sprigs parsley
1 orange, sliced with skin on, to
   garnish

If you are using a whole fish, ask the fishmonger to descale it for you. Wash the fish well on the outside, rinse the inside, then rub all over with the lemon half, squeezing the juice as you go. If you are using cod fillets, skin them by holding on to the tail end and placing a sharp knife at an angle between the flesh and the skin, and working the knife against the skin. If the fish is too slippery to hold, rub some salt on it to give you a grip, washing it off afterwards. Remove all the bones you can find, and cut out the bony section in the thick-fleshed end of each fillet. Wash the fillets and pat dry with absorbent kitchen paper. Sprinkle all over with the lemon juice, salt and pepper.

Place half the sauce and all the orange juice in an ovenproof dish, then add the fish, pepper, onion, capers, olives, Worcestershire sauce, oregano, bay leaf, chillies and parsley. Pour over the remaining sauce. Cover with foil and bake in a preheated oven at 180°C, 350°C, Gas Mark 4 for about 40 minutes, then test for readiness. The whole fish is cooked if the flesh comes off the bone easily; the fillet will be cooked in this time, it should separate easily. Bake uncovered for a further 15 minutes, basting frequently to prevent it from burning. Serve hot, garnished with sliced orange.

Bacalao a la Vizcaina

Salted cod in tomato sauce

A rich main course that must be prepared a day in advance, *Bacalao* is a dish of Spanish origin and is considered a delicacy in Mexico, where it is served with pride on Fridays—a day when meat is not eaten, but when people do still like to entertain. *Bacalao* is also a delicious filling for *Empanadas de Bacalao*. Salted cod is available from good fishmongers and some European and West Indian food shops.

SERVES 6

275 g (10 oz) pack salted cod
50 g (2 oz) butter
½ onion, finely sliced
1 red pepper, thinly sliced
15 stuffed green olives, sliced
250 ml (8 fl oz) Salsa para
   Enchiladas

1 tablespoon tomato purée
225 g (8 oz) new potatoes,
   cooked and diced
¼ teaspoon dried oregano
¼ teaspoon sugar

Soak the fish in cold water for 8 hours or overnight. Discard the water, cover with fresh water and bring to the boil. Simmer for 15 minutes, then discard the water and cover with more water. Bring to the boil, simmer for 10 minutes and drain. Allow to cool, then use your fingers to shred the fish as finely as possible, picking out any sharp bones. Heat the butter in a frying pan and fry the onion and red pepper for 3 minutes, then add the fish and remaining ingredients, mixing well. Cover and simmer for about 5 minutes, or until it starts to dry out. Serve hot with rice, a mixed salad and white crispy rolls.

Empanada de bacalao

Salted cod and tomato turnover

For this unusual turnover I use rough puff pastry which is quick and easy and very effective. The self-raising flour makes them puff even better. This turnover may be served as a main course

184

accompanied by an assortment of vegetables and a green salad. But if you prefer to serve it for a cocktail party or a starter, all you have to do is make *Empanaditas* (little turnovers) using a small biscuit cutter, making about 36 rounds. Garnish with lots of parsley. An alternative filling is *Picadillo*.

SERVES 6

Rough puff pastry

175 g (6 oz) self-raising flour
50 g (2 oz) unsalted butter,
   cubed
50 g (2 oz) lard or vegetable
   shortening

juice of ½ lemon
85 ml (3 fl oz) cold water
beaten egg yolk, to glaze

For the filling

1 quantity Bacalao (see
   page 184)

Sift the flour into a bowl and toss the fats in, coating them with flour. Using a knife or spatula, mix the lemon juice and water into the flour mixture without breaking the lumps. Now add just enough extra liquid to bind the ingredients into a soft dough. With floured fingers, gather the mixture into a soft ball and place it in the middle of a floured board. Using a floured rolling pin, shape it into a rectangle about 2.5 cm (1 inch) thick. Lightly mark the dough with 2 crosswise lines, dividing it into thirds. Fold the lower third towards the centre, trapping as much air as possible, and seal the edges. Now fold the top half towards the centre and repeat the sealing. Repeat the rolling and folding process 3 times, then wrap the dough in cling film and refrigerate for at least 1 hour. Meanwhile, prepare and cool the filling.

On a floured board, and with a floured rolling pin, roll out the dough to a rectangle 3 mm (⅛ inch) thick. Place on a greased baking tray and spread the filling over half of it. Fold over the other half to cover the filling. Seal with a fork, prick all over, and brush with beaten egg yolk. Bake in a preheated oven at 220°C, 425°C, Gas Mark 7 for about 15 minutes or until golden. Serve hot, or cool on a wire rack.

Seviche Acapulqueño

Marinated fish with honeydew melon sauce

This marinated fish dish makes a colourful starter for a cold buffet. *Seviche* is one of Mexico's most famous dishes, with many local variations. Traditionally, the only 'cooking' of the fish is as it marinates in the acidic lemon juice—but this variation comes from Acapulco, where there are a lot of tourists, who I suspect prefer to know their fish is cooked!

SERVES 4

½ honeydew melon
4 fillets lemon sole
250 ml (8 fl oz) dry white
  wine
2 tablespoons olive oil
6 spring onions, thinly sliced
1 carrot, peeled and grated

4 tablespoons tomato ketchup
salt and freshly ground black
  pepper
juice of 1 lemon
1 orange, pineapple, or other
  fruit, to garnish

Discard the seeds from the melon, mash the flesh with a fork and sieve it. Place the fillets in an ovenproof dish with the wine and bake, uncovered, in a preheated oven at 160°C, 325°F, Gas Mark 3 for about 15 minutes or until the fillets turn white. Carefully drain off most of the liquid from the dish. Heat the oil in a frying pan and fry the spring onions and carrot for 5 minutes, stirring often. Add the melon purée, ketchup, salt, pepper and lemon juice. Cook for about 5 minutes and spoon over the fish. Allow to cool before serving. Garnish with sliced oranges or pineapple or any fresh fruit.

Aguacates rellenos de sardina

Avocados stuffed with sardine

This is a tasty and economical starter, which is light and a little unusual.

SERVES 6

8 radishes
2 × 100 g (4 oz) cans
  sardines in tomato sauce
4 tablespoons soured cream
1 tablespoon lemon juice
½ teaspoon Worcestershire
  sauce

¼ teaspoon salt
¼ teaspoon ground black
  pepper
3 ripe avocados
sprigs of parsley
1 small lettuce, finely shredded

Top and tail the radishes and make small cuts around each one. Cover with cold water and refrigerate for about 1 hour, until the radishes have opened out into flower shapes. Drain off half the tomato sauce from the sardines. Remove the bones from the fish then mash with the soured cream, lemon juice, Worcestershire sauce, salt and pepper.

Halve the avocados and remove the stones. Fill with the sardine mixture and garnish with parsley. Arrange the avocados in a circle on a bed of shredded lettuce and decorate with radish roses.

Pastel de salmón

Baked salmon fishcake

This glorified fishcake is a good supper dish. It's prepared all in one go, freezes well and children love it. Serve accompanied by a green salad and *Calabacitas con Rajas*.

SERVES 4

225 g (8 oz) potatoes, cooked,
  peeled and mashed with
  50 g (2 oz) butter
200 g (7 oz) tinned salmon,
  drained, skin and bones
  removed
1 egg
1 teaspoon Worcestershire
  sauce

1 chicken stock cube
¼ teaspoon ground black
  pepper
2 tablespoons chopped parsley
½ teaspoon baking powder
sprigs of parsley, to garnish

Mix all the ingredients together well and place in a greased ovenproof dish. Bake in a preheated oven at 190°C, 375°F, Gas Mark 5 for 20–30 minutes. Garnish with parsley and serve hot.

■

Torta navideña de salmón

Cold salmon slices with Christmas decoration

The very attractive decorations for this dish make it perfect for a Christmas party. It is also ideal for a cold buffet dinner party, a lunch or a starter. Poinsettias grow wild in Mexico, where they are known as Christmas flowers because they bloom at Christmas-time, creating a mass of brilliant colour in the hedgerows. Cook this dish several hours before you need it.

SERVES 4

200 g (7 oz) can salmon
2 cheese crackers, made into
  crumbs
1 small onion, finely chopped
3 eggs, beaten
salt and ground black
  pepper
dash of Worcestershire sauce

dash of Tabasco sauce
1 small lettuce, shredded
2 tablespoons mayonnaise
2 red peppers, grilled and
  peeled, or 2 tinned pimentos
1 egg, hard-boiled, coarsely
  sieved
juice of ½ lemon

Drain the salmon and remove any skin and bones. Mix thoroughly with the crumbs, onion, eggs, Worcestershire sauce and Tabasco and season with salt and pepper. Wrap tightly, in a fat sausage shape, in kitchen foil lined with buttered greaseproof paper. Steam for 1 hour, allow to cool, then unwrap and cut into 1 cm (½ inch) thick slices. Place some of the shredded lettuce in the centre of a serving dish and arrange the slices of salmon in a circle touching each other, on top. Spread the slices with mayonnaise.

To make the poinsettia, cut the peppers or pimentos into petals, each about 5 cm (2 inches) long, 1 cm (½ inch) across and tapered at both ends. Arrange 5 of the petals in a circle on the salmon and make the centre of the flower with the sieved egg. Surround the salmon with the remaining lettuce. Season the lemon juice and pour it over the lettuce just before serving.

Jaibas en su concha

Savoury baked crab

This is a very good starter, which is sure to impress. It is especially attractive baked in crab shells, which can be washed and re-used. You can use individual ramekins or scallop shells instead.

This dish always brings back special memories for me. When I was expecting my first baby, I craved Mexican dishes and it was this one that I absolutely had to have. Not so extravagant in itself . . . except at that time we were living, not in Mexico, but in Jamaica. With its traditional colonial status, the food I could get was either Jamaican or English—hardly Mexican! Then I discovered that the most expensive restaurant in town served a very similar dish as a starter. I can still remember my husband's face when I asked the waiter to give me this dish for starter and for main course as well! After that, I only had to sit at the table for the same smiling waiter to say, 'Crab again, Ma'am!' See what you think of it.

SERVES 4

175 g (6 oz) crab meat, fresh, frozen or tinned
50 g (2 oz) butter
6 spring onions, finely chopped
6 sprigs parsley, finely chopped
¼ teaspoon Tabasco sauce

1 teaspoon Worcestershire sauce
½ chicken stock cube
¼ teaspoon ground black pepper
3 tablespoons tomato purée
50 g (2 oz) fine breadcrumbs

To garnish

sprigs of parsley

4 slices lemon

If you are using fresh crab, plunge it into boiling water for 10 minutes. Crack the shell and carefully pick all the white meaty flesh from the shell and claws. If using frozen or tinned meat, drain it carefully and search for small bones and pieces of shell.

Melt the butter in the frying pan and fry the onions and parsley for about 3 minutes, stirring constantly. Add the crab meat and remaining ingredients except the breadcrumbs, and fry gently, stirring occasionally. When the mixture starts to dry out, remove from the heat and spoon into the well-scrubbed and buttered shells. Place on a baking tray and cook in a preheated oven at 180°C, 350°F, Gas Mark 4 for about 15 minutes. Sprinkle over the breadcrumbs and return to the oven for another 10 minutes or until lightly browned on top. Serve hot, garnished with parsley and lemon slices.

■

Rosca de camarones en escabeche

Prawns and rice ring with red chilli sauce

This hot rice ring is tasty and also colourful, featuring, as so many other Mexican dishes do, the green, white and red of the national flag. Serve it as a main course along with salad and *Esquites*.

The origin of this dish could be Veracruz or the southeast of Mexico, near the Caribbean. Many Mexican dishes were adopted by the nearby Caribbean islands, and in turn a number of Mexico's coastline delicacies originally came from Jamaica and the Turtle Islands (now called the Caymans) and Cuba, which is where Cortés sailed from when he first touched the coast of the Yucatán Peninsula.

SERVES 4

1 kg (2 lb) fresh raw prawns
900 ml (1½ pints) water
1 teaspoon salt
2 tablespoons cooking oil
1 clove garlic
175 g (6 oz) long grain rice
1 chicken stock cube

2 sprigs parsley
1 medium-size onion, finely
  chopped
2 green chillies
1 quantity Salsa Adobada
½ lettuce, finely shredded

Rinse the prawns in running water. Bring the water to the boil in a saucepan, add salt, then add the prawns and simmer, uncovered, for 5 minutes. Remove from the heat and strain, reserving the liquid. Shell and devein the prawns.

In a heavy saucepan with a tight-fitting lid, heat the oil and fry the garlic until black, then discard it. Add the rice and fry for about 4 minutes, stirring, until it has changed colour. Drain off all the excess oil, and add 450 ml (15 fl oz) of the reserved prawn liquid. Stir in the chicken stock cube, parsley, onion and chillies. Cover and bring to the boil, then reduce the heat and simmer slowly for 15 minutes, or until all the liquid is absorbed. The rice will double in volume and become fluffy. Discard the parsley and chillies.

Bring the sauce to the boil, add the prawns and cook for 2 minutes. Now put half the rice in a greased 23 cm (9 inch) ring-mould, pressing down gently to make it firm. Add half the mixture of sauce and prawns, then cover with the remaining rice, pressing firmly. Invert the mould on to a serving dish, pour the remaining sauce over it and decorate with the prawns. Garnish with shredded lettuce around the ring.

VARIATION:

If you prefer to eat this dish cold, substitute *Salsa Típica* for the *Salsa Adobada*.

Cocktail de camarones almendrados

Prawn and almond cocktail

A delicate starter, ideal before a heavy main course. It's simple to prepare and entirely different, fresh and tasty. Prepare it several hours before you need it.

SERVES 4

200 g (7 oz) canned prawns
50 g (2 oz) stuffed green
  olives
4 spring onions, finely
  chopped
1 tablespoon olive oil
1 tablespoon tomato purée
50 g (2 oz) flaked almonds
juice of ½ lemon

pinch of sugar
¼ teaspoon salt
¼ teaspoon ground black
  pepper
4 tablespoons water
2 tablespoons tomato ketchup
dash of Worcestershire sauce
½ lettuce, shredded

Drain the prawns, reserving the juice. Reserve 4 whole olives for garnish and slice the rest. Fry the onions in the olive oil, then add the juice from the prawns and the remaining ingredients, except whole olives. Simmer for 5 minutes and allow to cool. Meanwhile, divide the shredded lettuce between 4 chilled cocktail glasses, cover with the prawns and pour the sauce over them. Serve chilled, garnished with whole olives and accompanied by cheese biscuits.

Camarones al mojo de ajo

Prawns in garlic and parsley

This is one of my favourite ways to eat prawns. Serve them in a scallop shell as a starter, or as a main course accompanied with rice, *Guacamole* and *Ejotes con Huevo*. If you love garlic, you may add one or two more cloves; otherwise the amount suggested is quite enough. Large uncooked prawns are best, but tinned or frozen ones will do.

SERVES 4

2 tablespoons olive oil
25 g (1 oz) butter
2 cloves garlic, finely chopped
½ onion, finely chopped
50 g (2 oz) parsley, finely chopped

1 green chilli, finely chopped (optional)
450 g (1 lb) raw shelled prawns
½ chicken stock cube
¼ teaspoon ground black pepper
juice of ½ lime or lemon

To garnish

lime or lemon slices
sprigs of parsley

Heat the oil and butter in a large, heavy-based frying pan. Fry the garlic, onion, parsley and chilli over high heat, stirring until the onion is golden and the mixture starts to dry. Add the raw prawns, crumbled stock cube, pepper and lime juice. Fry for another 5 minutes, stirring occasionally. Serve hot in scallop shells or ramekins, garnished with sprigs of parsley and some lime or lemon slices.

Ensalada de camarón

Shrimp salad

Salads are popular in Mexico. A salad like this one would be used as a starter for a lunch, which is usually the main meal of the day. It would also make a delicious light lunch in itself, accompanied by cheese biscuits.

SERVES 4

*1 small lettuce, finely
    shredded
200 g (7 oz) can shrimps,
    drained
2 sweet gherkins, finely
    chopped
3 tablespoons mayonnaise*

*juice of 1 lemon
dash of Worcestershire sauce
pinch of salt
pinch of ground black pepper
2 eggs, hard-boiled
2 ripe avocados
parsley, to decorate*

Arrange the shredded lettuce on a serving dish. In a bowl, mix together the drained shrimps, chopped gherkins, mayonnaise, half the lemon juice, Worcestershire sauce, salt and pepper; taste and add more salt if required. Pile the mixture in the centre of the dish. Peel the eggs and cut them in half lengthwise, then arrange around the shrimp mixture. Halve the avocados, remove stones and slice thickly lengthwise, taking care not to break them. Arrange around the shrimp mixture. Season the remaining lemon juice and spoon over the avocados.

■

Romeritos

Spinach in chilli sauce with shrimps and nopales

This is a main course that goes well with rice and soft warm tortillas. Exotic as it sounds, this dish is common fare in Mexico and is often served on Fridays when meat is not allowed to be eaten by the Catholic church. *Romeritos* is similar to rosemary in appearance, but soft and luscious dark green. If it is not available, you can use finely chopped spinach instead. The dried shrimps can be bought from Chinese or Indian shops. If you cannot obtain the ingredients for *Salsa Adobada*, you could substitute *Salsa para Enchiladas* and a tablespoon of ground chillies; and if you cannot obtain the *nopales*, substitute French beans.

SERVES 4

450 g (1 lb) romeritos or
  finely chopped spinach
300 ml (½ pint) water
100 g (4 oz) dried shrimps
1 egg white
oil for shallow frying

¾ quantity Salsa Adobada
275 g (10 oz) nopales,
  prepared as on page 134
  (optional)
225 g (8 oz) new potatoes,
  boiled, peeled and quartered

Clean the *romeritos*, removing any roots. Wash and place in a saucepan with the water and boil for 10 minutes. Drain and squeeze the water out. If using spinach, wash and cook for 5 minutes in only the water clinging to the leaves.

Clean the dried shrimps, discarding the shells, heads and whiskers, and purée in a blender for 30 seconds. Whisk the egg white until stiff peaks form, then fold in the shrimps. Heat the oil in a frying pan and fry the shrimp mixture, a tablespoon at a time, on both sides. Drain on absorbent kitchen paper and keep warm. Heat the sauce and add the *romeritos* or spinach, *nopales*, shrimp fritters and potatoes. Bring slowly to the boil and serve hot.

Postres, Panes y Galletas

Desserts, Breads and Biscuits

Desserts do not occupy a very prominent place in the Mexican meal, partly because fresh fruit is abundant, cheap and easy, and partly because so much attention is given to the main course. The net result is that often people are so satisfied after their savoury course that there is little room left for sweets.

Fresh fruit salads, sliced fresh pineapple, watermelon, mangoes, plums, prickly pears, fresh figs, paw-paw and many other delicious fruits all militate against complicated sweets.

There are some delicious native fruits which complete the kaleidoscope of the Mexican fruit market. There is the *mamey*, *zapote chico, zapote negro, granada china, pitaya, chirimoya* and an entire family of bananas, from the large plantain which is used for cooking, to the smallest Dominico, which is the size of your little finger and very sweet.

Desserts are seldom eaten hot, with the exception of *Buñuelos*, *Churros* and *Crepas con Cajeta*. Most are served well chilled—even fruit. Cream is not usual either, fruit salads and fresh fruits being eaten by themselves (except strawberries). We do, however, make milky desserts galore! Milk, eggs and sugar were introduced into Mexico by the Spaniards, and have been enjoyed ever since.

These sorts of desserts are often sweeter than they need be, probably to compensate for the very hot dishes that went before, and a small amount is quite enough. Also, sweet crystallized fruits such as pumpkin, figs, tangerines, spaghetti vegetal, tamarind, guava and others are often offered after the meal.

Cakes and biscuits are taking a more important place in the modern way of life, partly because of their availability in the shops and partly because more homes have conventional ovens. Nuts, especially pecan nuts, are very popular and are used in everything, including fruit salad. They are less oily than walnuts, smaller in size and more difficult to peel, but you can buy them shelled.

With all this in mind, I have carefully chosen those recipes for which the ingredients are easily available and which I have considered my favourites over the years. As a general rule, you can serve fresh fruit as it is an excellent ending to a heavy meal.

Ensalada de frutas

Fruit salad

Nothing is more refreshing than this salad served cool, especially after a meal featuring hot chillies. Basically any fruit can be used, but the fruit used in this recipe is the most common in Mexico.

SERVES 4

75 g (3 oz) strawberries, hulled and halved
½ cantaloup melon, cubed
100 g (4 oz) watermelon, seeded and cubed
1 large banana, peeled and sliced
2 oranges, peeled and sliced
100 g (4 oz) papaya, peeled and cubed

1 mango, peeled and cubed
juice of ½ lemon
150 ml (¼ pint) water
100 g (4 oz) granulated sugar
25 g (1 oz) pecan nuts, chopped, to garnish
150 ml (¼ pint) double cream (optional)

Mix all the fruits in a heat-resistant bowl with the lemon juice. Dissolve the sugar in the water over low heat, bring to the boil and strain over the fruits. Refrigerate until cold. Garnish with pecan nuts and serve with cream.

■

Dulce de higo verde

Green figs in syrup

This very unusual dessert is one of my favourites. In fact I like it so much I have gone to the trouble of growing a fig tree in my garden, since green figs are hard to find in Britain. Fig trees in colder climates seem to bear plenty of fruit which hardly ever ripens—so this is ideal if you wish to use up your own figs! Unfortunately I have never seen them for sale in Britain.

MAKES 1.2 litres (2 pints)

1½ kg (3 lb) green hard figs　　*1½ kg (3 lb) granulated sugar*
3 litres (5 pints) water　　*30 cloves*

Cut a cross in the head of each fig to allow the syrup to penetrate. Place in a saucepan, add the water, cover and simmer for 1½ hours or until they are very soft, skimming off the foam that appears on the surface. When the figs are soft enough, add the sugar and the cloves and simmer for 45 minutes. Serve cold with cream.

■

Crema de mango

Mango cream with hazelnuts or almonds

This is my own version of a delicious dessert, suitable for a dinner party. It will keep in the refrigerator for up to two days, and it freezes extremely well.

Mangoes are cultivated abundantly in Mexico, having been introduced from the Philippines after the Spanish conquest. The most popular kinds grown in Mexico are the Manila which has a pale yellow skin and is very sweet, and the commonly known Petacon, a type of Alfhonso mango with a rosy red skin, which is more readily found in Britain. If you can't find fresh mangoes, however, don't hesitate to use tinned mango. Or make this dessert with peaches, strawberries or raspberries instead. Easy and tasty, it's a great success with any of these fruits.

SERVES 8

1 kg (2 lb) fruit pulp (see
  below)
400 g (14 oz) can sweetened
  condensed milk
600 ml (1 pint) double cream
juice of 1 lemon

2 oranges, peeled, segmented
  and halved or 200 g (7 oz)
  can pineapple cubes
100 g (4 oz) chopped hazelnuts
  or flaked almonds, to
  decorate

Mash the fruit to a purée and rub through a sieve. Whip the sweetened condensed milk and double cream together until light and fluffy, then stir in the lemon juice. Fold in the fruit pulp, orange or pineapple pieces and pour into individual serving dishes. Decorate with the nuts just before serving.

■

Helado de fruta

Fruit ice-cream

Fresh fruit is plentiful in Mexico and mangoes are everyone's favourite. But as the price of fresh mangoes in Europe is so high, I recommend using tinned mango slices or you could use other soft fruit purées, like strawberries, blackberries, raspberries or peach. You might have to adjust the sugar according to the acidity of the fruit. Preparation starts the day before.

SERVES 10. Makes 2 litres (3½ pints)

400 g (14 oz) can evaporated
  milk
175 g (6 oz) icing sugar
juice of ½ lemon
1 litre (1¾ pints) mango
  purée, strained, or
  2 × 400 g (14 oz) cans
  sliced mangoes

50 g (2 oz) chopped nuts or
  flaked almonds

Place the unopened tin of evaporated milk in a saucepan and cover with water. Bring to the boil and simmer for 15 minutes. Remove the tin from the water and allow to cool for about 4 hours, then refrigerate for 24 hours still unopened. (It is dangerous to open the tin when it is hot.)

Cool all your equipment in the freezer for a few minutes, then open the tin and pour the evaporated milk into a chilled bowl. Beat with an electric mixer at top speed for about 3 minutes, until doubled in bulk and the consistency of egg whites. Add the sugar and lemon juice, and whisk just enough to blend well. Now add the fruit purée and whisk at the lowest speed just long enough to incorporate it.

Pour the mixture into a chilled container, seal and freeze for about 5 hours. This ice-cream does not need any more whisking; it will be nice and fluffy as it is, but it helps to put it in the refrigerator for about 30 minutes before serving to soften it a little. Serve garnished with chopped nuts or flaked almonds.

Helado de vainilla con Kahlua

Vanilla ice-cream with coffee liqueur

Ice-cream is never better than when it is made at home. This recipe is so simple, that my 14-year-old daughter and her friends often make it. It can be used as the base for any flavour of ice-cream such as chocolate chips and mint, which is made by simply substituting mint flavouring for the vanilla and adding 1 packet of chocolate chips. Or try rum and raisins—there are many more you can invent! One of my cookery class pupils enthusiastically tried 30 different flavours, one by one!

This ice-cream is actually lower in calories than ordinary ice-cream, despite the fact that it is made with dairy produce, and it is economical too, yielding almost half a gallon. One vital thing to keep in mind is that all your equipment should be chilled before use. Preparation starts 2 days before.

YIELDS about 1¾ litres (3 pints)

400 g (14 oz) can evaporated milk
175 g (6 oz) icing sugar
juice of ½ lemon

¼ teaspoon vanilla essence
10 tablespoons Kahlua coffee liqueur
10 sponge finger biscuits

Place the unopened tin of evaporated milk in a saucepan and cover with water. Bring to the boil and simmer for 15 minutes. Remove the tin from the water and allow to cool for about 4 hours, then refrigerate for 24 hours still unopened. (It is dangerous to open the tin while it is hot.)

Cool all your equipment in the freezer for a few minutes, then open the tin and pour the evaporated milk into a chilled bowl. Beat with an electric mixer at top speed for about 3 minutes, until doubled in bulk and the consistency of egg whites. Add the sugar, lemon juice and vanilla, and whisk just enough to blend well. Pour into a chilled container, seal and freeze for about 5 hours. This ice-cream does not need any further whisking; it will be nice and fluffy as it is, but it helps to put it in the refrigerator for about 30 minutes before serving to soften it a little. Pour 1 tablespoon of Kahlua over each helping just before serving and garnish with a sponge finger biscuit.

■

Gelatina blanca

Vanilla jelly

Jelly is a popular dessert in Mexico and I can remember the little man carrying his colourful jellies in a glass box and selling them in the streets. They had a base of greaseproof paper and were half milk, half strawberry or lime, with one raisin in the middle. This is an all-milk jelly which is especially popular with my family.

SERVES 6

200 g (7 oz) can sweetened
  condensed milk
2 egg yolks
2 tablespoons sugar
½ teaspoon vanilla essence

500 ml (18 fl oz) milk
1½ tablespoons powdered
  gelatine
25 g (1 oz) chopped nuts

Put all the ingredients, except the nuts, in a liquidizer and blend at top speed for 1 minute. Pour into a saucepan and stir continually over medium heat until the mixture comes almost to the boil. Remove from the heat and pour into a 1.2 litre (2 pint) mould. Cool, then refrigerate for 4 hours or until firmly set. To serve, dip the mould into hot water for a few seconds, invert on to a serving dish and garnish with nuts.

■

Flan

Crème caramel with a difference

A popular dessert throughout Mexico. Often served in individual bowls, it is a good example of the French influence. There are various old-fashioned recipes calling for twelve egg yolks, but this modern version is my favourite for its taste, texture and economy.

SERVES 6

*225 g (8 oz) granulated
  sugar*
120 ml (4 fl oz) water
4 egg yolks
*400 g (14 oz) can sweetened
  condensed milk*

300 ml (½ pint) milk
1 teaspoon vanilla essence
25 g (1 oz) flaked almonds

Heat the sugar and water in a small saucepan over low heat, stirring, until the sugar is dissolved. Increase the heat and boil for about 5 minutes, without stirring, until turning golden brown. Remove the pan from the heat, and immerse the base in cold water to reduce the temperature quickly. Pour the contents into a 15 cm (6 inch) pudding basin, tipping it slowly to ensure the caramel covers the sides and bottom. On a piece of buttered paper, drop a little caramel to use as decoration later.

Mix the milks, egg yolks and vanilla gently—do not whip. Strain into the caramel-coated bowl, cover with a damp cloth and tie the cloth in place. Put the bowl in a baking tin half-filled with warm water, allowing the edges of the cloth to touch the water, and place it in the centre of a preheated oven at 150°C, 300°F, Gas Mark 2 for 2½–3 hours, topping up with boiling water when necessary.

The flan is ready when it has set all the way through, and separates from the sides of the bowl when the bowl is tilted. Allow to cool, then refrigerate for at least 5 hours. To serve, run the tip of a pointed knife all around the edge of the bowl and invert the flan onto a deep serving dish, allowing the caramel to run over the top and sides. Remove the hardened caramel from the buttered paper, break it into fine pieces and sprinkle onto the flan with the flaked almonds.

VARIATION:

For a mocha-flavoured *Flan*, mix 1 tablespoon cocoa powder and 1 teaspoon instant coffee granules into the milk and continue as directed.

Cajeta de Celaya

Goats' milk caramel

Cajeta de Celaya is very popular in Mexico, particularly with children. Like many Mexican desserts, it is very sweet by European standards. However, a little goes a long way and it keeps almost indefinitely in a screw-top jar in the refrigerator. It is tasty as a topping for vanilla ice-cream and also makes a delicious dessert when mixed with dry sherry, spread on pancakes and sprinkled with chopped nuts (see recipe on page 207).

SERVES 6

*750 g (1½ lb) granulated
  sugar
2 litres (3½ pints) goats'
  or cows' milk
½ teaspoon bicarbonate
  of soda*

*2 × 10 cm (5 inch) sticks
  cinnamon or 1 teaspoon
  cinnamon
¼ teaspoon vanilla essence*

Place all the sugar and half the milk in a 4 litre (7 pint) saucepan. Bring to the boil, stirring occasionally to dissolve the sugar. Simmer for about 20 minutes until the milk turns light brown, then remove from the heat. Pour the rest of the milk into another saucepan, and add the bicarbonate of soda, cinnamon and vanilla. Bring to the boil, then very gradually add to the caramel, stirring constantly with a wooden spoon. Be careful, as the mixture will bubble furiously. When all the milk has been mixed in, keep stirring to ensure there are no brown sugar specks.

    Return the pan to the heat and simmer gently for about 1 hour, skimming off any froth that appears, and stirring occasionally. (If you have a sugar thermometer, the mixture should be ready when it reaches 120°C, 225°F.) Discard the cinnamon sticks, cool and bottle.

■

Dulce de chocolate Morelia
Chocolate blancmange

This cold dessert has always been my favourite. It is a simple blancmange-style sweet but the cinnamon gives it a special Mexican flavour. Morelia is the town where the best chocolate is made in Mexico.

SERVES 4

600 ml (1 pint) milk
175 g (6 oz) caster sugar
50 g (2 oz) cornflour
50 g (2 oz) cocoa powder
  or 100 g (4 oz) cooking
  chocolate

½ teaspoon cinnamon
¼ teaspoon vanilla essence
25 g (1 oz) flaked almonds, to
  garnish

Blend all the ingredients except the nuts for 45 seconds at top speed in a liquidizer. Pour the mixture into a saucepan and cook over low heat, stirring constantly with a wire whisk for about 5 minutes or until it starts to thicken.

Strain into a serving dish before it comes to the boil. This must be done quickly as the mixture thickens as it cools. Garnish with the flaked almonds and serve hot or cold.

■

Chongos Zamoranos
Junket in a cinnamon syrup

This is a very popular dessert all over Mexico, but in Zamora, which is the place this recipe is named after, they pride themselves on making the best *chongos* in all Mexico. This is a mild dessert, and youngsters particularly love the golden colour, mild flavour and squeaky, chewy texture, which comes from long simmering. The only disadvantage is that, after having to simmer for at least 4 hours, it disappears so quickly! Preparation starts the night before.

SERVES 6

1.2 litres (2 pints) milk	*2 egg yolks*
250 g (9 oz) granulated	*3 teaspoons rennet*
sugar	*15 cm (6 inch) stick cinnamon*

Mix the milk, sugar and egg yolks thoroughly in a large saucepan. Cook over a low heat for about 5 minutes, stirring, until it reaches body temperature (36°C, 98°F on a sugar thermometer). It is better to have it a little too cool than too hot. Add the rennet, cover and remove from the heat and leave in a warm place overnight.

The next morning, cut the curd in the pan into 2½ cm (1 inch) squares, then break up the cinnamon stick and insert a piece in each square. Simmer, uncovered, over a very low heat for about 1 hour, increasing the heat slightly as the curds toughen, but watch that it does not boil too hard or the curds will disintegrate. As it heats, the solids will separate from the buttermilk and thus boil in it. After about 4 hours, when the curds are a nice rich golden colour, and the liquid has been reduced by half and is quite thick and syrupy, remove from the heat and cool. Serve cold.

Cocada con crema

Grated coconut dessert

Cocada is sold in Mexico in many different forms. One version, well known in many parts of the world, consists of coconut and sugar mixed together then eaten as a snack. This recipe is a glorified *Cocada* which I find very tasty.

SERVES 6

250 g (9 oz) granulated	*85 ml (3 fl oz) sherry*
sugar	*150 ml (¼ pint) double cream*
250 ml (8 fl oz) water	*drop of vanilla essence*
225 g (8 oz) grated or	*1 tablespoon icing sugar*
desiccated coconut	*25 g (1 oz) flaked almonds, to*
3 egg yolks, well beaten	*garnish*

Dissolve the sugar in the water over a low heat. Increase the heat and boil to the soft ball stage (115°C, 238°F), when a small amount of syrup dropped into cold water can be moulded into a soft ball with the fingers. Remove from the heat and add the coconut, beaten egg yolks and sherry. Mix well, then return to a very low heat for about 10 minutes to dry out the mixture. Stir occasionally, until you can see the bottom of the pan. Turn out onto a serving dish and allow to cool. Whip the cream with the vanilla and icing sugar until stiff, and spoon over the coconut mixture. Garnish with the flaked almonds and refrigerate. Serve cold.

■

Dulce de calabaza

Stewed pumpkin with cinnamon and orange

Pumpkin grows very easily in Mexico. It is not used as a vegetable, however, but eaten in a sugar syrup which is very popular. It is also sometimes crystallized as are sweet potatoes, figs and *tejocotes* (similar to crab apples), and of course pumpkin seeds are popular in their own right. This dessert is usually cooked with the pumpkin seeds left unshelled, but these can be a problem to eat. For this reason, I have included shelled pumpkin seeds instead, which not only add colour to the dish, but are easy to chew and they can be obtained at most health food shops. Unless you are already familiar with muscovado sugar, I suggest you try this recipe first using granulated sugar, because although muscovado is delicious, it looks less appetizing. Preparation should start two days in advance.

SERVES 8

750 g (1½ lb) pumpkin flesh
2 litres (3½ pints) water
1 tablespoon garden lime
juice and coarsely chopped
  rind of 2 oranges
750 g (1½ lb) granulated or
  muscovado sugar

2 × 10 cm (4 inch) sticks
  cinnamon
75 g (3 oz) shelled pumpkin
  seeds

Cut the pumpkin into 5 cm (2 inch) squares and prick them with a fork. In a non-metal container dissolve the lime in half the water and soak the pumpkin in this solution overnight. Drain the pumpkin and rinse under running water. Boil the orange peel in the remaining water until soft, about 30 minutes. Add the pumpkin, orange juice, sugar, cinnamon and shelled pumpkin seeds, and simmer for 10 minutes until the pumpkin softens. Remove the pumpkin and place in a heat-resistant dish. Boil the syrup for another 30 minutes or until reduced by half, then pour immediately over the pumpkin. Allow to cool and serve at room temperature.

This dessert freezes extremely well and will keep in the refrigerator for up to 5 days.

Borrachitos

Tipsy meringues

These meringues with their beer flavour are quite irresistible, having a sticky soft texture like marshmallow. They can be eaten on their own or over pineapple rings.

MAKES about 20 small meringues

2 egg whites	*1 teaspoon cornflour*
100 g (4 oz) caster sugar	*2 tablespoons beer*

Whisk the egg whites until they form peaks, then add half the sugar and whisk again for 1 minute. Mix the rest of the sugar with the cornflour and add with the beer, whisking just enough to blend them in.

Line a baking tray with a double layer of nonstick baking paper. With a tablespoon, spoon out 20 individual meringues, using another tablespoon to ease them on to the paper. Bake in a preheated oven at 140°C, 275°F, Gas Mark 1 for 15 minutes. As soon as they start going brown around the edges, remove from the heat, cool and eat immediately. The meringues will not keep longer than a couple of hours.

Crepas con cajeta

Banana and milk caramel pancakes

This is a hot dessert, which is quite a rarity in Mexico, where desserts are generally cold. It is a glorious combination of Spanish and French cuisines, with a Mexican accent! In restaurants they often pour brandy over the pancakes and flame them. You can also add half a banana before rolling the pancakes to make it an even bigger and better dessert.

SERVES 6

2 tablespoons dry sherry or rum
½ quantity Cajeta de Celaya (see page 202)
1 quantity Crepas (see Crepas de Cuitlacoche, page 71)

3 bananas (optional), *sliced lengthwise*
50 g (2 oz) pecan nuts, finely chopped (or walnuts, hazelnuts or almonds)
150 ml (¼ pint) double cream, to serve

Mix the sherry or rum with the *Cajeta de Celaya*. Grease an ovenproof dish and cover the bottom with 5 tablespoons of *cajeta*. Make the pancakes, and as each is finished place in the middle of it 1 tablespoon of the remaining *cajeta*, a few nuts and the sliced banana, if used. Roll up each pancake and place in the dish.

Pour over the remaining *cajeta*, cover the dish with kitchen foil and bake in a preheated oven at 220°C, 425°F, Gas Mark 7 for 15 minutes. Remove from the oven, sprinkle with nuts and serve hot with cream.

■

Buñuelos

Crispy tortillas with muscovado sugar syrup

Buñuelos are very popular all over Mexico. In the south, they serve large *Buñuelos* with hot muscovado sugar syrup poured over and fresh cream and nuts added to taste. In the north, they cut the *Buñuelos* into 8 pieces and toss them in caster sugar and cinnamon after frying. Prepared in this manner they go well with coffee or tea. Whichever way you prefer, they are simple to prepare, provided you already have the wheat tortillas.

SERVES 4

4 wheat tortillas   *oil for deep frying*

Syrup

225 g (8 oz) muscovado   *7½ cm (3 inch) stick cinnamon*
  sugar   *rind and juice of 1 orange*
150 ml (¼ pint) water

To garnish

150 ml (¼ pint) double   *25 g (1 oz) chopped nuts*
  cream

Heat the oil in a deep-fryer to 180°C, 350°F. For southern-style *Buñuelos*, fry each tortilla in the oil for 3 minutes or until golden brown, then stand it on its side to drain on absorbent kitchen paper. Mix the remaining ingredients together in a saucepan and bring to the boil, stirring occasionally. Simmer over medium heat for 5 minutes, strain and pour over the fried tortillas just before serving. Garnish with double cream and nuts.

If you prefer to try the northern style, cut the tortillas into 8 pieces, and fry half of them until golden. Drain off as much oil as possible, before shaking in a brown paper bag with 100 g (4 oz) caster sugar and 2 teaspoons ground cinnamon.

■

Sopaipillas

Puff fritters with honey and rum syrup

These are the American interpretation of Mexico's well-known *Muéganos*. *Sopaipillas* are especially popular in the southern states of the U.S., where they are served with warm syrup. In Mexico *Muéganos* are sold in the streets, being much smaller and clustered together with very thick syrup. But they can quite easily pull out your fillings if you are not careful! The American idea of making larger puffs and simply pouring warm honey over them just before serving is still very tasty and much kinder to your teeth.

It would have a more Mexican flavour if you use muscovado sugar syrup (see *Buñuelos*, page 207).

SERVES 4

Batter

75 g (3 oz) plain flour
1 teaspoon baking powder
pinch of salt

15 g (½ oz) lard
50 ml (2 fl oz) warm water
oil for deep frying

Syrup

2 tablespoons honey
1 tablespoon rum

½ teaspoon cinnamon
15 g (½ oz) butter

Sift the flour, baking powder and salt together, add the lard and rub in lightly until the mixture resembles breadcrumbs. Add the warm water slowly. Turn the dough on to a lightly floured board and knead until smooth. Roll it out to the thickness of a thin coin, and cut into 5 × 7½ cm (2 × 3 inch) rectangles. Place on waxed paper, cover and refrigerate for 2 hours.

Heat the oil in a deep-fryer to 190°C, 375°F and fry 1 rectangle at a time until golden. They will puff as they fry. It is important to maintain the temperature of the oil in between frying. Drain on absorbent kitchen paper and keep warm. Before serving, re-heat in a very hot oven for a few minutes.

To make the syrup, heat the honey, rum, cinnamon and butter in a saucepan, stirring until well mixed. Pour over the fritters and serve immediately.

■

Campechanas

Pastry puffs with sugar topping

Campechanas are one of the multitude of *biscochos* (sweet buns) sold at bakeries in Mexico. They have always been one of my favourites; they are simple and quite different, and can be made large as in the recipe, or half the size, and served with *Chocolate Caliente* (see page 226) or coffee.

SERVES 4

1 quantity Rough Puff
   Pastry (see *Empanadas de*
   Bacalao, page 184)

40 g (1½ oz) lard, melted
65 g (2½ oz) caster sugar

Roll out the pastry and cut into 16 strips, each 10 × 5 cm (4 × 2 inches). Place on a greased baking sheet, brush with melted lard and sprinkle with sugar. Bake in a preheated oven at 200°C, 400°F, Gas Mark 6 for about 15 minutes. Eat cold.

Churros

Fried choux pastry

Churros are another example of the influence of Spain in the Mexican way of life. They are sold in paper bags, for passers-by to eat as they stroll round the parks. They are easy and tasty but must be served at once. They are ideal to serve with *Chocolate Caliente*.

SERVES 4

50 g (2 oz) butter
150 ml (¼ pint) water
65 g (2½ oz) plain flour,
   sifted

2 eggs, lightly beaten
oil for deep frying
100 g (4 oz) caster sugar
1 teaspoon cinnamon

Melt the butter in a large saucepan, add the water and bring to the boil. Add the flour in one go, and beat until the mixture leaves the sides of the pan. Cool a little, beating continually, then add the eggs, one at a time, beating vigorously. Spoon the mixture into a piping bag fitted with a fluted 1 cm (½ inch) nozzle.

   Heat the oil in a deep-fryer to 180°C, 350°F. Pipe the dough straight into the oil, allowing about 15 cm (6 inches) for each *churro*. Fry for 3–4 minutes until golden brown, then drain and shake in a brown paper bag with the caster sugar and cinnamon. Eat while still warm.

Pastel de elote

Corn bread

This corn bread can be offered as a vegetable with a main course. It is quite sweet, and goes well with pork (see *Pierna de Carnero Adobada*, page 158) or any meat with a substantial gravy or sauce. It is a simplified version of *Tamales de Elote* which have to be wrapped in individual portions. It is ideal for using up corn on the cob which is not tender enough to eat just boiled.

SERVES 6

450 g (1 lb) fresh or frozen corn kernels, thawed
100 g (4 oz) butter, softened
100 g (4 oz) granulated sugar
1 teaspoon salt
100 g (4 oz) masa harina or cornflour
1 tablespoon baking powder
3 eggs separated

Blend the corn to a paste in the liquidizer. Cream the butter and sugar together until pale, add the corn paste, then add the salt, flour and baking powder. Beat the egg yolks until they change colour and fold them into the mixture. Beat the egg whites until they form peaks and fold them into the mixture. Turn into a well-greased 20 cm (8 inch) square cake tin and bake in a preheated oven at 160°C, 325°F, Gas Mark 8 for about 1 hour.

■

Pan de muerto

Halloween bread

This bread, literally translated as Bread of the Dead, is traditionally served in Mexico on or around 1st and 2nd November, All Saints Day and All Souls Day, which are national holidays. It could also be made for Halloween. In Mexico on these 2 days, the graves are tended to, the monuments are scrubbed clean, and the cemetery has a thorough 'spring cleaning' which turns it into a festival of flowers, beautiful aromas, colour everywhere, tears, laughter and even music. Far from being a sorrowful occasion, it is more like a family picnic.

All Saints Day is the day for the *muertos chiquitos*, the souls of dead children, reserving All Souls Day for the adults. Candles are lit in the churches for every member of the family that has died, and altars are carefully built in the corner of the family room. Food, drink, flowers and *Pan de Muerto* are left among the candles and the portraits of Saints and relatives, the idea being that the spirit of the dead will feast on the spirit of the food and drink. However, what sometimes happens is that by the evening of the second day, the spirit of the living have had it all—drinking more than they should and causing brawls, which can finish up with adding a few dead to next year's celebrations! Yellow is the traditional colour for the dead, and is not a popular colour to wear. The *zempazuchitl* (marigold) is the flower used for the occasion and so is stewed pumpkin.

To complete the festivity, every bakery in town will paint its windows with dancing skeletons. The skeletons are depicted eating *Pan de Muerto* and playing the guitar. On the shelves of shops and supermarkets, sugar skulls make their appearance with brightly coloured eyes made of brilliant-coloured foil and 'your name while you wait' painted on in coloured sugar. These skulls are happily nibbled away at, serving if anything ever did as an excellent reminder of our inevitable future!

Pan de Muerto is a round bun with dough in the shape of bones and knuckles forming a cross over the top. There is one round knob of dough in the middle, surrounded by small bits of dough—'tear drops'. All these knobs are particularly tasty as they are more crispy and they often have more sugar on them than the rest of the bread. It is enjoyed in every home on or around *Día de Muertos*, rather as Hot Cross Buns are eaten on or around Easter Sunday. Preparation should start the night before.

SERVES 6

350 g (¾ lb) strong plain
  flour
pinch of salt
15 g (½ oz) fresh yeast or
  2 teaspoons dried yeast
100 g (4 oz) granulated
  sugar
120 ml (4 fl oz) warm milk

1 teaspoon aniseed
2 tablespoons grated orange
  rind
6 tablespoons water
150 g (5 oz) butter
2 eggs, beaten
1 egg yolk

Topping

1 egg white
50 g (2 oz) caster sugar

25 g (1 oz) pink sugar crystals
(optional)

Warm bowls and utensils and grease a baking tray. Sift 225 g (8 oz) of the flour with the salt into a mixing bowl, reserving the rest for rolling. In a small basin, cream together the yeast and ½ teaspoon of the sugar. Add the warm milk and about one third of the flour from the mixing bowl. Beat well and leave in a warm place for 15 minutes or until it doubles in size.

Put the aniseed, orange peel and water into a saucepan, bring to the boil and cook for 1 minute. Strain and cool. Rub the butter into the remaining flour, then add the sugar, beaten eggs and yolk, 3 tablespoons of the aniseed liquid and finally the yeast batter. Mix well. Turn the dough onto a floured surface and knead thoroughly for about 10 minutes, then place in a greased bowl and cover with a damp tea-towel. Leave to rise overnight in a cool place; it should have doubled in size by the morning.

Turn the risen dough onto a floured board and knead for about 5 minutes until smooth. Divide in 8 equal portions to make individual breads. Place 6 of the portions on a well-greased baking tray, spacing them well apart. The other 2 portions are for the 'bones' and 'tears'. To shape the bones, divide 1 portion into 2 and roll each half between your floured hands, allowing it to hang down so that its own weight makes it stretch, until about 1 cm (½ inch) in diameter. Roll the strips gently on a floured board. Brush 1 strip with a little water on one side, place it across the bun, pressing with your thumbs at each end to form the 'knuckles'. Repeat with the remaining strip to form a cross on the top, then flatten the bones on top and brush with water. Using the remaining portion, make a round ball the size of a large grape and press it gently on the top. Then make the 'tear drops', wetting them and placing them at random between the rolled 'bones'.

Cover with a warm damp tea-towel and leave in a warm place for about 40 minutes to rise again. Bake in the centre of a preheated oven at 200°C, 400°F, Gas Mark 6 for 10 minutes, then reduce the heat to 160°C, 325°F, Gas Mark 3 and bake for 10–15 minutes. Lightly beat the egg white and brush it over each bun, then sprinkle with caster sugar. Sprinkle over with pink sugar crystals, if using. Cool and serve with *Chocolate Caliente*.

Rosca de reyes

Three kings ring

This spiced fruit bread is perfect for coffee mornings or tea parties. In Mexico it is traditionally served on 6th January, Epiphany, a date which the little children eagerly await. At that time, invitations go out for sharing a *Rosca*, at a sort of afternoon tea party at which coffee, hot chocolate and limeade, rather than tea, are served. Few *Roscas* are actually baked at home these days in Mexico, but the bakeries make magnificent ones which are displayed for the public to make their choice from.

Epiphany being the time when the Three Kings reached Nazareth bearing their gifts, every *Rosca* must contain special surprises which are placed inside before baking. First and foremost, is the *niño*, a tiny china doll about 5 cm (2 inches) long which looks rather like a jelly baby. There are other surprises too, such as a ring or coin, and the decorations include symbolic 'jewels' in the shape of crystallized fruit. The *Rosca* is circulated among the guests so that each can cut their own piece in hopes of coming across the gifts, but trying to avoid the *niño*. If you get the *niño* in your slice, you are committed to holding a party for everyone present on Friendship Day (2nd February). If you don't happen to like the people, bad luck—you can hardly swallow the *niño*! On the other hand, if you find a ring, there will be a wedding in the family . . . and if you get the coin, good luck and prosperity are on their way for the new year.

SERVES 10

350 g (12 oz) strong flour
10 g (¼ oz) fresh yeast (or
  1 teaspoon dried
  yeast)
100 g (4 oz) granulated
  sugar
120 ml (4 fl oz) warm milk
100 g (4 oz) butter
pinch of salt
¼ teaspoon cinnamon
2 eggs, beaten

2 egg yolks, beaten
grated rind of 1 lemon
50 g (2 oz) candied orange peel,
  roughly chopped
50 g (2 oz) candied pineapple,
  roughly chopped
50 g (2 oz) glacé cherries,
  roughly chopped
25 g (1 oz) flaked almonds,
  roughly chopped

Topping	Surprises
25 g (1 oz) granulated sugar	*1 jelly baby, wrapped in foil*
	1 small coin, sterilized
25 g (1 oz) butter	
25 g (1 oz) plain flour	*75 g (3 oz) icing sugar*
1 egg white, lightly beaten	*2 tablespoons milk or water*

Warm bowls and utensils and grease a 25 cm (10 inch) baking tray. Place 225 g (8 oz) of the flour in a mixing bowl, reserving the rest for rolling. In a small basin cream together the yeast and ½ teaspoon of the sugar. Add the warm milk and about one-third of the flour from the mixing bowl. Beat well and leave in a warm place for 15 minutes. Meanwhile, rub the butter into the remaining flour and stir in the sugar, salt and cinnamon. Make a well in the centre, add the beaten eggs and yolks, lemon rind and yeast batter and mix well. Turn the dough onto a floured surface and knead thoroughly for 10 minutes. Place in a greased bowl and cover with a damp cloth. Leave to rise for about 5 hours in a warm place, or overnight in a cool place, until it doubles in size.

Turn the dough onto a floured surface and knead until smooth. Add the candied fruits and almonds, reserving some for decoration, and knead until well mixed. Roll the dough with your hands into a sausage shape about 56 cm (22 inches) long. Join ends to form a ring and place on the greased baking sheet. Cover and allow to rise in a warm place for about 30 minutes.

Make cuts around the ring with a pair of scissors, about 5 cm (2 inches) deep and 7½ cm (3 inches) apart. To make the topping, cream the butter and sugar together until light and fluffy, then add the flour to form a paste. Roll the paste into small fingers and place them across the ring starting in the centre, in between the cuts made. Glaze the *Rosca* with the lightly beaten egg white. Bake in the centre of a preheated oven at 200°C, 400°F, Gas Mark 6 for 25–30 minutes until golden brown. Cool and cut 2 small triangles from the top and insert in one a 'jelly baby' wrapped in foil, and a sterilized small coin in the other. Mix together the icing sugar and the milk or water and use to glaze the ring, making sure the incisions are covered. Decorate with the remaining candied fruit and almonds. You now have a *Rosca de Reyes* with a *niño*, a 'surprise' and jewels! *Buen provecho!*

Biscochos para chocolate

Small cakes for hot chocolate

Another simple but tasty way of making *biscochos*. These little cakes can be offered with tea or coffee as well as *Chocolate Caliente*. They have the added attraction that they contain no fat.

MAKES 12

2 eggs, separated
100 g (4 oz) granulated
  sugar
¼ teaspoon vanilla essence

75 g (3 oz) plain flour
1 teaspoon baking powder
25 g (1 oz) chopped nuts
25 g (1 oz) icing sugar

Beat the egg yolks with the granulated sugar until pale in colour. Stir in the vanilla essence. Sift the flour and baking powder together into a large bowl and fold in the egg yolk mixture. Beat the egg whites until they form peaks, and then fold them into the mixture with the nuts. Spoon into greased individual bun tins and bake in a preheated oven at 150°C, 300°F, Gas Mark 2 for 15 minutes. Serve warm, sprinkled with icing sugar.

'Hot cakes' Mexicanos

Corn dough hot cakes

This, for a change, appears to be an adaptation of the American 'hot cakes', which has been introduced into the Mexican kitchen. It makes a very substantial breakfast or tea, served with butter and syrup flavoured with cinnamon. Muscovado sugar is also very good used in place of the granulated sugar.

SERVES 4

1 egg
150 ml (5 fl oz) milk
50 g (2 oz) plain flour
25 g (1 oz) cornflour

25 g (1 oz) masa harina
2 teaspoons baking powder
2 teaspoons sugar
15 g (½ oz) butter, melted

Syrup

150 ml (5 fl oz) water
75 g (3 oz) granulated sugar

10 cm (5 inch) cinnamon stick

To make the dough, lightly beat the egg and milk together. Sift the flours and baking powder together into a mixing bowl. Make a well in the centre, add the egg and milk mixture, sugar and melted butter and beat with a wooden spoon to make a batter.

Heat an 18 cm (7 inch) heavy-based frying pan and grease it with a little butter. Make sure the entire surface of the pan is greased, and discard any butter left over. Put 3 tablespoons of the batter, spaced well apart, in the frying pan and cook the hot cakes over moderate heat until small holes appear on the surface and the cakes double in size. Turn over and cook until golden. Cover and keep warm, and repeat frying in batches of 3 until all the batter is finished. To make the syrup, dissolve the sugar in the water over low heat, add the cinnamon and boil for about 10 minutes. Remove the cinnamon and pour over the hot cakes just before eating.

■

Polvorones de boda

Shortbread biscuits

Polvorones is the name given to sweet shortbread of different sizes and flavours, which literally melt in the mouth! The *Polvorones* in this recipe are the smallest, and are often served at wedding receptions because being covered in icing sugar, they look as 'pure and innocent' as a bride. They are best eaten an hour or two after cooking, but will keep in an airtight container for a few days.

MAKES 20 × 2½ cm (1 inch) biscuits

*100 g (4 oz) butter or
    margarine, softened*
25 g (1 oz) caster sugar
100 g (4 oz) plain flour

50 g (2 oz) cornflour
¼ teaspoon almond essence
20 blanched almonds
25 g (1 oz) icing sugar

Cream the butter and sugar together until a creamy colour. Sift the flour and cornflour together and work them into the creamed mixture with a wooden spatula, then add the almond essence. Knead the mixture until smooth.

Take about 1 teaspoon of mixture, roll it into a ball in the palm of your hands and place it on a greased baking tray. Repeat until all the mixture is used up. Insert one almond in the centre of each biscuit so that only half the almond is showing. Bake in a preheated oven at 160°C, 325°F, Gas Mark 3 for 30 minutes. While still hot, dust with sifted icing sugar. Cool on a wire rack.

Bebidas

Drinks

Mexico has such an incredible variety of drinks that there is something for everyone, whatever their age. On hot sunny days as you stroll through the parks, drinks of all colours and flavours are being sold. For instance, there are early morning drinks for anyone who is hungry. A good *Atole* will more than satisfy those hunger pangs. There is also the delightful chocolate, the word coming from the Aztec *xoco* and *lati* (cocoa and water). Another drink, *Café de Olla*, is a strong coffee boiled with cinnamon and muscovado sugar, which is drunk from early morning till nightfall.

For the children there are innumerable colourful and tasty cool drinks made from fresh fruits. They range from the well-known *Limonada* (lemonade) to any other kind of fruit 'ade', as well as fresh fruit juices like orange juice, coconut milk, sugar cane juice, etc. For the old or ailing, there are teas which are said to cure anything from back-ache to shattered nerves or broken love-affairs.

For the more demanding, Mexico offers Tequila, both white and golden (aged), which has gained popularity the world over. White Tequila is primarily an aperitif, but hardened drinkers will drink it all night long. For beginners and people like me, there are a variety of Tequila cocktails which add to the fun without being quite so lethal. The gold Tequila can be offered as you would port, after the meal. Mezcal, like Tequila, is made from the *agave* and is an unrefined type of drink. It is often sold with a maggot in the bottle (more for sensationalism than for taste, since the poor maggot only lived in the plant and is so well preserved in the alcohol that it is totally sterilized). A more native alcoholic drink is *Pulque* (also made from the *agave*) which is popular with the working classes but it is now quickly losing ground to the excellent Mexican beer.

Finally, Mexico offers the popular clear and dark rums which are of good quality and of course Kahlua, a coffee liqueur flavoured with vanilla which has also gained international popularity.

Margarita cocktail

Tequila mixed with lime juice

Margarita Cocktail appears to have made its name so quickly that you can even buy it pre-mixed and bottled now. But the fresh version is by far my favourite. It is a potent drink, as the alcohol content in the Tequila is deceptively high. It is also an unusual drink, as the rim of the glass is moistened with lime juice and then salted (which sounds strange but is quite delightful). This, I imagine, has the virtue of cooling down the effects of the *Margarita* itself. Lime in this case is essential for the best flavour—do not be tempted to substitute either bottled lime juice or lemon.

SERVES 4

2 limes, halved
1 tablespoon salt
250 ml (8 fl oz) Tequila
4 tablespoons Triple Sec or
　Cointreau
8 ice cubes

Moisten the rim of 4 cocktail glasses by rubbing with lime, then dip the rim on to a saucer containing the salt. Chill the glasses. Squeeze the limes into a liquidizer, add the Tequila, the liqueur and ice cubes and blend at high speed for 30 seconds. Pour into the chilled glasses and serve.

Cocktail de tequila

Tequila sunrise

A popular cocktail, which is a beautiful colour and reminiscent of Mexican sunrises. It can be made with almost any fruit juice, plus a touch of grenadine syrup if desired.

SERVES 4

250 ml (8 fl oz) Tequila
4 tablespoons unsweetened
  orange or pineapple juice
4 teaspoons egg white

4 tablespoons grenadine syrup
  (optional)
4 pieces fresh fruit, to garnish

Mix the Tequila, fruit juice and egg white in a blender at high speed for 20 seconds and pour into chilled glasses. Tilting the glass, spoon in the grenadine if used, and drop a piece of fruit into the drink. The flavour of the egg does not come through and you have a lovely bubbly drink.

■

Tequila con limón

Tequila with lime

Tequila is the best-known alcoholic drink in Mexico and is served as an aperitif rather than after meals. Well-hardened drinkers can drink half a bottle in one night, but one or two drinks are quite sufficient for anyone I know.

Traditionally it is served at room temperature and with squares of lime and coarse salt. The idea is that you lick the salt, then swallow 25 ml (1 fl oz) of Tequila in one go, and finally suck the lime. You can actually feel the Tequila going down your throat all the way down to your tummy! There are different types of Tequila, the white one being better for cocktails and mixes, whilst the golden or *añejo* (mature) Tequila is better to drink on its own.

SERVES 4

1 tablespoon coarse salt
1 lime, quartered

120 ml (4 fl oz) Tequila

Serve the salt and the lime on a plate. Pour the Tequila into 25 ml (1 fl oz) glasses and instruct your guests on what to do.

■

Tequila matador

Tequila and tomato juice

The literal translation of this drink is 'killer' . . . but it actually resembles a Bloody Mary, so its effect could be to revive you from a hangover.

SERVES 2

50 ml (2 fl oz) Tequila
100 ml (4 fl oz) tomato juice
dash of Worcestershire sauce

dash of Tabasco sauce
juice of ½ lime
4 ice cubes

Shake all the ingredients together and strain into cocktail glasses.

■

Ponche de tequila

Tequila punch

One good way of getting the party going once and for all! The trouble is that this punch is so good, my guests are in the habit of drinking it all through the night!

SERVES 20

750 ml (1¼ pint) bottle
  Tequila
225 g (8 oz) caster sugar
600 ml (1 pint) fresh orange
  or pineapple juice
juice of 6 limes

dash of Angostura bitters
2 × 500 ml (18 fl oz) bottles
  American ginger ale
500 ml (18 fl oz) soda water
500 ml (18 fl oz) tonic water
40 ice cubes

Mix the Tequila, sugar, orange juice, lime juice and Angostura bitters together and refrigerate. Just before serving, mix in the ginger ale, soda and tonic waters, and add 2 cubes of ice to each drink.

Rompope

Home-made advocaat-type drink

Rompope is the first alcoholic drink I ever remember tasting. When I was a child in Mexico, it was a drink offered to ladies instead of *Jerez* (sherry). It is well loved by all.

SERVES 6. Makes 600 ml (1 pint)

400 g (14 oz) can sweetened
  condensed milk
300 ml (½ pint) milk, chilled

4 egg yolks
¼ teaspoon vanilla essence
150 ml (¼ pint) rum or vodka

Place all the ingredients in a blender and mix at top speed for 45 seconds. Strain into chilled glasses. This drink will keep in the refrigerator for several days.

■

Limonada

Fresh lemonade

Limonada and similar fruit 'ades' are common in Mexico and are served in most homes at lunchtime. In fact they are more often made from limes, strawberries, oranges, grapefruit, tamarind or pineapples rather than lemons. *Limonada* differs from *Licuados* in that it contains a much larger proportion of water. But whichever is used, a big cold jug of it is refreshing and appealing in the middle of a hot day. In this recipe I have called for lemons instead of limes, because lemons are more readily available in Britain and they are ideally suited to the recipe—in fact limes cannot be used instead because they have a bitterness when used with pith and skin.

SERVES 6. Makes about 1 litre (1¾ pints)

1 lemon, quartered
1 litre (1¾ pints) cold water

6 tablespoons granulated sugar

Place the lemon quarters, skin and all, in a liquidizer. Cover with 300 ml (½ pint) of the cold water and the sugar. Liquidize at top speed for 40 seconds only, then strain into a water jug. Now pour the rest of the water through the lemon peel in the strainer to catch any remaining flavour and natural oils. Refrigerate. Serve with ice cubes.

■

Sangría

Red wine cup

The perfect antidote to long hot days, *Sangría* is just as popular in Mexico as it is in Spain and Portugal. It is light and refreshing and ideal for summer parties.

SERVES 8

1 quantity Limonada
  (see page 223)
1 apple, finely sliced

1 orange, peeled and finely
  sliced
½ bottle red wine, chilled

Place whole or crushed ice cubes in each glass, and half-fill with lemonade. Drop in a few pieces of the fruit and fill the rest of the glass with red wine, tipping the glass and pouring the wine carefully down the inside of it so that it will remain on top of the lemonade rather than blending with it.

■

Licuados

Blended fruit drinks

Licuados are drinks made from fresh fruits, blended in the electric blender with either milk or water. The choice of fruits you can use is quite mind-boggling. *Licuados* take the place of orange juice for breakfast, or a mid-morning coffee break. Of course, when you are walking along the street in Mexico City under the blazing sun and you come by one of these *licuado* stalls, you are compelled to stop and have a cool drink. Here are some ideas.

Licuado de plátano

Milk and banana

MAKES about 300 ml (½ pint)

1 banana
250 ml (8 fl oz) cold milk

2 teaspoons granulated sugar

■

Licuado de nuez

Nut and milk

MAKES about 300 ml (½ pint)

50 g (2 oz) pecan nuts,
  walnuts or hazelnuts

250 ml (8 fl oz) cold milk
1 teaspoon granulated sugar

■

Licuado de fresas

Strawberries and orange juice

MAKES about 300 ml (½ pint)

225 g (8 oz) strawberries
150 ml (¼ pint) fresh orange
  juice

2 tablespoons granulated sugar

Blend the ingredients for each drink for 30 seconds at top speed and serve with ice cubes in tall glasses. Drink straight away.

■

Agua de Jamaica

Sorrel drink

Sorrel, or flower of Jamaica, is the flower of a wild plant; it is not related to the wild sorrel leaves which grow in Britain. Deep red in colour, it produces a very tasty drink which is also rich in vitamin

C. Sorrel blooms at Christmas and with its appropriate red colour, it is a popular children's drink during the festivities. The flowers are generally sold dried, but I have occasionally found fresh sorrel flowers at West Indian shops in Britain. If you are lucky enough to find fresh flowers, you will need double the quantity given. Preparation should start 4 hours ahead of time.

SERVES 8

100 g (4 oz) dried flor de   *1¾ litres (3 pints) water*
   Jamaica (sorrel flower)   *100 g (4 oz) caster sugar*

Wash the flowers in a sieve under a running tap. Place them in a saucepan with half the water, bring to the boil, and simmer for 5 minutes. Cool and strain into a water jug. Stir in the remaining water, reserving 8 tablespoons for the syrup. Mix the reserved water with the sugar in a saucepan, stir over moderate heat until the sugar dissolves, then add to the drink. Serve well chilled, with ice cubes.

■

Chocolate caliente

Hot chocolate

Hot chocolate is the most popular breakfast drink among Mexican children. Though electrical gadgets have now revolutionized the process, the traditional way of making hot chocolate with a nice thick foam is by using a *molinillo*, which is an elaborately decorated piece of wood carved into several rings. The *molinillo* is placed in the chocolate then rolled between the palms of the hands, causing the wooden rings to whirl round, drawing in air and producing the frothy bubbles. Egg is occasionally added to the hot chocolate in order to make it a 'meal in one', but it is mostly made with boiled milk, producing a thicker drink than milk that has just been warmed up.

In pre-Columbian times, *cacao* (cocoa) seeds were used in Mexico as money. The infuriated Spaniards in search of the Aztec Emperor's silver and gold, simply refused to believe that the treasure consisted of room after room in the Palace filled with cocoa beans. Gold and silver were only treasured for their beauty by the Aztecs. Because of the obvious value of *cacao*, only the very privileged could afford literally to 'drink' their money—so it was considered the drink of the Emperors. But as there was no milk in Mexico, the hot chocolate consisted of a bitter-sweet mixture of ground cocoa seeds, water, vanilla and honey. When milk and sugar became available, they were such an improvement to this that I doubt if it is ever drunk with water now.

Mexican chocolate is coarsely ground, and the sugar, cinnamon and vanilla are already in it when you buy it. By adding these flavourings to dark cooking chocolate you can make an excellent version of the Mexican drinking chocolate.

SERVES 4

200 g (5 oz) dark plain
chocolate
900 ml (1½ pints) hot milk

¼ teaspoon cinnamon
¼ teaspoon vanilla essence
sugar to taste

Put the chocolate in a saucepan and melt it over a pan of hot water. Add the hot milk slowly, stirring all the time until well mixed. Add the cinnamon and vanilla. Place the saucepan directly on the heat and bring the mixture to the boil. Lower the heat and whisk briskly with an egg beater or balloon whisk for 1–2 minutes. Remove from the heat and carry on whisking until bubbles form about 2½ cm (1 inch) above the liquid. Serve hot in individual cups, being sure to divide the foam equally. *Biscochos* or a sweet bread is always offered with hot chocolate.

Alternatively, leave the mixture until cold, whisk again and pour into individual glasses.

■

Café de olla

Coffee with cinnamon and sugar

Café de Olla is the drink of the peasants. Very delicious too, if you like sugar in your coffee. However, because so many people prefer to avoid sugar, I make a syrup which I offer separately to those who wish to try this spicy coffee. It tastes best served in a pottery mug.

SERVES 4

5 tablespoons water
4 tablespoons muscovado
  sugar
13 cm (5 inch) stick
  cinnamon or 1 teaspoon
  cinnamon

4 mugs freshly brewed hot
  coffee

Heat the water, sugar and cinnamon, stirring until the sugar is dissolved. Boil for 2 minutes, then pour it into a jug, to serve as an alternative to cream.

Atole

Maize drink

Atole has a deceptively mild flavour, but it is a very filling and calorie-loaded drink. It has an extremely thick consistency and is served piping hot for breakfast, instead of porridge. It is often flavoured with fresh fruit purée, such as strawberries, mango, pineapple or raspberries. Chocolate is also sometimes used to flavour *Atole*, which is then called *Champurrado*.

SERVES 4

50 g (2 oz) masa harina or
  cornflour
600 ml (1 pint) water
1 litre (1¾ pints) milk

175 g (6 oz) caster sugar
225 g (8 oz) fresh fruit, puréed
pinch of cinnamon, to garnish

Dissolve the *masa harina* or cornflour in the water. Bring the milk to the boil and pour the milk over the dissolved *masa harina*, stirring constantly. Pour the mixture back into the saucepan and simmer for 3 minutes, stirring constantly, then add the sugar and fruit purée. Serve in individual mugs garnished with a little powdered cinnamon.

VARIATION:

Champurrado—Chocolate drink

Substitute the fruit purée with 100 g (4 oz) grated plain cooking chocolate and heat the milk with a 13 cm (5 inch) cinnamon stick. Remove the cinnamon before stirring in the chocolate.

Te de yerbabuena

Mint tea

Garden mint is called 'good weed' in Mexico because it is believed to cure almost any malady in the digestive system. With food being so hot and alcoholic drinks so strong, having a cure-all tea to serve instead of coffee after a meal comes in very handy. This is a nice mild tea, which I prefer to conventional tea; it can be served hot or cold.

SERVES 2

10 leaves garden mint   *sugar to taste*
350 ml (12 fl oz) water

Boil the mint in the water for about 5 minutes, strain into tea cups and drink very hot, sweetened to taste. For a cool drink, strain, allow to cool and garnish with fresh mint leaves.

Pronunciation Guide

achiote	*a-CHYO-te*	annatto
adobado	*a-tho-BA-tho*	in chilli sauce
agrio	*A-gryo*	sour
agua, aguado	*A-gwa, a-GWA-tho*	liquid
aguacate	*a-gwa-KA-te*	avocado
ajo	*A-ho*	garlic
ajonjolí	*a-hon-ho-LEE*	sesame seeds
albóndigas	*al-BON-dee-gas*	meatballs
almendra	*al-MEN-dra*	almond
antojito	*an-to-HEE-to*	lit. 'what you fancy', appetizer
arroz	*a-RROS*	rice
asado	*a-SA-tho*	grilled
atole	*a-TO-le*	maize drink
aves	*A-bes*	poultry
bacalao	*ba-ka-LA-o*	salted cod
barbacoa	*bar-ba-KO-a*	steamed lamb (barbecue)
bebida	*be-BEE-tha*	drink
biscocho	*bees-KO-cho*	sweet buns
bistec	*bees-TEK*	beef steak
blanco	*BLAN-ko*	white
bolillo	*bo-LEE-yo*	french bread
borracho	*bo-RRA-cho*	tipsy
botana	*bo-TA-na*	hors d'oeuvre
budín	*boo-THEEN*	casserole
buñuelo	*boo-NYWE-lo*	type of biscuit
burrito	*boo-RREE-to*	wheat tortilla with a filling
cacahuates	*ka-ka-WA-tes*	peanuts
cacahuazintle	*ka-ka-wa-SEENT-le*	type of maize kernels
cacao	*ka-KA-o*	cocoa
cajeta	*ka-HE-ta*	milk dessert
calabacita	*ka-la-ba-SEE-ta*	courgettes
calabaza	*ka-la-BA-sa*	pumpkin
caldo	*KAL-do*	stock
caliente	*ka-LYEN-te*	hot

camarones	*ka-ma-RO-nes*	prawns
camote	*ka-MO-te*	sweet potato
campechana	*kam-pe-CHA-na*	type of sweet bun
canela	*ka-NE-la*	cinnamon
capeado	*ka-pe-A-tho*	covered in egg and fried
carbón	*kar-BON*	charcoal
carne	*KAR-ne*	meat
carnitas	*kar-NEE-tas*	fried pork
cazuela	*ka-SWE-la*	clay pot
cebolla	*se-BO-ya*	onion
chalupa	*cha-LOO-pa*	boat-shaped
chayotes	*cha-YO-tes*	cho-cho
chilaquiles	*chee-la-KEE-les*	tortilla chips with sauce
chile	*CHEE-le*	chilli
chilpotle	*cheel-POT-le*	smoked jalapeño chilli
chirimoya	*chee-ree-MO-ya*	sweet-sop
chivichango	*chee-bee-CHAN-go*	fried burrito
chongos	*CHON-gos*	curds in syrup
chorizo	*cho-REE-so*	spiced minced pork
churro	*CHOO-rro*	fried batter
cilantro	*see-LAN-tro*	coriander
cocada	*ko-KA-tha*	coconut dessert
col	*kol*	cabbage
coliflor	*ko-lee-FLOR*	cauliflower
compuesta	*kom-PWES-ta*	assembled
conserva	*kon-SER-ba*	preserve
costillitas	*kos-tee-YEE-tas*	spare ribs
crema	*KRE-ma*	cream
crepa	*KRE-pa*	crepe
cuitlacoche	*kweet-la-KO-che*	corn fungus
deshebrada	*des-e-BRA-tha*	shredded
dulce	*DOOL-se*	sweet or dessert

ejote	*e-HO-te* runner bean	
elote	*e-LO-te* sweetcorn	
empanada	*em-pa-NA-tha* turnover	
enchilada	*en-chee-LA-tha* rolled tortilla with sauce	
enfrijoladas	*en-free-ho-LA-th-as* tortilla with beans	
ensalada	*en-sa-LA-tha* salad	
epazote	*e-pa-SO-te* Mexican herb used mainly with black beans	
escabeche	*es-ka-BE-che* marinated	
espárragos	*es-PA-rra-gos* asparagus	
espinaca	*es-pee-NA-ka* spinach	
esquites	*es-KEE-tes* fried corn	
estilo	*es-TEE-lo* style	
flan	*flan* crème caramel	
flor	*flor* flower	
frijoles	*free-HO-les* beans	
fruta	*FROO-ta* fruit	
galleta	*ga-YE-ta* biscuit	
gelatina	*he-la-TEE-na* jelly	
guacamole	*gwa-ka-MO-le* avocado dip	
harina	*a-REE-na* flour	
helado	*e-LA-tho* ice-cream	
hígado	*EE-ga-tho* liver	
higo	*EE-go* fig	
hoja	*O-ha* leaf	
horno	*OR-no* oven	
huachinango	*wa-chee-NAN-go* red snapper	
huevo	*WE-bo* egg	
jaiba	*HIE-ba* crab	
jalapeño	*ha-la-PE-nyo* type of chilli	
jerez	*he-RES* sherry	
jícama	*HEE-ka-ma* Mexican tuber	
jitomate	*hee-to-MA-te* tomato	
jugo	*HOO-go* juice	
kahlúa	*ka-LOO-a* name of coffee liqueur	
legumbres	*le-GOOM-bres* vegetables	
licuados	*lee-KWA-thos* liquidized	
limón	*lee-MON* lime	
macarrón	*ma-ka-RRON* spaghetti	
maíz	*ma-EES* maize	
mamey	*ma-MEY* brown, thick-skinned fruit with sweet pink flesh	
manteca	*man-TE-ka* lard	
marisco	*ma-REES-ko* shellfish	
masa	*MA-sa* dough	
menudo	*me-NOO-tho* name of tripe soup	
metate	*me-TA-te* type of dried chilli	
mexalpilli	*me-zal-PEE-yee* stone rolling pin	
milpa	*MEEL-pa* maize plant	
molcajete	*mol-ka-HE-te* mortar made of lava	
mole	*MO-le* chilli sauce	
molinillo	*mo-lee-NEE-yo* wooden whisk	
moyetes	*mo-YE-tes* french bread with beans	
muéganos	*MWE-ga-nos* carameled fritters	
nachos	*NA-chos* fried tortilla chips with cheese	
nogada	*no-GA-tha* sauce made with nuts	
nopales	*no-PA-les* cactus paddles	
nuez	*nwes* nut	
olla	*O-ya* pot	
ostiones	*os-TYO-nes* oysters	
pambacitos	*pam-ba-SEE-tos* type of bread	
pan	*pan* bread	
papa	*PA-pa* potato	
papaya	*pa-PA-ya* paw-paw	
pavo	*PA-bo* turkey	
peneques	*pe-NE-kes* type of tortilla	
pepita	*pe-PEE-ta* pumpkin seeds	
perejil	*pe-re-HEEL* parsley	
pescado	*pes-KA-tho* fish	

pib	*pee(b)* type of oven	sardina	*sar-DEE-na* sardine
pibil	*pee-BEEL* annatto seasoning	sazón	*sa-SON* seasoning
picadillo	*pee-ka-DEE-yo* minced beef	seco	*SE-ko* dry
picante	*pee-KAN-te* spicy-hot	sencillo	*sen-SEE-yo* simple
pimiento	*pee-MYEN-to* red capsicum pepper	seviche	*se-BEE-che* marinated fish
		sopa	*SO-pa* soup
piñones	*pee-NYO-nes* pine kernels	sopaipilla	*so-pie-PEE-ya* fried pastry
pipián	*pee-PYAN* ground pumpkin seeds	sopes	*SO-pes* maize flour rounds
pitaya	*pee-TA-ya* type of fruit	taco	*TA-co* cigar-shaped tortilla with filling
plátano macho	*PLA-ta-no MA-cho* plantain		
poblano	*po-BLA-no* originating in Puebla	tamales	*ta-MA-les* maize dumplings
		taquito	*ta-KEE-to* small corn tortilla with filling
pollo	*PO-yo* chicken		
polvorones	*pol-bo-RO-nes* crumbly biscuits	tejocotes	*te-ho-KO-tes* type of crab apple
ponche	*PON-che* punch	tejolote	*te-ho-LO-te* pestle made of lava
poro	*PO-ro* leek		
postre	*POS-tre* dessert	tequila	*te-KEE-la* alcoholic drink
pozole	*po-SO-le* pork soup	ternera	*ter-NE-ra* veal
puerco	*PWER-ko* pork	tomate verde	*to-MA-te BER-the* tomatillo
pulque	*POOL-ke* native drink	tomatillo	*to-ma-TEE-yo* green husk tomato
quesadilla	*ke-sa-DEE-ya* tortilla folded in half with filling	torta	*TOR-ta* french bread filled like a sandwich
queso	*KE-so* cheese	tortilla	*tor-TEE-ya* flat maize or wheat pancake
raja	*RA-ha* strips of chilli		
ranchero	*ran-CHE-ro* ranch-style	tostado	*tos-TA-tho* toasted
refrito	*re-FREE-to* re-fried	totopo	*to-TO-po* tortilla chip
relleno	*re-YE-no* stuffed	vainilla	*bie-NEE-ya* vanilla
robalo	*ro-BA-lo* type of fish	verde	*BER-the* green
rollo	*RO-yo* roll	verdolagas	*ber-tho-LA-gas* purslane (type of vegetable)
romerito	*ro-me-REE-to* type of green vegetable		
		verduras	*ber-DOO-ras* vegetables
rosca	*ROS-ka* sweet bun in ring shape	vinagre	*bee-NA-gre* vinegar
		vinagreta	*bee-na-GRE-ta* vinaigrette
salmón	*sal-MON* salmon		
salsa	*SAL-sa* sauce	xoco-latli	*cho-ko-LAT-lee* chocolate
sangría	*san-GREE-a* lemonade and red wine drink	zapote	*sa-PO-te* type of fruit

Index